FURTHER RESEARCHING
BENEATH THE SURFACE

Contributions in this volume cover ways of knowing, the dynamics of research encounters, new methods of psycho-social inquiry, and the first-hand experience of being a researcher. Since the first volume of *Researching Beneath the Surface* was published by Karnac in 2009, psycho-social research has become more established but is also more scrutinised by a new generation of researchers, practitioners, and clinicians. This volume offers a timely exploration of the latest developments in psycho-social research, bringing together a series of papers in which both longstanding contributors to the field and new researchers explore tensions, possibilities, and innovations in psycho-socially inspired research.

Showcasing advances in psycho-social research methods, the book focuses on methodological dilemmas, innovations in method and methodology, and on experiences of conducting psycho-social research in challenging contexts. It also focuses on the contested but pivotal role of psychoanalysis in psycho-social research and explores what can be added by transdisciplinary use of deep ecology, continental philosophy, and relational approaches as alternative or supplementary ways of knowing.

Further Researching Beneath the Surface: Psycho-social Research Methods in Practice offers fresh insight into the practical and emotional issues of conducting oneself as a psycho-social researcher and learning from experience. It will be of great interest to psycho-social, qualitative, organisational, and psychoanalytically-oriented researchers, as well as postgraduate students in these fields.

Anne-Marie Cummins is a Senior Lecturer in Sociology at the University of the West of England, a founder member of the Centre for Psychosocial Studies (now the Psychosocial Studies Research group) and former UK editor of the journal *Organisational and Social Dynamics*. She has taught on and co-led the UWE Psychosocial Doctoral programme. Anne-Marie has a background in Group Relations, Group Analysis and Organisational Consultancy.

Nigel Williams is a Senior Lecturer in Psychology, and a member of the Psycho-Social Studies Research Network at the University of the West of England. He is engaged in Psycho-social research that reaches across boundaries to deepen and inform professional practices. He lectures in Psycho-social and Beneath the Surface Methodologies, Systems and Complexity Theory, Groups and Organisations, and Intergenerational Memory. He is an organisational consultant and is a registered psychotherapist and supervisor with the United Kingdom Council for Psychotherapy.

FURTHER RESEARCHING
BENEATH THE SURFACE

Psycho-social Research
Methods in Practice

Volume 2

Edited by

Anne-Marie Cummins and
Nigel Williams

Routledge
Taylor & Francis Group

LONDON AND NEW YORK

First published 2018
by Routledge
2 Park Square, Milton Park, Abingdon, Oxon OX14 4RN

and by Routledge
711 Third Avenue, New York, NY 10017

Routledge is an imprint of the Taylor & Francis Group, an informa business

British Library Cataloguing-in-Publication Data
A catalogue record for this book is available from the British Library

Library of Congress Cataloging-in-Publication Data
A catalog record has been requested for this book

ISBN: 978-1-78220-412-1 (pbk)

Typeset in Palatino
by The Studio Publishing Services Ltd
email: studio@publishingservicesuk.co.uk

CONTENTS

PART II: DOING

PART III: EXPERIENCING

ACKNOWLEDGEMENTS

We would like to acknowledge the inspiration and hard work of our two now retired professors in psychosocial studies, Simon Clarke and Paul Hoggett. They have, in their very different ways, been formative and inspirational figures for us and our students and without their vision, creativity, and drive, this second generation of psychosocial writing would have been less adventurous and less wide ranging.

ABOUT THE EDITORS AND CONTRIBUTORS

The editors

Anne-Marie Cummins is a senior lecturer in sociology at the University of the West of England and also a group analyst in training. She is ex-UK editor of the journal *Organisational and Social Dynamics*, former award leader of the UWE Masters in Group Relations and an experienced group relations consultant. Her principal research interests are: emotional and political resistances to current educational regimes in HE and organisational renewal and development in the psychotherapeutic and psychoanalytic sector. She is a member of the UWE Psycho-social Studies Research group and is currently researching the social, psychoanalytic, and group-analytic reception of transgenderism. Anne-Marie is also a member of OPUS and the Listening Post Steering Group, which was set up in 2017.

Nigel Williams is a senior lecturer in psychology and sociology, and a member of the Psycho-Social Studies research network at UWE. He is engaged in in psycho-social research that reaches across boundaries to deepen and inform professional practices. He lectures in psycho-social and Beneath the Surface methodologies, systems and complexity theory, and intergenerational memory. He is an organisational consultant and is a registered and qualified psychotherapist and supervisor with United Kingdom Council for Psychotherapy. His has recently published an essay, "The Anglo-German diaspora", in *The Ethics of Remembering and the Consequences of Forgetting: Essays on Trauma, History and Memory* (2014) edited by Michael O'Loughlin (Rowman & Littlefield).

The contributors

Louisa Diana Brunner, PhD, is an organisational and leadership development consultant, executive coach, and independent researcher. She is a certified family business adviser and a Family Firm Institute mentor. She has long experience in coaching and selection at Bocconi School of Management and for graduates at Bocconi University. She has been on the staff of many Group Relations Conferences, and has published and presented papers at conferences. Currently, she is the Treasurer of PCCA (Partners for Confronting Collective Atrocities), Honorary Member of Il Nodo Group, a member of FFI, ISPSO, OFEK, and OPUS. She is on the International Advisory Board of the journal *Organisational and Social Dynamics*.

Lita Crociani-Windland, PhD., is senior lecturer in Sociology and theme leader for Psycho-Social Studies at the University of the West of England. She is co-chair of the Association for Psychoanalysis, Culture and Society. Her research interests concern affective dynamics, continental philosophy, group relations tradition and experiential learning, social pedagogy, and disability. Her publications include: "Learning, duration and the virtual" in Clarke and Hogget's *Researching Beneath the Surface* (London: Karnac, 2009); *Festivals, Affect and Identity* (London: Anthem Press, 2011); "Politics and affect" (with Paul Hoggett) in *Subjectivity* (2012) 5, 161–179; "Old age and difficult life transitions: a psycho-social understanding", in *Psychoanalysis, Culture & Society* (2013), 18(4); "Towards a psycho-social pedagogy as a relational practice and perspective", in *Organisational and Social Dynamics* (2013), 13(2).

Julian Manley, PhD., is a researcher based at the University of Central Lancashire (UCLan). His research has been focused on the development and use of affective, visual, and imaginative methods, with special expertise in the area of social dreaming. He is Trustee and Vice Chair of the Gordon Lawrence Foundation and Director of the Foundation's academic research committee. He is a member of the Executive Committee of the Climate Psychology Alliance. He combines group-based work with other psychosocial methods and has a special interest in the application of Deleuzian perspectives to psycho-social studies.

Rose Redding Mersky, PhD, has been an organisational development consultant and executive coach for over twenty-five years. She offers workshops in various socio-analytic methodologies, such as organisational role analysis, social dream-drawing, organisational observation, social photo-matrix, and social dreaming. She is an Honorary Trustee of the Gordon Lawrence Foundation for the Promotion of Social Dreaming. She has been a member of the International Society for the Psychoanalytic Study of Organizations (ISPSO) for almost thirty years and served as its first female president. Her publications have focused primarily on the practice of consultation and the utilisation of these methodologies in both organisational and research practice. She recently received her doctorate from the University of the West of England in Bristol. She lives and works in Germany.

Nadine Riad Tchelebi, PhD, is a senior lecturer at the Bristol Business School. Her research interest focuses on unconscious group dynamics and how these conglomerate to shape organisational decision-making. She is currently engaged in numerous regional and international consultancy projects where she explores exactly that. Her PhD enquiry led her to temporarily living in a convent community. Nadine regularly works with individuals and groups in experiential workshops that she designs and runs herself. She is a member of OPUS and ISPSO, on the board of PCCA, and the UK Editor of the international journal *Organisational and Social Dynamics*. Her latest publication is titled "Taking Bion 'back to basics': let us stop counting—'oneness' as the only basic-assumption mentality", *Organisational & Social Dynamics*, 17(1): 50–70.

Jem Thomas is a psychotherapist registered with the British Psychoanalytic Council. He is a member of the Severnside Institute for

Psychotherapy, a former academic, and one of the founders of the Association for Psycho-Social Studies.

Jane Woodend, PhD, following her earlier career as an occupational therapist and NHS manager, qualified as a psychodynamic counsellor in 2000 and then completed a postgraduate training in 2002. She has been in practice since then and worked with a wide variety of presenting problems in individuals and couples. Jane has an MSc in Applied Psychology (Learning Disabilities) and completed her PhD in 2014, where her research into endings in psychodynamic counselling broke new ground in terms of both psycho-social methodology and findings. She is co-director of Five Valleys Counselling Practice Ltd in Stroud, Gloucestershire.

Rembrandt Zegers lives in the Netherlands. He was a development manager with Greenpeace International, working on the governance and organisational development portfolio of Greenpeace offices worldwide. He is associated to the University of the West of England (UWE) as a part-time PhD student. He is particularly interested in critique to (Western) thinking about environmental problems and how leaders can contribute to ecocentric practices as he is consulting to leaders and communities. He sees psycho-social research methods as very relevant to researching this field, as they provide deep insight to being human and human emotions. Also, his research allows him to become involved with people he otherwise would not meet or could engage with. He finds that to be a very important and inspiring aspect of doing research.

Introduction: researching beneath the surface—a continuing journey

It has been almost a decade since the first volume of *Researching Beneath the Surface* was published. The book reflected developments and innovations in psycho-social scholarship and research methods in the first decade of the twenty-first century. Much has happened since that time, both in the psycho-social research community here at the University of the West of England, and nationally and internationally. At a UK level, the national network attained official status as the Association for Psycho-Social Studies in 2013 and has now adopted the online *Journal for Psychosocial Studies*, which was started at UWE Bristol and hosted here until very recently. The National Association for Psycho-Social Studies had an inaugural launch with a one-day symposium in 2014 and has gone from strength to strength with longer conferences at the University of Central Lancashire (UCLAN) in 2015, at UWE, Bristol in 2016, and a third is to be held in 2018 at the University of Bournemouth. While originally envisaged as national Association conferences, the membership turned out to be international, drawing people from different countries across the world. Across the Atlantic, the Association for Psychoanalysis, Culture and Society has also gone from strength to strength, continuing to host an annual conference in Rutgers University in New Jersey and to run the successful and, by now, very well established international journal, *Psychoanalysis Culture and Society*. This conference and journal have been a worldwide locus for psycho-social and cultural ideas and publications for well over two decades.

The reason to focus on psycho-social methods once more is that this is a fundamental need in this new field of studies. Indeed, it is sometimes said that the field is defined *by* its methods and its innovative approach to social research. Psycho-social research claims not only to be able to produce "hard to get" or new forms of data, but also to change our relationship to data itself and to redefine what data might be as the research develops and unfolds. This is underpinned by a view that all social research is, like it or not, a relational activity. In some ways, then, what is happening in psycho-social research is typical of the relational turn across the social sciences, as well as within psychotherapy and counselling, and group and organisational work (Clarke et al., 2008).

In 2009, Clarke and Hoggett wrote, in Volume 1 of *Researching Beneath the Surface*, the companion to this book,

> Psycho-social studies is also informing the development of new methodologies in the social sciences, including the use of free association and biographic narrative interview methods, the application of infant observation methodologies to social observation, the development of psychoanalytic ethnography/field work and attention to transference–countertransference dynamics in the research process. (2009, p. 2)

But what has happened since? When we commissioned this volume, we were particularly interested in hearing about experiences of, and responses to, methodological dilemmas, in relation to developments and innovations people had trialled, and about experiences of conducting psycho-social research in challenging contexts. Contributions could be about ways of knowing, about the dynamics of research encounters, about psycho-social methods of enquiry or analysis—or any combination of these things. Here at UWE, another generation of psycho-social research students, we might call them the post-FANI generation (free association narrative interviewing), had matured and not only produced new developments in methods, but had their own reflections on more established ways of doing psycho-social research.

Some of this very rich and innovative work is showcased here, together with long-standing contributors to the field. This volume is a continuation of the process of documenting new methods and the further elaboration of existing ones. In that spirit, it focuses on the contested but pivotal role of psychoanalysis in psycho-social research, while also engaging in transdisciplinary explorations taking in inter-subjectivity, deep ecology, Deleuzian and continental philosophy, as well as a commitment to innovative research methods and ways of conceptualising the psycho-social research journey.

The reader might or might not by now have noticed our use of the hyphenated spelling of "psycho-social". This is not by accident or mere preference. As Hoggett put it (2008, p. 379), "The hyphen in psycho-social studies signifies both the irreducibility of the psycho-logical to the social (and vice versa) and their complementarity, that is, the impossibility of there being the one without the other". Fol-lowing debates on the usefulness (or not) of distinguishing the psycho and the social realms as separate, the hyphen has disappeared from the preferred spelling of "psychosocial" adopted by the official Asso-ciation for Psychosocial Studies. However, in this volume, we wish largely to retain it and offer a case for its possibilities and creative capacities. We contend that the presence of the hyphen signifies a dif-ferent and more complex duality than *just* the psycho and the social: we might, for instance, want to think about different modalities of process: for instance, quantity and quality, in Bergson's (1946) sense, "K" and "O" in Bion's (1970) sense, or the place where thirdness is formed, as discussed by Benjamin (2004). Or, we might want to think about the hyphen as the place which is "both–and" as well as "neither–nor" (Hoggett, 2008, p. 384), a place where the interrelations that form the reality we encounter and want to happen and are worth holding on to for that precise reason.

This book is divided into three parts, though the reader will find that, as is to be expected in a field like this, these divisions are some-what artificial given the unity of theory, practice, and experience. In Part I, some of the epistemological and ontological questions which are raised in psycho-social research, whether this be from explicitly psychoanalytic or non-psychoanalytic approaches, are explored under the heading "Knowing". In Part II, a series of psycho-social interven-tions are described under the heading "Doing": these chapters take in a variety of topics: doing research in challenging circumstances, exploring the limitations of old psycho-social paradigms, developing new ones, and linking the psycho-social with the ecological. In the final section of the book, Part III, we present a series of theoretically informed reflections ("Reflecting") on the vicissitudes of being a psycho-social researcher and the way in which examination of this process can lead to academically rigorous theory as well as a re-thinking of "third spaces" in the research journey.

Part I: Knowing

In this section, we introduce a series of chapters which concern themselves with the platforms from which psycho-social research can be established. There has always been a tension in the psycho-social world between psychoanalytically orientated exponents of the work and others who, for various reasons, reject psychoanalytically informed approaches. The views expressed in these chapters reflect that tension to some degree. Our three contributors, a psychodynamic therapist and practitioner (Jem Thomas), an academic (Lita Crociani-Windland), and an activist (Rembrandt Zegers), tackle the topic of what it is to know and how one comes to know from a variety of these platforms.

Jem Thomas leads off the book with a review of the recent academic literature and debate around the role and relevance of psychoanalytic insight and methods to social research in general and psycho-social research in particular. He is concerned that we have been too quick to assume that psychoanalytic insight and methods are directly relevant to psycho-social research, given that psychoanalysis is itself a form of research but one with epistemic goals. He gives a series of lively and challenging vignettes drawn from clinical work and from infant observation to begin to show how, in the key areas of interpretation and working through, psychoanalysis is a very different project to the research encounter.

In thinking about infant observation as a metaphor for research, he suggests that psychoanalysis and psycho-social research can share a commitment to participatory observation. He is concerned to identify how the process of "wild research" can begin and discusses the problem of both the defended subject and the defended researcher. He draws some parallels between the triangulation of data that psycho-social researchers aim for through joint data-processing groups, and to the role of supervision in psychoanalysis, but he suggests that the long-term nature of the psychoanalytic relationship and the complex training of the psychoanalyst marks it apart from psycho-social research. The area of convergence he suggests is in the encounter with the other and the effect that discovering new experience has on reorganising the psyche of both parties. Psychoanalytic psychotherapists and social researchers share this underlying relational theme, while needing to be aware of, and open to exploring, very significant differences in approach and goals. The chapter makes a case, then, for caution and conservatism when claiming that psycho-social work is "psycho-analytically informed".

Lita Crociani-Windland draws on the work of Bergson (1913, 1935), developments in neuroscience (McGilchrist, 2009; Schore, 2003), and relationally informed ideas of thirdness (Benjamin, 2004) to explore the role and place of the researcher's subjectivity in psycho-social ways of knowing. By mapping a trajectory from thinking in the late nineteenth century to the early twenty-first century, she is able to show how converging and overlapping philosophical, neuroscientific and psychoanalytic frameworks are available as a basis on which to build a more intellectually rigorous, creatively synthesised, and, arguably, more fully psycho-social account of the nature of being and ways of investigating it.

Her account takes us beyond a narrow transference–countertransference reading of the researcher's subjectivity and into one that is more rounded, rich, and, possibly, more ethical. Qualitative aspects of reality—with all of their unconscious, embodied, intuitive, and affective processes—must be apprehended via the researcher's careful and reflexive use of subjectivity. Of particular use, she argues, is Bergson's approach to what is sometimes called intuition and the way in which a researcher's (or anyone's) intuitive responses can be examined methodically, in particular by framing the issue at hand in terms of time and duration (defined here as profound qualitative aspect of time) rather than simply space. Behind much of the chapter is a reminder of the limitations of dualism and a plea for the kind of thirdness typified by Winnicott's (1971) helpful concept of transitional space, or Benjamin's (2004) account of intersubjectivity. Not only does this take us away from a drive-based psychoanalytic reading of research material, one which sees repression and resistance every-

where, but it makes possible a more ethical use of researcher subjectivity in a way that goes beyond "do-er–done to" dynamics and is
sensitive to inter- and intrasubjectivity. In effect, this is about paying
attention to (research) relationship, attunement, curiosity, and interest;
this is the terrain on which good psycho-social work is done. The
researcher nust be aware of his or her subjectivity, but unless this
subjectivity is based on interest and curiosity there is no possibility for
thirdness to emerge. This point is also explored later in in this volume
in the chapter by Brunner, who discusses the need for empathy and
some level of identification with one's research subjects, even in the
face of overwhelming differences in power and status.

The theme of the ecological crisis, global warming, and sustainable
living are issues central to our current and future lives, but what kinds
of research and leadership might need to emerge alongside them?
Rembrandt Zegers gives a fascinating and groundbreaking foray into
ways of researching leaders and leadership in the ecology movement.
His argument is that a paradigm shift is required in research methods
in order to study leadership in a meaningful way as exercised in relation to nature, ecology, and issues surrounding human relationships
to the natural world. This involves an inclusion of embodied awareness and of the idea that nature also needs to be seen as possessing
agency, a quality often reserved only for humans. He argues that the
human relationship to nature is largely unconscious and mediated via
the body. However, psychoanalysis itself has, until recently, stopped
looking at the link between nature and unconscious processes.

He suggests that we need to adopt what he calls a relational view
of nature. Combining free association narrative interviewing (FANI)
with Gendlin's (2003) "bodily knowing" method, he discusses choice
of research subjects via the lens of systems and complexity, thereby
showing us how decisions in research that are normally thought of as
individual choices of design can be located and chosen from the point
of view of a system or systems. He shows how his interviewing
method brings a different kind of data, shot through with sensation
and non-human themes. In so doing, he offers us a different object for
psycho-research: that of the field. This is a challenging and fascinating
read that takes us to the edges and limits of our contemporary cultural
ideas about leadership and about research.

To conclude this section, as supervisors of psycho-social research
projects, it has been our experience that the application of a range of

"beneath the surface concepts", coupled with this theoretical eclecticism and a loyalty to the values of practice and/or activism, is what will most help people to be reflexive. Whatever the differences in background or allegiance to particular political or theoretical positions, it is precisely the "beneath the surface" concepts that allow researchers to be more aware that the emotional information disguised in affect and/or strange and uncanny states of mind can greatly enrich the research process. We would also wish to hi-light that this comes with a commitment to the idea that subject and object are always trying to exchange places, that research and intervention, and social healing, are in this sense always inextricably bound together. In this book we suggest that it is the role of the psycho-social researcher to embody, via appropriate personal and social valences, varying degrees of these three vital components; the therapeutic, the commitment to research, and social engagement and intervention.

Part II: Doing

In this section we present a series of chapters in which psycho-social practitioners explore the tensions and possibilities in their work, tensions which have been lived through first hand as they struggled to put method into action. Finding that one has "fallen out" with an established method for researching under the surface provokes both oedipal anxiety (to find one's self pitched against, or in tension with, established "names" and institutions) but also excitement and curiosity in the possibilities of methodological hybridisation. Part of that excitement is perhaps in the realisation that psycho-social research methods by now have their own "establishment" big names and preferred methods. In the chapters outlined below, Brunner and, later, Cummins describe their experiences of running up against some of the limitations and challenges of, to use the phrase at its most general, "doing research differently", and Manley describes the way in which the doing of psycho-social research is enriched by arts-based practice and Deleuzian concepts. For each of these authors, there is something new to be learnt by taking established methods to their limits and by losing one's bearings to some degree.

There is a tendency for psycho-social research, and, indeed, social science research in general, to occupy itself with giving voice to the less powerful. What happens when we try to apply the insights and methods of psycho-social research techniques to researching the rich and powerful? How do psycho-social methods need to be thought about and adapted for these circumstances? Louisa Diana Brunner discusses her experiences of interviewing powerful people using the FANI method.

As well as the key issues one would normally expect to see discussed when researching these groups from *any* research perspective (access, gatekeepers, the personal credibility and connectedness of the researcher), she describes the way in which the sometimes overwhelming affects evoked in the researcher in these encounters with the powerful can be managed and understood. The "allure of power" and the researcher's own reactions to great wealth can put psycho-social researchers in the kinds of defensive positions to which they are unaccustomed, ones where collusion and seduction (and powerful feelings of exclusion) have to be recognised and worked with. Brunner argues that some degree of empathic identification with one's research subjects and their values is crucial for building trust and working alliance. In a similar way to Crociani-Windland (also in this volume), Brunner argues that an understanding of thirdness and a grasp of the dynamics of mutual recognition is crucial to the success (or not) of researching powerful people, as in a full and frank admission and understanding of the social and cultural position of the researcher. She concludes that when interviewing powerful people, concepts we are familiar with in psycho-social methods—the defended subject, the defended researcher, intersubjectivity, the third position, the dynamics of trust—all need to be "stretched a bit more" and that without some level of shared social background and some level of an identification or empathy with the values of the researched group, properly psycho-social research cannot take place.

Julian Manley begins by revisiting the chapter he wrote in 2009 on social dreaming for Volume 1 of *Researching Beneath the Surface*. In that chapter, Manley was keen to develop a more Deleuzian underpinning for social dreaming, taking it beyond its (psychoanalytic) foundations to a place which allowed more access to the affective and embodied realms of human experience. Along with others at the Psychosocial Research Unit at UCLAN, Manley has been instrumental in developing a new and increasingly significant psycho-social methodology—that of the visual matrix.

In this new chapter, Manley draws our attention to the way in which a specifically Deleuzian perspective can make a fresh contribution to developing the method and methodology of the visual matrix in psycho-social research. He shows how use of the matrix as a method can be brought from the world of psychoanalytically informed consultancy and practice into a thorough-going version of psycho-social *research*. There follows a substantial empirical example of a visual matrix in action based on an artwork and exhibition created by artist William Titley on the theme of urban demolition and the enforced eviction of tenants from their homes. Manley maintains that the Deleuzian ideas of deterritorialisation and reterritorialisation, that is, moving things, images, and fragments from one territory to another, is not only the essence of artistic endeavour, but is also a way of understanding what happens to people in the visual matrix when their own individual and collective creativity to thinking and exchange is activated. He goes on to illustrate the way in which it is possible to think of affect in the matrix as giving rise to unfixed, mobile and rhizomatic intensities as one image resonates with, and triggers, another. Within these processes, the individual is subsumed into the social, or, to put it in a Deleuzian way, into the "body without organs". These ideas are illustrated with verbal and visual research materials collected for the research matrix, all of which illustrate a complex relationship and interconnectedness between psyche and society.

What does it mean to *listen socially*? Or to think together? Can a group or an individual in some way detect or express the social unconscious or affective undercurrents? In her chapter, Anne-Marie Cummins takes critical look at Listening Posts, a method derived from the Tavistock Group Relations tradition and in the tradition of applied psychoanalysis. She suggests that while the idea that a small group can in some ways reflect, channel, or express society's wider social processes has some purchase, there are major limitations and flaws in Listening Post methodology as currently constituted. Listening Posts are a "top-down" method of interpreting findings: they have a narrow social base of self-selected participants and they work from the problematic position that unconscious social processes can be somehow "revealed" by the method itself and rendered into convenor-led and theory-driven hypotheses. The Listening Post tradition is steeped in Kleinian and post-Kleinian interpretative repertoires that tend to rule out the more creative and playful aspects of the primary process thinking, which can also be present in "listening socially".

Cummins suggests ways of refreshing the Listening Post model into something which is more reflexive, more attuned to power and authority relations, and more and more keyed in to the dynamics of intersubjective meaning making. Much of this can be achieved by substituting the idea of a metaphorical Listening "post" with the idea of a listening matrix. This allows the emergence of shared thinking and affect which, in turn, tells us something about the socio-cultural and the trans-subjective realms as manifest in everyday life and preoccupations. These meanings can remain open to multiple interpretations rather than being hierarchically ordered into a series of once and for all fixed "hypotheses", as with the typical Listening Post. An example is given of a variation of Listening Post methodology where this more open approach has been trialled and where "social poetry" is collectively created and interpreted. Such developments link Listening Posts with the more associative and creative processes typical of other psycho-social methods, such as the visual matrix or the social photo-matrix. All three emphasise the non-hierarchical, the trans-subjective, and the link between intersubjective meaning-making and socio-cultural sources of meaning.

Overall, the reader will note the way in which the chapters in this section have in common a concern with expanding "traditional" psycho-social methods, whether this be beyond British or American psychoanalytic frames of reference which privilege anxiety or relationality (Manley), or beyond the familiar position of being "one-up" when one conducts FANI-type interviews (Brunner), or, beyond any attempts to regularise and discipline researching the unconscious via the production of post-Kleinian-inspired "hypotheses" (Cummins). The notion of the matrix as a forum for social research, as opposed to organisational consultancy, is an especially significant development, though one which, like all forms of exploration of the unconscious, comes with its own problems of interpretation and validity.

Part III: Experiencing

The importance and significance of personal insight and self-discovery during the research process had often been thought of as a confusing factor and, at best, a by-product of the research process.

Given the emphasis on relational methods, reflexivity, and the role of intuition in research, it is incumbent on psycho-social researchers to develop and clarify their ideas about issues concerning objectivity and what it is to know. Psycho-social methods need to be located in thorough and thought-through philosophical and epistemological arguments, but they also need to be sensitive to experiential learning.

Research, while almost always occurring inside a system of the university or commissioning body, also becomes a system in itself, perhaps like a temporary learning community, a term originally coined to describe group relations conferences. These networks of learning involve researchers and their research subjects, their supervisors, and other collaborators, as well as friends and family, all of whom entwine and inform the more formal aspects of research. Each of the following chapters tells us more about this deeply relational and experiential process in research.

Rose Redding Mersky talks about how support systems can develop into "third spaces" that provide containers for different aspects of learning while conducting research. Using Mitchell's (2014) ideas on family and social processes, she reflects on the importance of horizontal (social, collegial) and vertical (pseudo-familial, supervisory) "third spaces" in the research process, particularly as they apply to older doctoral students. This way of thinking about horizontal and vertical third spaces moves beyond the usual transference–countertransference axes of the tangle of (non-field, university-based) research relationships doctoral students find themselves in. It moves us into a way of thinking which takes seriously the idea of "identity workspace"' and the necessity of a capacious "holding social skin" while one traverses the doctoral journey and the development and integration of a (new) professional identity. Drawing on Mitchell's work about siblings (2014) and on Teitel's (2002) work on skin and identity, Mersky shows how "researching beneath the surface" entails a commitment to seeking out third spaces between oneself and one's research topic. Reporting on her experience as an older doctoral student, she offers frank advice to both older students and their supervisors about the transferential dynamics of the relationship and goes on to consider the practical implications of taking third spaces seriously in the planning and organisation of doctoral programmes.

Sometimes, the new student attempting research, perhaps for the first time, can feel confused. Students trying to choose a research method and to know something about what to expect as researchers are often left to learn by making mistakes. The debates over how to do research and how to develop confidence and acquire a new role and identity can seem daunting. Jane Woodend has given a first-person account of her journey to becoming a researcher. She writes in the spirit of giving first time research students an insight into the vicissitudes of constructing and conducting psycho-social research. The chapter offers a view into an academic process and gives a refreshing reminder of the problems both of choice of methods and dealing with prosaic events, such as being late for interviews, or keeping up morale in the face of low response rates.

Like Mersky (also in this volume) she explores the subtle and sometimes confusing transition from previous professional identity to that of researcher, and the ways in which growing confidence in the multi-layered role of psycho-social researcher can bring about new insight into the research data. She reflects on many of the specific identifying features of psycho-social methods and gives a series of helpful vignettes on data processing, supervision, and interviewing. This account might be helpful for beginning researchers, as well as a reminder for those more established, of the problems that can crop up and sometimes derail research.

Research, then, can change us. Our encounter with new people, groups, and organisations can profoundly challenge who we think we are. This can be disturbing and confusing, but, if responded to in creative and methodologically informed ways, new insights can arise that lead back into the research process. This can be thought about as the researcher's subjectivity as a research instrument (see Crociani-Windland in this volume). It also relates to the idea that the affective level of research meetings or encounters can be the place where these new experiences begin. The skill is then to recognise this, rather than personalise the experience as "faulty". The following piece is an excellent example of an experienced researcher doing just this.

Nadine Tchelebi, with her background in organisational research and consultancy, brings our attention to the fascinating and often neglected area of developments that occur for the researcher during the course of research that can be both life-changing and also subtly feed back into research itself. She conceptualises this type of development in terms of "finding self when looking for other" and, more generally, on the value of creating a focus for intrasubjectivity in the research encounter. She explores the idea that social science research is, at a deeper level, always "me search" in which a capacity to process the lived experience of the researcher becomes an essential quality of psycho-socially informed research. Her case studies and vignettes give a lively and absorbing insight into research as it unfolds in real time. She allows us to see both what we might ordinarily think of as "outcome" or "findings" *and* the road travelled or journey undertaken in which something crucial has changed for the researcher. She shows us that intrasubjectivity is a potent and subtle concept allowing us to explore the "other-in-mind" in various settings, some of which are mundane, such as the industrial works canteen, and others which are sacred, such as the life of Sisters in a convent.

In this, she is able to take us to the interplay of "us and them" at various levels—in her family of origin, and in her identity spanning several cultures—and to show how something that might otherwise remain hidden or, at best, "autobiographical" can become a deep part of the research when the researcher reconceptualises herself as a "research instrument" attuned to conflicting identity. She develops a theoretical frame that allows us to think about the relationships between objectivity and subjectivity in research, and elaborates on how it is only when conflict or frame breaking occurs that deeper insight arises. This is allied to the systems psycho-dynamic idea that the emergence of conflict is a key source for insight and creativity if it can be recognised and worked with appropriately.

Subjectivity, as spoken about in these last three chapters but also as touched on in all contributions in this book, are part of a grand introspective tradition that takes the human capacity to reflect, intuit, and observe as a fundamental part of scientific and artistic activity. It is a tradition that revels in, and quietly reveals, the truth that the inner and outer worlds belong together, and that the human psyche is unusually freighted with analytical and intuitive capacities that can make reliable, accurate, and creative navigation of internal and external worlds eminently possible. It invites us to trust in human experience and collaboration as both dependable and innovative ways of coming to know about the world. In this sense, the psycho-social offers a riposte to the current evidence based reductionism of what our current age takes as knowledge.

It now only remains for us to thank all the contributors for their time and thoughts and for their enthusiastic engagement with this volume. We do not claim that this volume can represent all innovations, challenges, or dilemmas encountered by this generation of psycho-social researchers. Nevertheless, we maintain that it has an important contribution to make to ongoing conversations in this relatively new field, as well as to explorations of qualitative social science research in general. Finally, we hope that some of the experiences, the reflections, the new thinking, and the methodological innovations described will act as sources of encouragement and interest for a generation of psycho-social researchers in the making.

Anne-Marie Cummins
Nigel Williams

References

Benjamin, J. (2004). Beyond doer and done to: an intersubjective view of thirdness. *Psychoanalytic Quarterly, LXXIII*: 5-46.
Bergson, H. (1913). *Time and Free Will: An Essay on the Immediate Data of Consciousness*. Minneola, NY: Dover [reprinted 2001].
Bergson, H. (1935). *The Two Sources of Morality and Religion*. Notre Dame, IN: Notre Dame University Press [reprinted 1977].
Bergson, H. (1946). *The Creative Mind*. New York: Citadel Press [reprinted 1974].
Bion, W. R. (1970). *Attention and Interpretation*. London: Tavistock.
Clarke, S., & Hoggett, P. (2009). *Researching Beneath the Surface*. London: Karnac.
Clarke, S., Hahn, H., & Hoggett, P. (2008). *Object Relations and Social Relations: The Implications of the Relational Turn in Psychoanalysis*. London: Karnac.
Hoggett, P. (2008). What's in a hyphen? *Psychoanalysis, Culture and Society, 13*: 379–384
Gendlin, E. (2003). *Focusing: How to Open Up Your Deepeer Feelings and Intuition*. London: Rider.
McGilchrist, I. (2009). *The Master and his Emissary. The Divided Brain and the Making of the Western World*. New Haven, CT: Yale University Press.
Mitchell, J. (2014). Siblings and the psychosocial. *Organisational & Social Dynamics, 14*(1): 1-12.

Schore, A. (2003). *Affect Regulation and the Repair of the Self*. New York: W. W. Norton.

Tietel, E. (2002). Triangular spaces and social skins in organisations. *Socio-Analysis*, 4: 33-52.

Winnicott, D. W. (1971). *Playing and Reality*. London: Routledge.

PART I
KNOWING

CHAPTER ONE

"As easy as to know . . .": on the tensions between psychoanalysis and psycho-social research

Jem Thomas

"If to do were as easy as to know what were good to do . . ."

(Shakespeare, *The Merchant of Venice*, I(ii) 13–14)

Introduction: psychoanalysis and research

The key claim of this chapter is that psychoanalysis is a form of research. It is other things, too, but it is a way of creating, of generating, of "having" knowledge, rather than, say, being just a perspective on knowledge. That raises the question of what its relation might be to other forms of research in the human sciences and the associated question of what might happen when other forms of research try to borrow from psychoanalysis, as in psycho-social studies. This chapter, then, is an attempt to reflect on the relationship between insight in psycho-social research and insight in the consulting room. I use "psychoanalysis" here very broadly to include all those forms of thought and therapy with a family resemblance that derives ultimately from Freud but does *not* include medical psychiatry, behavioural therapy, and so on. My epigraph from Shakespeare is because, for some time now, psychoanalysis has been much interested in the idea of "research". In the epigraph, Portia feels that the knowing is easy, the doing hard. In some ways, the situation with regard to psychoanalysis and research is the reverse. Methods in psychoanalysis or in qualitative research, the "doing", can be acquired quite simply (although mastery is another matter altogether), at least in comparison with the natural sciences. On the other hand, the status of what is discovered, the "knowing", can be deeply problematic. In saying psychoanalysis is a form of research, I am maintaining that many of its core concepts—free association, transference and countertransference, projective identification, the reflexive use of subjectivity—are ways of forming knowledge, of getting close to someone's experience. They also, however, give rise to knowledge whose status is contestable and something in the current psychosocial literature and the psychoanalytic interest in research makes me, at least, uneasy.

The interest in research is almost impossible to avoid. It is prominent on the websites. The International Psychoanalytic Association's (IPA) website has a drop-down menu under the heading "Research" with sections on current research, research training, university links and the like, and it claims that "The IPA's Board, at its July 2012 meeting in Toronto . . . reaffirmed its commitment to research funding" (2016). The British Psychoanalytic Council, for its part, has a website section called "Research and evidence" with various further links with titles such as, "Where and how to find useful research" and "Developmental neuroscience" (2016). Add to that journals with names such as *Counselling and Psychotherapy Research: Linking Research with Practice*, or major reviews of research evidence such as Roth and Fonagy's magisterial *What Works for Whom? A Critical Review of Psychotherapy Research* (2005) and it appears as if there is a whole new rapport, a very concordat, between the world of psychoanalysis and the world of the academy.

The idea of a concordat, however, necessarily implies the idea of a previous split. Indeed, the literature on psychoanalysis and psychological research is full of a rhetoric of splitting—of theory and practice, of the researcher and the therapist, of "knowing" *vs.* "treating". This perhaps echoes the idea of a split (and its overcoming) that has been around in academic psychology for a long time: in fact, since 1949. The "Boulder model" or "Colorado model" (Shapiro, 2002) of the "scientist–practitioner" advocated clinical psychologists who would be trained in both spheres, the practical and the theoretical. In recent years, there has been some scepticism about the model, with research seen as having little relevance to practice, but equally there have been calls for the model's renewal (Shapiro, 2002). For Fonagy (2000), there is a deep fault-line between psychology as a natural science and psychoanalysis as a practice of individual insight, which precious few authors can bridge. Smithson and colleagues (2015) highlight some of the tensions generated in making therapists familiar with qualitative research methods. So, what we are presented with is first a split and then the call for it to be bridged or healed. Why? Why should it be healed? Well, partly, we are told (Blomberg et al., 2001; Taylor, 2010), because, in the competitive world of modern therapies, psychoanalysis needs to show it is effective. Even more, though, because the two "sides" apparently have much to learn from each other (Knox, 2013; Olds, 2006). Fonagy claims a closer integration with research-based biological psychology could yield "a great deal of increased sophistication" in psychoanalysis' use of concepts" (2000, p. 8), which, he implies, are rooted in folk-psychology.

A lot of the traffic seems one-way. Academic psychology, mostly, seems to have little interest in psychoanalysis, and the attacks on psychoanalysis typical of the Freud Wars, as a pseudo-science, have not altogether gone away; the Department of Psychoanalysis and Clinical Consulting, at Ghent University, led by the Lacanian psychoanalyst, Paul Verhaeghe, for example, was explicitly attacked as pseudoscientific by other academics in the pages of *De Standaard* in December 2011 (Boudry, 2011). The IPA might be keen on research but something like 70% of its research funding goes on promoting psychoanalysis as a form of treatment (2016) and it is hard to avoid the thought that there is an element of *Torschlusspanik*, that wonderful German word for the "Oh, my God! It might be too late . . ." feeling, about psychoanalysis's sudden interest in the academy and research.

Psycho-social studies

However, there is one highly significant example of the influence going the other way, *from* psychoanalysis *to* research and the academy. That example is psycho-social studies, a branch of academic work and research explicitly proclaiming the influence of psychoanalysis.

Psycho-social studies has been noticeably successful. There is a book series published by Palgrave Macmillan, "Studies in the Psycho-social", there is a national Association for Psychosocial Studies in the UK, and a closely allied body, the Association for the Psychoanalysis of Culture and Society in the USA; there are journals, websites, conferences, and a great deal of excitement about how qualitative research can be transformed by learning from, and drawing on, psychoanalytic method (Hollway & Jefferson, 2013).

In practice, psycho-social studies has proved harder to define than its defenders might like. The website declares that psycho-social studies, as a discipline,

> studies the ways in which psychic experience and social life are fundamentally entangled with each other. Psychological issues and subjective experiences cannot be abstracted from societal, cultural and historical contexts, nor can they be deterministically reduced to the social. Similarly, social and cultural worlds have psychological dimensions and are shaped by psychic processes and intersubjective relations. (APS, 2016)

This extract is unobjectionable but does little to distinguish the real hallmark of this new disciplinary focus, which is the emphasis on new research methods, methods that draw heavily on the psychoanalytic tradition. This focus is perhaps best exemplified in the Clarke and Hoggett collection, *Researching Beneath the Surface* (2009) and the Hollway and Jefferson text, now in its second edition, *Doing Qualitative Research Differently* (2013, first edition 2000). All sorts of new research methods have appeared under the broad umbrella of the: the social dreaming matrix (Manley, 2014), the photo matrix, especially in psycho-social Germany (Sievers, 2006, 2007), biographic-narrative interpretive method (Wengraf, 2013). However, by far the most influential are the free association narrative interview (FANI) and the growing interest in techniques derived from the psychoanalytic tradition of infant observation. Both are strongly associated with the work(s) of Hollway (2015), Hollway and Jefferson (2013), and Urwin (2011).

So, if psychoanalysis is seeking closer links with research and at least some researchers are drawing on psychoanalytic method, what could possibly be the source of my unease? What I want to argue in the rest of this chapter is that the split I have touched on is—in common with all splitting—somewhere misleading and illusory. However welcome the developments I have just sketched might be, and they are, indeed, welcome, I want to assert that psychoanalysis *is* a research method and that attempts to borrow from it, or to supplement it, create tensions that are difficult to manage and easy to overlook.

Free associative research

One starting point for the idea that research can borrow methods from the practice of psychoanalysis is that there is something similar, a resemblance, between the two. The research interviewer listens, the therapist listens; the research interviewer gives a gentle prompt (it is gentle in this tradition, at least), the therapist gives a gentle prompt. For both the aim is discovering or uncovering something. Hollway and Jefferson are explicit about it,

> There are, also, similarities between these fields. For example when Frosh, describing clinical psychoanalysis, writes "in few other places does a person have the opportunity to engage in a largely uninterrupted flow of talk with an attentive listener, whose role it is to try to understand what is being said and to help the speaker make sense of it" (2010: 1), the role of qualitative research interviewers comes to mind. (2013, p. 150)

However, what is more important than the similarities in listening style is the similarity in the way psycho-social studies and psychoanalysis both conceive of the subject: as an "unreliable narrator". An unreliable narrator is not a judgement of the person, but of their narrative. The term was introduced in 1961 by the literary critic, Wayne Booth, to refer to those narrators in fiction who do not have the god's-eye-view omniscience of the "universal" narrator. Shortly after, in 1965, Ricoeur's idea of a "hermeneutics of suspicion" (Ricoeur, 1970), referring specifically to psychoanalysis, also emphasised the idea of an account whose meaning is neither transparent nor necessarily trustworthy. The patient or research subject might lie, or distort, or self-dramatise; they might aggrandise or belittle themselves; they could fantasise or confabulate, or grab for the lowest common denominator of public opinion. Above all, he or she might simply not know the answer to the question or how to put into words experiences that are literally unthinkable. In other words, their talk just cannot be taken at face value. Hollway and Jefferson refer in particular to the "defended subject" (2013, p. 4 and passim), a term that now has acquired a wide currency. The interviewee is someone whose basic anxiety must at all times be taken into account. This does not mean just that they might be anxious in their encounter with the interviewer or the therapist, but, rather, that their defences against their fundamental anxieties in life affect how they construe the world and so, of course, how they answer questions. For Hollway and Jefferson, four features of the defended subject stand out: they might interpret a question through a different meaning frame to that of the interviewer; they might be strongly invested in particular discursive positions to protect vulnerable parts of their selves; they might simply not know why things are experienced by them in certain ways and they might also be powerfully disposed to disguise some feelings and actions (Hollway & Jefferson, 2013, p. 24). In her more recent work, Hollway has added a point which is, to my mind, of huge importance: that the interviewer must somehow listen also to what is *not* said; the things that are emotionally present precisely in the kinds of spaces they leave (2015, p. xi).

One option, when confronted with an unreliable narrator, is to focus on analysing the discourse and simply to bracket off the question of its validity. The psycho-social approach, again like the psycho-analytic tradition, with some notable exceptions (e.g., Phillips, 1994, 2000, and Eagle, 2000), has rejected this option, as the task is to understand the subject through their discourse, rather than the discourse *tout court*. The counter-idea that the subject might be constructed entirely in and through their discourse simply begs the point at issue, the transparency of the accounts people give of themselves (Gabriel, 2015, pp. 38–44; Hollway, 2015, p. 21).

The free associative narrative interview has at its heart, as the name implies, the idea that the interviewee is not interrupted in his or her narrative flow and, further, that the free associations of the researcher are themselves relevant. The free association is, just as in psychoanalytic practice, both "theirs" and "mine". The result is that the narrative given has an emotional logic rather than, or as much as, a cognitive one. And, even more, its particular associative impact on me, the researcher, is of great significance. Both Hollway and Jefferson (2013)

and the various contributors to Clarke and Hoggett (2009) are generous with examples of the way in which they used their subjectivity,
their own emotional and associative responses to their subjects' own
uninterrupted narrative flow, to generate their results. However, there
is a danger, one that is readily apparent. The psychoanalyst Sonny
Davidson was once in supervision with Melanie Klein. Sensitive to his
own subjectivity, he commented to her that a patient had put his confusion into him, the analyst. "'No, dear" said the redoubtable Mrs Klein,
"that's not it, *you* were confused" (Grosskurth, 1986, p. 449).

Klein was herself deeply ambivalent about the use to which the
notions of countertransference and projective identification were put,
even though they arose from her work. The problem that they pose so
acutely, of course, is the difficulty of verifiability. How do we know
that this or that view is the subject's, not mine? How do I know that
my feeling is a clue to the subject's? Does it matter? After all, we are
in dialogue. Well, it does indeed matter if the stated aim of the
research, or of the psychoanalysis, is the understanding of the subject.
There is an inherent epistemic risk, to use Hook's phrase (2008, p. 399),
in making use of free association and our own subjectivity as a
research tool. To be fair, this risk is well known both in psychoanalysis and in psycho-social studies. It is the risk known to Freud as "wild
analysis", the idea that an interpretation would somehow lack the
discipline acquired by the long training psychoanalysis involves.
Hollway and Jefferson are acutely aware of this problem.

Rachel Thomson had referred to the "defended researcher", one
whose own defences against anxiety are at work, and the problem of
"over interpretation" in the 2010 bi-annual British ESRC research
methods festival. The need to find an adequate answer animates the
introduction and afterword to the second edition of Hollway's and
Jefferson's book (2013, pp. x–xi, 145). Their answer is couched mainly
in terms of the importance of triangulation: the second research interview, the discussion with well-informed co-researchers. But these last
might, unfortunately, themselves be well-defended researchers. The
discussion with and among well-informed co-researchers is partly
reminiscent of Balint groups. These were set up in the 1950s as puta-
tively long-term, stable, facilitated groups in which collective reflection would, it was hoped, produce a deeper understanding of doctor–
patient relationships. There are huge advantages to such groups but,
as Kjelmand and Holmström (2010) note, they are open to the same

sorts of group dynamics that can occur in any group, destructive as well as constructive.

Consider two brief examples from my own clinical practice. They are both of the same patient, whom I have anonymised. I gave these same examples to three different groups of students to reflect on, in a free-associative manner, to see whether what they made of it resembled what I had made of it in the actual therapeutic session. One group of students were undergraduates in the social sciences, another comprised postgraduates in psycho-social research methods, and the third group were trainee psychotherapists. All the exercises were conducted in the Spring of 2016 but the clinical examples were taken from several years earlier. All three groups reacted rather differently. The patient was a divorced woman in her thirties, with multiple diagnoses of quite severe illnesses. This is taken from very early in her treatment.

> Tanya comes to her therapy extremely bad-tempered. In the previous week, she says, since I last saw her, her washing machine has broken down, flooding her kitchen with dirty, sudsy water. She is very dependent on her washing machine, as her job requires her to wear a uniform that gets dirty and she washes it regularly. She called in a repairman and he had fixed the machine. However, she thinks it is still not quite right; it might break down again. She feels hugely irritated and bothered by it. What are we to make of this?

The social science undergraduate students focused on the idea of the straw that breaks the camel's back—they spoke of stress, the difficulties facing people with demanding manual jobs. (Incidentally, I had not specified whether or not the job was manual and had not supplied any more information than is here.) The postgraduate students had similar thoughts, except that they also considered the possibility that the repairman might, in some way, represent me. The trainee therapists also made that last point in a big way: I was the repairman; could I "fix" her? For my part, in the session, I had seen things almost wholly transferentially. I do not mean that I doubted whether or not her washing machine had broken; I believed her, but I also thought I was being told, "Can you repair me or will I break down?" In addition, I thought the ideas of dirt and flooding significantly referred to her anxieties about herself. This was the main issue I took up in the session, rather than the transferential material.

I then presented the students with a second example, from the same patient, a couple of weeks or so later in the treatment. There was, again, no more detail than that I am giving here. This time their interpretations diverged much less from each other's, though more from mine.

> It's two or three weeks later and Tanya arrives *very* cheerful. Over the preceding weekend she has had a one-night stand with a man she picked up in a café. She knows nothing about him, including whether or not he is married. She found the sense of riskiness of the whole encounter really exciting. At the end of our session, she is still in very good humour.

This time all three groups of students immediately focused on the idea of risk. The idea that the man was unknown and the sex risky was what they came back to again and again in their conversation. One of the students in the trainees' group speculated about whether or not it might be a form of self-harm. All three groups were surprised when I said that, at the time, I had been inclined to think, as with the previous example, that there was perhaps something here about the analysis itself. She had decided somewhere to take a risk, to "couple" with a "strange" man (me) and had hopes that there would be something exciting and positive about this.

Now, thinking back here to free association and the use of one's own subjectivity as investigative tools, how on earth can any of these interpretations be shown to be "right", if, indeed, any are? They all have merit and, no doubt, other interpretations are possible, too. But here is the problem: how are we to ground any of the interpretations? For instance, my initial interpretation of both scenarios was that they were about her, me, and therapy. But at no point does she mention either me or therapy. How could a discourse or narrative analysis identify these scenarios as being "about" therapy, or "about" our interaction? The actual words give so little anchorage. It is a far cry from the way in which, in qualitative analysis, including psycho-social analysis, themes or topics are identified. If we look at the words in the discourse, they are, moreover, different in each example. If we look at the emotional tone, that, too, differs, from irritation to joy. Incidentally, why did no one notice her joy, her sheer delight in her sexuality? Perhaps because, in our culture, it comes with alarm bells, flashing lights, and health warnings left, right, and centre. The students, even the trainees, could not see past the anxiety inscribed into sex in modernity; defended researchers indeed. Equally, perhaps, I could not see past the mechanics of the beginnings of therapy. I might have directly given her my interpretation; it was very early in the therapy and I confined myself to the remark, in each session, "Perhaps some of the things you're thinking about apply here, too." A few months later, when I made a more overt transference interpretation, I got the wonderful response, "It's not all about you, you know!" A defensive response that nicely pricked my narcissism and reminded me of the difficulty of seeing ourselves, and the therapeutic task, through the patient's eyes. It reminded me also not to rush too hastily to understand or hypothesise. How varied, too, were the associations and responses in the three groups, how quickly panicked by controversial matters (sex). This is perhaps where the impulse comes from to "check" psychoanalytic insight, to use group reflection and consensus, or outcome studies, or discourse analyses in an attempt to "ground" the insights.

Observing, interpreting, checking

One obvious feature of the narrative interview is that it is dependent on speech. Habermas suggested narrative analysis could illustrate how the mechanisms of defence—the defended subject—disclose themselves in the very structures of narration. However, this insight is vitiated by his own recognition of the differences between the life narrative in research and in psychoanalysis. In the research context there is no "fully developed transference", the narrative is isolated from an ongoing dialogic context and abstracted from the non-verbal aspects of communication (Habermas, 2006, pp. 501–502). Increasingly, psycho-social researchers have attempted to get around or behind the deceptiveness of speech, partly by a growing emphasis on embodiment, the physical expression of emotional and mental states. This has been associated with greater emphasis on the visual (Froggett et al., 2015; Sievers, 2006, 2007) and there has been a striking growth in interest in the methodology of infant observation as a psycho-social tool (Urwin, 2011). Rustin, in the key text on infant observation, describes it as a "naturalistic method" (2002, p. 54); its emphasis is on watching, rather than listening, and on careful looking, not on theoretical interpretation. Any recording/noting is not mechanical and includes the emotional impact of the material on observer and observed. It is this emphasis on the sensitive awareness of the emotions of the observer that makes it so valuable. Hollway notes, for instance, that,

> Although the FANI method is usually capable, through free associations, of eliciting the kind of experience-near accounts that afford psychological depth . . . the method necessarily relies on language and elicits a mode of communication that is to a significant extent under conscious control. There is a tendency to reproduce the image of a rational, unitary, language-based subject, a premise on which interview methods were traditionally based. (2015, p. 43)

By contrast, the observation method is more sensitive to affect, more able to see, literally, what is embodied. It takes us closer to the world described by Bion (1962a) in which therapist and patient together echo the way in which the mother assimilates and processes her infant's experience and gives it some sort of voice.

However, the interest in infant observation is not only because it gets us closer to unconscious, embodied emotional states. It is also because the method includes organised reflection, usually in the form of a regularly held seminar. In the reflection, the observer presents the raw data of her observation and the other participants give their own comments in a process that Rustin describes

> as an extension of the process of observation . . . These discussions often lead to the recall and understanding of unnoticed aspects of a situation, whose significance had previously escaped observers, or which has been suppressed from consciousness completely. (2002, p. 67)

This emphasis on the reflective group is precisely the thing that, it is hoped, can both extend and deepen the emotional insight of the researcher and also provide the correlative corrective, the triangulation, that will help regulate or obviate any "wild analysis", any unwarranted or idiosyncratic interpretation. Whether it can do both tasks seems doubtful to me, as each pushes the reflective group in a slightly different direction. A not dissimilar point is made by Kjelmand and Holmström in their reflection on Balint groups, which call, they say, for participants with "psychological stability and an open mind"

(2011, p. 808) and which still run the risk of group dynamics that "are sometimes malicious" (2011, p. 808). Trying to tune in to the emotional resonance is not the same as trying to wonder whether someone has got it quite right. Of course, this double thinking, emotional and analytical, is precisely what is typical of psychoanalysis, but I shall come back to that below.

Rustin states that infant observation is a form of ethnography and, therefore, "observers are unavoidably *participant* observers to a certain degree" (2002, p. 61). This is an extraordinary understatement. To observe is to enter into a relationship and, therefore, at once to be subject to all the vicissitudes of relationality and intersubjectivity that are the homeland of psychoanalysis. There is a lovely episode of the popular television comedy, *Friends* (1996), in which one character, Chandler, awakes to find his new flatmate sitting at his bedside staring at him. When Chandler demands to know what he is doing, he gets the answer, "Watching you sleep." When the seriously freaked-out Chandler objects, he is told, "What about all the other nights when you don't see me?" He, of course, had not known about them—he had been asleep. The comedy of the situation lies precisely in the nature of watching, its potential for perversity. The gaze, especially the unsolicited gaze, cannot be a neutral thing. Indeed, anyone involved in infant observation, a crucial element in most psychoanalytic training, feels the pull of some sort of transference or another. It might be the transference of a version of the medical gaze: perhaps the mother sees the observer as a helpful health official. This is implicitly conceded in Rustin's claim that the observed babies are found "making use of Health Visitors, GPs, neighbourhood acquaintances, or the National Childbirth Trust" (Rustin, 2002, p. 53).

Since observers are usually women, another transference is to sisterhood or to the benign role of grandmother, aunt, or family friend. Should the observer help if the mother is overwhelmed? If she does, she is pulled out of role; if she does not, what role has she entered? For men doing infant observation, there is the added element of voyeuristic awkwardness. Usually only the husband/father is present when the half-dressed mother breastfeeds the baby, changes its nappy, expresses milk. The observer, transferentially then "becomes" the husband or "becomes" a sister/mother/aunt, and so on. All this is without considering the transference proto-thoughts of the baby himself. Consider these extracts from two infant observations of a five-month-old baby boy.

His breathing was slow and quiet, and I watched him, with little really to report for about ten minutes. I was willing him to wake up and gradually his sleep appeared to lighten . . . He woke up suddenly and looked around. He didn't see me immediately, but then he saw me, fixed his gaze on me and smiled. I smiled back and said, "Hello Henry". He smiled again. I left the room and went downstairs . . .

. . . he suddenly woke up: there was no gradual lightening of his sleep as on previous occasions, he was just awake, staring at me and he surprised me. He gave me a big smile. I smiled back and he smiled back again. He suddenly seemed to get very excited and started thrashing his legs around releasing them from the blanket . . . I desperately wanted to talk to him, didn't want to ignore him, so I said quietly "Hello Henry." He smiled and started thrashing his legs about in response . . . I was feeling awkward being with him and not engaging with him.

(I am deeply grateful here to one of my colleagues for her generous permission to use these extracts from her work; I have changed the baby's name to protect the family's confidentiality.)

Why did the observer go downstairs? Partly because Henry, by smiling and provoking a response from her, was drawing her into a relationship, one which felt to her like a transgression of the observer's role. In the first session cited, the observer was later drawn into helping the mother with the detritus of a problematic nappy change and again wondered how far she could transgress "pure" observation. The leader of her observation group commented that her dilemma would not have occurred if she had been observing mother and baby together, the whole point of infant observation, rather than the baby sleeping alone. But, surely, the mother had left the baby sleeping (on the floor in the second example) precisely because the observer was there "to keep an eye on him". My point here is that in the observation, the observer cannot help but be caught up in the transferences and phantasies of both mother and baby and anyone else present. Just as the psychoanalytic session, although structured to be very unlike a normal conversation, generates distinctive patterns of transference and countertransference, so, too, does infant observation. In both cases, these and other emotional aspects of the work are the subject of discussion, in the clinical supervision in one case, the observational seminar in the other, but both are zones of complex interaction.

Psychoanalysis as research

As we have seen, then, the problem for psycho-social research is that its research instruments in fact pose the very difficulties psychoanalysis faces: the inherent subjectivism of emotional sensitivity, the hall-of-mirrors quality of transference, countertransference, and projective identification. Hollway and Jefferson revert to splitting and have sought to reassert the difference between therapy and research, insisting psychoanalytic interpretation's "purpose is largely therapeutic" and that "clinicians interpret into the encounter, whereas researchers will save their interpretations for outside it" (2013, p. 72), and that the aims are different: "the expression of repressed material is not the central aim of the use of free association in research interviewing" (2013, p. 151). In so doing, though, they compound the problem, for it is *precisely in interpreting into the encounter that psychoanalysis finds its verification*, if that is the term.

I am not the first person to insist that psychoanalysis is itself a form of research. It is not an application of knowledge generated and validated elsewhere, it is precisely the instrument for making and validating certain sorts of discovery; notably discoveries about the unconscious mind and its working in experience and relationships. A similar position is taken, say, by Hinshelwood (2013) or Green (2000). The discoveries psychoanalysis makes are, moreover, not only about this or that individual patient, though that is the prime focus. Whatever their merits, the idea of the Oedipus complex, or of affect regulation in maternal reverie, or of the homology between structures of group authority and family structure, all have their origins in psychoanalysis.

The processes used in psycho-social studies to check and validate insights, the triangulation through another's opinion and the use of a reflective group in which provisional hypotheses and insights can be absorbed, reflected on, and discussed emotionally and cognitively, have their counterpart in psychoanalysis. The counterpart is the supervision session and the clinical seminar(s) that are both part of the training and of the ongoing work. No psychoanalyst would want for a minute to downplay their significance. But, and it is a really big "but", they are not where the validation or falsification of psychoanalytic insights lie.

In the case I discussed earlier, Tanya, I did say to her, however tentatively, that she might be talking about her anxieties and hopes

about me and the therapy. In short, I made a transference interpretation "into" the therapy. The result was a significant shift in our working alliance, towards greater trust. On the other hand, with some other
patient and on some other day, the effect might have been resisted, as
she later did with her warning-me-off remark that "It's not all about
you." Precisely these sorts of points were made by Freud as long ago
as 1918 in relation to Sergei Pankejeff, the Wolf-Man. Freud said that
neither confirmation of an interpretation by the patient, nor his or her
disagreement with it, really means that much: it neither confirms nor
refutes. After all, this particular patient, the Wolf-Man, was sunk in an
"obliging apathy" (Freud, 1918b, p. 11) that made him happy to
concur with most of Freud's suggestions. Instead, Freud notes, what
really matters is the effect of the analyst's remark. For instance, one
suggestion of Freud's "had to be dropped. The material of the analysis did not react to it" (1918b, p. 80). By contrast, Freud says, the
suggestion of the reality of his oedipal feelings had real effects in the
patient's life. Freud thinks it is "unjust" (1918b, pp. 89–90) to attribute
thoughts or changes in the patient to suggestion from the analyst's
imagination. In fact, says Freud, it is almost the opposite: "There is no
danger at all in communicating constructions of this kind to the
person under analysis; they never do any damage to the analysis if
they are mistaken" (1918b, p. 19). If the patient agrees with the
analyst's interpretation, that might be evidence only of compliance, if
they disagree, that might be evidence only of resistance. Neither
agreement nor disagreement by the patient attests to the validity of
the interpretation or insight. Freud famously declared that you have
to experience psychoanalysis to be convinced by it (1909b, p. 103), a
point echoed in a different way by Bion when he claimed that when
the unconscious emotional thinking is married to conscious thought
in the consulting room, it "gives to psychoanalytic objects a reality
that is quite unmistakable, even though their very existence has been
disputed" (Bion, 1962b, p. 310).

In short, Freud and Bion were saying that when a comment by the
analyst aligns with the patient's unconscious, there is an effect, and
there is not when there is no such alignment. We could look at this by
saying Freud had a pragmatic theory of truth, as opposed to a corre-
spondence one. But that seems to me to take us into unnecessarily
murky philosophical waters. The dilemma facing the psycho-social
researcher is what Zahavi called the "egocentric predicament" (2014,

p. 110), that is to say, the possibility that what I think of as the "other" person is no more than my projections, or a simulacrum of my own thoughts and feelings. Against this, we can suggest, in both psycho-social research and in psychoanalysis, that there is a primacy to the face-to-face being with someone. Experiencing them is not the same as imagining them or thinking of them. What we do in this face-to-face moment is to grasp the other with some sort of immediacy. In my example from my colleague above, when the little baby Henry smiles at her and she smiles back, something has been grasped and under-stood by them both. But to describe this as "observation" or "associa-tion", or as anything cognitive, is misleading. It is more direct than that. In the Germanic tradition it was called *Einfühlung*, usually trans-lated as empathy. It is not necessarily *sympathy*, fellow feeling, it is a "distinct form of other-directed intentionality, which allows the other's experiences to disclose themselves as other rather than as our own" (Zahavi, 2014, p. 151). The phenomenological tradition I am drawing on here recognises that there are limits to this. The experi-ence grasped might, perhaps, have to be supplemented with theoret-ical or contextual, social, political, or cultural knowledge (Zahavi, 2014, p. 168). More importantly, it has to be construed, worked over, wrestled with. This is what I meant earlier; psychoanalysis must both grasp emotionally and wonder if it has got things right, cognitively. But that is what takes time, a lot of time.

There is now a substantial literature on validity in qualitative research: see, for instance, Yardley (2007) or Shenton (2004). What they have in common with psycho-social research is the fact that the rela-tionship between researcher and research subject is invariably time-limited in a way that is far less true for psychoanalysis, where the insight can be proved (in the original sense) in the relationship itself. It takes conversation with the other, takes rupture and repair, and takes many of the other vicissitudes of relating. All these are available in ongoing, open-ended psychoanalysis but not in psycho-social research. Zahavi, thinking of a different problem, says that, "The deci-sive question is . . . to understand the link between early forms of perceptually grounded empathy and more sophisticated forms of interpersonal understanding" (2014, p. 187). Psychoanalysis does exactly this, in a double sense of "early". It links early, often prever-bal, childhood experience to the adult's construal of his world. It also links the forms of grounded understanding that come early in the therapy to the later, more complex and intersubjective, forms of understanding. To this extent, psychoanalysis is best seen not as an attempt to cure or treat, but as an attempt to know. Hollway (2015, pp. 69, 101) grasps this in her distinction, drawn from Bion, between knowing "of" and knowing "about". Knowing "of" is mutative—it transforms the knower. As Hinshelwood puts it, "Knowing something is the beginning and the end. New knowledge is an added element to the state of mind, and rearranges everything else" (2013, p. 1). Psycho-analysis, like research, is an act of discovering new knowledge and it is the new knowledge that engenders change in the patient and, often, the therapist, too. That knowledge and that change, however, arise from and in a face-to-face encounter that is ongoing, corrigible, and mutually defeasible.

The ethics of practice

What follows, I think, is that we can see psychoanalysis as a habitus, in Bourdieu's sense of a system "of durable, transposable disposi-tions" (1977, p. 72). There is a distinctive setting, the consulting room, a distinctive set of boundaries of time and behaviour, and a distinctive set of habits and practices, which are learnt by the analyst in his or her training and learnt and (re)negotiated by therapist and patient in the treatment. It is within this frame that the "knowing" is mutually generated and receives its confirmation in an ongoing process of change and development. This habitus is an ethical practice. It is ethi-cal in the simple, though important, sense that there is a code of proper conduct the therapist must follow, a system of supervision and a procedure for complaint in place in most, if not all, psychoanalytic associations. Equally importantly, it is ethical in the broader sense of an ongoing relationship in which the participants reflect on their changing relationship, habits, and feelings. The frame of the habitus is what holds this relationship and what limits the possibility of wild analysis and distorted understandings.

What, then, takes the place of this habitus when we are talking of the use of psychoanalytic ideas in research? As we have seen, this is the role taken by the reflective group for some psycho-social resear-chers. My own examples above were necessarily small scale, to illus-trate the variability in response that there can be to material extracted from the context in which it was generated. Both Wendy Hollway and the child psychotherapist Anna Fleming have stressed the importance of the stability of the reflective group and the regular repetition of its reflection on the materials (personal communications). However, this does not alter the fact that where there are groups, there are group dynamics. In fact, we can see this as an ethical practice, too, in that broader sense in which the researchers" relationships to each other, and to the subject matter of their material, change and develop as a consequence of the process of reflection. This takes us back to the question of the "split" mentioned in the introduction. Therapeutic practice and research have been seen as having a different focus, something like "treatment" *vs.* "enquiry". The implication of the reflections here is that this differentiation is hard to sustain when psycho-social research draws heavily on psychoanalytic method. Both are forms of enquiry, both are struggling for understanding, but, in the case of psychoanalysis, there is a recognition that that can be, perhaps will be, mutative—the participants will change. In the case of psycho-social research, the question arises of what changes might come about for research subjects and for researchers and whether those have yet been adequately thought through as an ethical practice.

Conclusion

In this chapter, I have argued that the recent interest in psychoanaly-sis and research too readily accepts the idea that psychoanalysis is something applied, a practitioner's field, and downplays (with some worthy exceptions such as Green or Hinshelwood) the fact that psychoanalysis is, in and of itself, a form of research, an instrument or methodology for the investigation of the unconscious mind and its ramifications. I have further been especially interested in psycho-social research as it explicitly borrows from psychoanalysis, respects it, and is interested in it. I believe psycho-social research is probably the most interesting research into human affairs currently going on in the UK, the USA, and Germany for just that reason; its output is excit-ing and fascinating. Yet, at the same time, there is a tension between psycho-social research and psychoanalysis located just exactly in that ever troublesome area, the epistemological query, "How do you know?" more traditionally put as a question about verification or falsification. For psychoanalysis, I have argued, the answer lies in a pragmatic area: the ongoing relationship between therapist and patient and their mutual and mutable efforts to understand. For a positivist, that would never be enough, but positivism long since turned from raging lion to toothless moggy. Nevertheless, psychosocial research, and other forms of psychological enquiry in the relevant areas, seem to me to have worse responses to this question than does psychoanalysis. That is the tension that gave rise to my unease.

This is not meant to underestimate either the difficulties in using psychoanalysis as research or the benefits inherent in the research–practice dialogue. One way to read Gabbard's (2000) now well-known article on preserving clients' confidentiality in publication is less as a "how-to" guide and more of a reflection on the tension between research and therapeutic aims. A patient who knows her therapist might publish about her is liable to be hugely affected in how she speaks and relates to her researcher–therapist. On the other hand, reflection by researchers on the nature of their confusion in the face of their material can be helped, and perhaps clarified, by a reflection on the history of the concept of countertransference in psychoanalysis.

So, what implications might all this have for psycho-social research, or for the relationship between psychoanalysis and academic research more generally? Perhaps not that much; I am trying to illustrate a tension, no more than that. Psycho-social studies and psychosocial research are hugely positive developments from the standpoint of anyone psychoanalytically minded. Equally, it is true that psychoanalysis needs to keep in touch with developments elsewhere. As I said at the outset, who is against dialogue? One way to look at these tensions benignly might be to say that we have different perspectives, different points of view, and what is needed is a synthesis of perspectives. After all, a hammer cannot cut wood and a saw will not drive a nail: what can be done by one form of research cannot be done by another and the different forms of knowing need to be put together.

However, I am unhappy with the way the "scientist–practitioner" model takes it for granted that psychoanalytic psychotherapy is a form of practice, of applying knowledge or insight discovered or "validated" elsewhere, when it is always a form of research, of uncovering something. Bluntly and crudely, psychoanalysis is the way that we discover what experience of the world this person and that person have, what form their suffering in the world takes, and how it is to be construed. It takes two to do it, as it is a difficult and commonly painful picking through the dense and distorting myriad experiences and mutual interpretations that is the stuff of any relationship. By the same token, all forms of enquiry—perhaps I should say all other forms of enquiry—are also relationships. To observe someone, to interview someone, to talk to someone, to record someone, to video someone, to set him a task such as taking a photo or being in a role-play, to get him to fill in a questionnaire, all the burgeoning stuff of modern qualitative methods, is establish a relationship with him. And establishing a relationship with him is exactly to get into the transference, countertransference, projection, mutual attunement, rupture, and repair that is the subject matter of psychoanalysis.

Psychoanalysis is painfully aware of the problems of wild analysis; equally painfully aware, too, of the problem of analysis terminable and interminable. Psychoanalysis is slow, it is lengthy and the relationship often fails or breaks down. Freud's first published case history was, after all, a report of a failure. It is in that slow maturing of the relationship and the difficult reflection on its successful moments and its failures that psychoanalysis finds its validation. That is not easily exported.

References

Association for Psychosocial Studies (2016). www.psychosocial-studies-association.org/about/ (accessed 17 April 2016).

Bion, W. (1962a). *Learning from Experience.* London: Karnac.

Bion, W. (1962b). The psycho-analytic study of thinking. *International Journal of Psychoanalysis, 43*: 306–310.

Blomberg, J., Lazar, A., & Sandell, R. (2001). Long term outcome of long term psychoanalytically oriented therapies: first findings of the Stockholm outcome of psychotherapy and psychoanalysis study. *Psychotherapy Research, 11*: 361–382.

Booth, W. (1961). *The Rhetoric of Fiction.* Chicago, IL: University of Chicago Press.

Boudry, M. (2011). Pseudo-wetenschap aan de universiteit. http://skepp.be/nl/psychologie-coaching/psychoanalyse/pseudo-wetenschap-aan-de-universiteit (accessed 22 July 2017).

British Psychoanalytic Council (2016). www.bpc.org.uk/ (accessed 16 April 2016).

Bourdieu, P. (1977). *Outline of a Theory of Practice.* Cambridge: Cambridge University Press.

Clarke, S., & Hoggett (Eds.) (2009). *Researching Beneath the Surface: Psycho-Social Methods in Practice.* London: Karnac.

Eagle, N. (2000). A critique of the postmodern turn in psychoanalysis: recent work of Mitchell and Renik. Paper presented on the 10th June 2000 to the Annual Meeting of the Rapaport–Klein Study Group: www.psychomedia.it/rapaport-klein/june2000.htm (accessed 17 April 2014).

Fonagy, J. (2000). Grasping the nettle: or, why psychoanalytic research is such an irritant. Paper presented to the Annual Research Lecture of the British Psychoanalytic Society, 1 March. http://psychoanalysis.org.uk/ sitres/default/files/documents/pages/fonagy_grasping_the_nettle.pdf (accessed 17 July 2017).

Freud, S. (1909b). *Analysis of a Phobia in a Five-Year-Old Boy. S. E., 10:* 5–149. London: Hogarth.

Freud, S. (1918b). *From the History of an Infantile Neurosis. S. E., 17:* 7–121. London: Hogarth Press.

Friends (1996). Season 2, episode 19 (43 overall). Entitled, "The one where Eddie won't go". First aired in the USA, 28th March 1996, production code 457319.

Froggett, L., Manley, J., & Roy, A. (2015). The Visual Matrix Method: imagery and affect in a group-based research setting. *Forum Qualitative Sozialforschung/Forum: Qualitative Social Research,* http://ww1.qualitative research.net/ (accessed 17th April 2016).

Frosh, S. (2010). *Psychoanalysis Outside the Clinic: Interventions in Psychosocial Studies.* London: Palgrave Macmillan.

Gabbard, G. (2000). Disguise or consent? Problems and recommendations concerning the publication and presentation of clinical material. *International Journal of Psychoanalysis, 81:* 1011–1086.

Gabriel, M. (2015). *Why the World Does Not Exist.* Cambridge: Polity Press.

Green, A. (2000). What kind of research for psychoanalysis? In: J. Sandler, A.-M. Sandler, & R. Davies (Eds.), *Critical and Observational Psychoanalytic Research: André Green and Daniel Stern* (pp. 21–26). London: Karnac.

Grosskurth, P. (1989). *Melanie Klein.* London: Karnac.

Habermas, T. (2006). Who speaks? Who looks? Who feels? Point of view in autobiographical narratives. *International Journal of Psychoanalysis, 87:* 497–518.

Hinshelwood, R. (2013). *Research on the Couch: Single-case Studies, Subjectivity and Psychoanalytic Knowledge.* Hove: Routledge.

Hollway, W. (2015). *Knowing Mothers: Researching Maternal Identity Change.* Basingstoke: Palgrave Macmillan.

Hollway, W., & Jefferson, T. (2013). *Doing Qualitative Research Differently: A Psychosocial Approach.* London: Sage.

Hook, D. (2008). Articulating psychoanalysis and psychosocial studies: limitations and possibilities. *Psychoanalysis, Culture and Society, 13:* 397–405.

International Psychoanalytic Association (2016). http://www.ipa.world/ (accessed 30 March 2016).

Kjelmand, D., & Holmström, I. (2010). Difficulties in Balint groups: a qualitative study of leaders' experiences. *British Journal of General Practice, 60:* 808–814.

Knox, J. (2013). The analytic institute as a psychic retreat: why we need to include research evidence in our clinical training. *British Journal of Psychotherapy, 29:* 424–448.

Manley, J. (2014). Gordon Lawrence's social dreaming matrix: background, origins, history and developments. *Organisational and Social Dynamics, 14:* 322–341.

Olds, D. (2006). Interdisciplinary studies and our practice. *Journal of the American Psychoanalytic Association, 54:* 857–876.

Phillips, A. (1994). *On Flirtation.* London: Faber and Faber.

Phillips, A. (2000). *Promises, Promises: Essays on Literature and Psychoanalysis.* London: Faber and Faber.

Ricoeur, P. (1970). *Freud and Philosophy: An Essay in Interpretation.* New Haven, CT: Yale University Press. First published in French as: *De l'interprétation. Essai sur Sigmund Freud.* Paris: Editions du Seuil, 1965.

Roth, A., & Fonagy, P. (Eds.) (2005). *What Works for Whom? A Critical Review of Psychotherapy Research* (2nd edn). New York: Guilford Press.

Rustin, M. (2002). Observing infants: reflections on methods. In: L. Miller, M. Rustin, M. J. Rustin, & J. Shuttleworth (Eds.), *Closely Observed Infants* (pp. 52–75). London: Duckworth.

Shakespeare, W. (1930). *The Complete Works of Shakespeare*, W. J. Craig (Ed.). London: Oxford University Press, Humphrey Milford.

Shapiro, D. S. (2002). Renewing the scientist–practitioner model. *The Psychologist, 15:* 232–234.

Shenton, A. (2004). Strategies for ensuring trustworthiness in qualitative research projects. *Education for Information, 22:* 63–75.

Sievers, B. (2006). Vielleicht haben Bilder den Auftrag, einen in Kontakt mit dem Unheimlichen zu bringen – Die Soziale Photo-Matrix als ein Zugang zum Unbewussten in Organisationen. *Freie Assoziation, 9:* 7–28.

Sievers, B. (2007). Pictures from below the surface of the university: the social photo-matrix as a method for understanding organizations in depth. In: M. Reynolds & R. Vince (Eds.), *Handbook of Experiential Learning and Management Education* (pp. 241–257). Oxford: Oxford University Press.

Smithson, J., Holmes, J., & Gilles, F. (2015). Integration, assimilation or transformation. Introducing therapists to qualitative research methods. A focus group study. *European Journal of Psychotherapy and Counselling,* 17: 296–313.

Taylor, D. (2010). Psychoanalytic approaches and outcome research: negative capability or irritable reaching after fact and reason? *Psychoanalytic Psychotherapy,* 24: 398–416.

Urwin, C. (2011). Infant observation meets social science. *International Journal of Infant Observation and its Applications,* 14: 341–344.

Wengraf, T. (2013). Critical realism and psycho-societal method: researching variable agency by using BNIM (available from tom@tomwengraf. com or via APS, 2016).

Yardley, L. (2007). Demonstrating validity in qualitative psychology. In: J. Smith (Ed.), *Qualitative Psychology: A Practical Guide to Research Methods* (pp. 235–251). London: Sage.

Zahavi, D. (2014). *Self and Other: Exploring Subjectivity, Empathy and Shame.* Oxford: Oxford University Press.

CHAPTER TWO

The researcher's subjectivity as a research instrument: from intuition to surrender

Lita Crociani-Windland

Introduction

The aim of this chapter is to introduce different frameworks from philosophy and psychoanalysis by which to approach an understanding of the role of subjective experience in psycho-social research and to link these frameworks so as to develop a sense of how the relation of researcher and research might be understood and developed according to these models. In other words, it is about ways of knowing that include the researcher's subjectivity as a necessary element in the research encounter.

As Frosh (2003, p. 1564) pointed out "the idea of the psycho-social subject as a meeting point of inner and outer forces, something constructed yet also constructing, a power-using subject that is also subject to power, is a difficult subject to theorise . . ." and therefore also to research. In addition, the psycho-social subject has an unconscious dimension and is not just a rational agent, which, by necessity, complicates the picture even further. Yet, if, as psycho-social researchers, we are to seriously engage with this ontological standpoint, we must engage with the complexity this entails, particularly in relation to research encounters. Here, we are confronted with ourselves and others as such subjects and this is where our subjectivity and reflexivity, as the attention given to it, is a crucial aspect of psycho-social research.

What I aim to demonstrate and offer, in this chapter, is a way of unpacking and grounding the idea of the psycho-social subject by giving a sense of the development of different frameworks and to arrive at an ontological understanding by which the psycho-social subject can be understood as constituted by encounters between internal and external milieus over time, both partaking of different modalities and processes by which they combine and express themselves in actual life. This chapter is, therefore, concerned with how we can understand in more detail what might be meant by subjectivity, what underlies it in theoretical and epistemological terms, and what its uses and principles for practice might be, starting with Bergson and Bion, then moving through psychoanalysis to changing notions of transference and countertransference to a relational perspective. The reason to start from here is, briefly and very selectively, to track a trajectory of some relevant development of ideas from the nineteenth to the twenty-first centuries.

Ontological duality and psycho-social studies: qualitative and quantitative aspects of reality

Henri Bergson (1859–1941) is known as a process philosopher, whose work has had a profound influence on Gilles Deleuze (1925–1995). Both these philosophers have an embodied, process-focused ontology. While they do not put nature and nurture in opposition, there is, none the less, a dualism in their way of thinking about reality. The focus is on different ways by which reality is constituted. Having trained as a mathematician, Bergson cannot be accused of being inimical to numbers, yet his interest in consciousness led him to argue that the nature of reality cannot be reduced to them. In *Time and Free Will* (1913), he makes the point that, to put it rather simply, intuition is deeper than intellect, and that there is a real difference between deep-seated psychic states and that which can be measured. I will return to his ideas later, but one of the key issues that comes from his (and Deleuze's) work and that frames this chapter is their interest in the differences between quality and quantity, and their focus on the qualitative, non-verbal, and fluid foundational aspects of reality.

While Bergson's interest in *Time and Free Will*, originally written as his doctoral thesis, was on consciousness and free will, what he and Deleuze offer is a different way of thinking about the unconscious, not as something just belonging to individual subjects or necessarily as the outcome of repression, but as an ontological basis for all of reality alongside those aspects that can be more easily observable and quantifiable. The term "virtual" is used by both Bergson and Deleuze to denote those aspects that are hard to quantify, or even qualify, except by a selective process that always leaves a remainder, though "duration" is the term first used by Bergson in his work on the nature of time and is the one to which I will restrict myself for present purposes.

In Bergson, the different foundational aspects of reality are viewed in terms of quality and quantity, as a way of distinguishing and characterising them in the early part of his work. In his last book (1935), they are identified in terms of static and dynamic processes working at social as well as individual levels. He gives the examples of laws and mysticism as, respectively, static and dynamic aspects of morality.

Bergson and Deleuze are seen as difficult thinkers, with a tendency to shift their terms and be imprecise in their definitions. This, in my view, has two main causes: it reflects developments in their thinking, but even more important is the fact that these shifts mirror the shifting quality, the lability of their object of study, which, in fact, is not an object at all, but the sum of the forces, tensions, and processes that underlie their effects and can merely be more easily quantified, qualified, and observed. I mention this at this juncture because I wish to follow their example and, rather than seek fixed definitions, try to evoke and characterise what I am attempting to set out, approaching it from different directions in an effort to point at topological (dis)guises or contextually determined depictions of similar dynamics. "Topology is the science of self-varying deformation" (Massumi, 2002, p. 134). What is beneath the surface, in other words, has many guises and is never exhausted by one definition, description, qualification, or characterisation. This logic allows me to think that the different theoretical understandings I am going to bring to bear are different facets of how we might characterise some principal aspects of getting to beneath the surface aspects of reality. To quote Eigen once more, (1999, p. 24): "My interest is not in "reconciling" (reducing?) so much as seeing ways they help set each other in motion". In what follows, I shall, therefore, first of all place some of Bergson and Bion's ideas side by side and relate them to each other, bringing out aspects fundamental to an appreciation of the need for researchers to engage with the unquantifiable, qualitative, and beneath the surface aspects and the criteria that might be a basis for doing so, all fundamentally requiring reflexive capacities and particular rules of method. This could be understood as a way of holding a "binocular vision" (Bion, 1961), which, in turn, is a fundamental basis for psycho-social studies with its Janus quality of looking both ways: towards both the psychic and the social, to understand their dynamic interactions.

Bergson's intuition as a method: Bion's "K" and "O", reflexivity, and research

> Coming to know means "to place oneself in a conditional relation to something"; to feel oneself conditioned by something and oneself to condition it—it is therefore under all circumstances establishing, denoting and making conscious of conditions . . . (Nietzsche, *Will to Power*, p. 555, cited in Abou-Rihan, 2008, p. 7)

The extract above tells us that consciousness and reflexivity are never separate from an external trigger. In other words, we are psycho-socially conscious, taking the social in an expansive sense to mean all the external conditions of our existence. The affective impact that external stimuli can have is, however, not something that can be unproblematically qualified and named. That requires a process of selection and discernment, which is culturally mediated and determined, rather than simply an effect of the external stimuli on the internal individual milieu. To put it another way, we can learn to distinguish pleasant and unpleasant, we have to be taught and/or learn by experience to think of some things as good or bad, but, as we all know, this is subject to cultural variation and can vary not just across different geographical cultural locations, but even in relation to group or class membership and organisational dynamics. What is given to us to begin with is simply a bodily capacity to affect and be affected; what we make of that, its qualifications, is open to interpretation. This is context-dependent and such context has to be factored in, not only in terms of its social conditioning and how it came to be so, but also in terms of our own individual response to it.

How things came to be so is about time. Time is a fundamental aspect of reality in its own right and partakes of the essential duality of Bergson's (1913) ontology: clock time is, in his view, a practical quantification and spatialisation of a more profound qualitative aspect of time, which he calls "duration". "Pure duration is the form which the succession of our conscious states assumes when our ego lets itself live, when it refrains from separating its present state from its former states" (Bergson, 1913, p. 100). Without delving too far into the philo-sophical complexity of "duration", let me translate this for present purposes as that aspect of time that makes present what I will call the "affective genealogy" of our subjectivity, but without dulling that affect by putting it in a sequence of separate states or events. What I mean by this is the origin of our consciousness, the way we have been formed by affective experience and responded to it, the necessarily uneven and, most of all, intense affective circumstances of our devel-opment, or, in Bergson's view of the world, the qualitative intense, rather than extended, homogenous and spatialised aspect of time. The difference is one of kind. The artificial evenness and practicality of clock time is obvious; it is a human social convention, which we are barely aware of most of the time, yet dissolves in the affectively intense moments when time seems to stop. The commonly reported slowing of time perception in very intense situations might be a per-ception of duration itself. The time disordering effects of trauma could be linked to us being thrown into an experience of duration by its intensity. The way psychoanalysis and other psycho-social method-ologies, such as social dreaming or visual matrices, invite one to relive, to make present, rather than just remember, affectively intense experiences is, in my view, about accessing that qualitative aspect of time, duration itself, in order for us to be able to reframe it with the help of a different significant other than the one/s involved the first time. Yet, here I am giving somewhat negative instances, whereas Bergson (1913) is far more positive in this and some of the emotions he deals with in *Time and Free Will* are of joy and aesthetic experience. For the purpose of accessing pure duration, our conscious state

need not be entirely absorbed in the passing sensation or idea: for then
... it would no longer endure. Nor need it forget its former states: it
is enough that, in recalling these states, it does not set them alongside
its actual state as one point alongside another, but forms both the past
and the present states into an organic whole, as happens when we
recall the notes of a tune melting so to speak, into one another.
(Bergson, 1913, p. 100, also cited in Crociani-Windland, 2009)

This last statement, in my view, speaks of a coming together of past
and present that resonates with what will be dealt with later in more
detail: thirdness.

Bion also distinguished a duality, or difference in kind in relation
to learning and knowledge. He posited a difference between the two,
which he indicated as "K" for knowledge and "O" for not knowing,
and, as French and Simpson (2000) have posited, learning occurs by
holding the two in tension. "O" stands for the ineffable, that which is
immanent, in a similar way to duration and quality (and the virtual,
as a development of the concept of duration) in Bergson's (and
Deleuze's) philosophy. "O" stands for the reality of the moment, its
truth. This is not an absolute truth: it is contingent. I have gone into
more detail about Bergson and Bion in the first volume of *Researching
Beneath the Surface* (Crociani-Windland, 2009), and will not expand on
this comparison here. Suffice to say that these dualities seem to me to
be attempting to characterise something profound and remarkably
similar in processes of learning and, therefore, also in research.

Bion (1970) advocated the withholding of memory and desire.
As a trained analyst, he would have wanted to know his patient's
biographical history, yet this was not his main focus. It seems to me,
to use my earlier formulation, his interest could be expressed as
being in the "affective genealogy" of his patients. His innovation in
how he conceived of accessing this is often referred to using the term
"negative capability", borrowed from Keats, and what he called
"faith" in "O". Faith in "O", according to Eigen (1999) is a faith in the
body and introspection. It seems to me that intuition could be seen as
a commonly used term that approaches some of these issues. This is,
in fact, the word Bergson used as key to his method for philosophy,
which presupposes duration and that I will return to shortly.

In Bergson's and Bion's binocular way of seeing things, it is
necessary to acknowledge the role of introspection in how we have
come to know, and how we can continue to learn about, the world.

Introspection is a part of what it means to use one's subjectivity in order to come to know; it is in the tension between "K" and "O" described by Bion and in the capacity to distinguish between differences in kind in Bergson. Yet, introspection needs to be practised, sharpened, and trained. Noticing and having faith in one's bodily responses is a part of that. This requires trust in our capacity to be affected (and to affect). Our bodies responding faster than we can register in any consciously precise way is a feature of this kind of intuition, itself deeply connected to our unconscious participation in duration or, to link all of the above, to the affective genealogy of the present moment, in other words, "O", the qualitative, immanent aspect of the necessarily psycho-social reality we try to learn about.

What Bergson offered was a way to approach intuition methodically that, in my view, goes beyond Bion's. Bergson's idea of intuition as a method is based is on three main rules: the attention to the positing of problems; the rediscovery of true differences in kind between quality and quantity; the framing of problems in terms of time, rather than space (Deleuze, 1991, chapter 1). For both Bergson and Deleuze, the nature of reality itself is problematic. This is not a negative view; both are known as vitalists, and the term "problem", in Bergson's view, is more a positive concept than a need. For example, a baby has a problem in that food (or other conditions to sustain health) is required that she cannot yet procure autonomously. She solves it by devising a particular sign of distress that tunes into a mother's affective response that prompts her to feed the baby. This gives a more positive perspective than portraying the baby as needy and demanding. Crying, in this perspective, is a way of life preserving itself, of solving a problem. This can be seen in itself as an example of a reframing of the problem of a crying baby. The solution is there already: the baby wants to live and be well, for this, the first solution that will address that problem is food, though it could be other sources of affective discomfort or any condition not sustaining of life and health. At a very simple level, thinking through time might tell us it has been a while since she was fed, but, given a particularly insistent baby, we might have learnt from experience that feeding and comfort have become a "composite" of material, quantitative (no food) and psychological aspects, and so offering one solution (food) might alleviate the other problems. On the other hand, crying might stop in the repeated absence of a solution being achieved, as in the case of neglect.

This way of approaching learning, which, in my view, is synonymous with research, means asking questions such as these: what was the problem to which this problem itself might have been seen as a (necessarily partial) solution? How is this problem constituted, in both conscious and unconscious ways? How did it come to be such? How do I use my own affective response in tension with my conscious knowledge and experience; in other words, my intuition or faith in "O" in conjunction with more cognitive analytical knowledge and capacities, in order to learn about it?

As already stated, the ontological duality outlined by Bergson is important as it opposes a split between mind and body. It is an embodied view that puts affective and qualitative dimensions at the centre of enquiry, while acknowledging their tensions in co-existence with more finite quantitative and material aspects of life; in reality, these aspects are always together, they are always mixed. Bion's distinction between "K" and "O" can be understood in similar terms of being different in kind. The body and consciousness, taken in their broadest sense, also partake of an important duality in that differences started to be recognised within the neurosciences in the workings of right and left brain (McGilchrist, 2009; Schore, 2003; Sperry, 1968). Our analytical and attunement capacities have been seen as a fundamental duality founded in our bodily constitution and more recent neuroscientific work points out the relationality and complexity of brain hemispheres. This, as I hope will become apparent, only strengthens the points that I am leading us towards. It will become clearer how this has been worked with in later sections dealing with Jessica Benjamin's work and relational approaches. The next step, therefore, is to go from duality to thirdness by way of a brief mapping of different notions of transference and countertransference.

It might be useful at this point to summarise the main points so far: what Bergson's, Bion's, or neuroscientific notions have in common is the acknowledgement of aspects of reality which require special conditions in order to be related to and researched. The researcher's subjectivity and introspectively derived material is vital to this. In general, these special conditions have to do with a particular attitude the researcher has to be willing and able to adopt, and some rules that feature the attention to the positing of questions and to time in its aspect of duration, not just in its usual spatialised, sequential aspect, as outlined earlier. Techniques from psychoanalysis lend themselves to this kind of enquiry. I will enter into this more fully later by examining Benjamin's notions of thirdness, itself similar to, and founded on, Winnicott's notion of "transitional space", and her ideas on "one, third and surrender". Suffice to say for now that both the psychoanalytic and philosophical perspectives of Bergson and, later, Deleuze make it imperative to enquire into what could be termed as either unconscious or preconscious aspects of reality.

Moving from duality to thirdness:
a brief history of transference and countertransference

This section offers a brief overview of how notions of transference and countertransference have transformed as they shift over time, from Freud's original formulation to later understandings, which allows us to move to a notion of thirdness and intersubjectivity. Let me begin with some very basic definitions of the terms: transference denotes the client's imaginings of the therapist influenced by their past, whereas countertransference denotes the therapist's reactions to the patient. Transferential processes have gone on to be seen as so central to psychoanalysis as to lead to the coining and widespread use of the catchphrase "transference: the total situation" (Joseph, 1985). They are also seen as central to psycho-social research (Hollway & Jefferson, 2000). In broad terms (Hinshelwood, 1999), and in spite of deeper analysis qualifying this and showing the pre-Heimann understanding to be more complex than the following outlines (Holmes, 2014), the shifts in understanding and operationalising these concepts can be summarised in terms of three basic models.

Model 1, Freud: the patient imagines, the analyst must be objective. Freud thought transference phenomena were ubiquitous and not unique to therapy, that transference could be a useful tool to understand the unconscious, and that this was, in fact, how the unconscious broke out. For him, however, countertransference was a hindrance, blocking the transference relation, and resulting from a lack of self-awareness, and/or insufficient analysis.

Model 2, Heimann and the Independents: both patient and analyst have feelings that are useful in accessing the unconscious. This reworking emerged after Freud's death, during and after the Second World War. It arose from the so-called "Controversial Discussions" (Klein's object relations theory *vs.* Anna Freud's classic Freudian instinct/drive based model). Although Klein held to the classic Freudian ideas on transference and countertransference, there were already germs of the new model in object relations theory. Klein's concept of projective identification created a bridge from seeing transference as a block to seeing it as an intelligible response. It was the so-called Independents (Fairbairn, Winnicott, Bowlby on and off) and, particularly, Heimann (1950), however, who redefined countertransference as a more positive, complex, and rich response to the patient's transference. In Heimann's own words:

> the analyst's emotional response to his patient within the analytic situation represents one of the most important tools for his work. The analyst's counter-transference is an instrument of research into the patient's unconscious. The analytic situation has been investigated and described from many angles, and there is general agreement about its unique character. But my impression is that it has not been sufficiently stressed that it is a relationship between two persons. . . . The aim of the analyst's own analysis, from this point of view, is *not to turn him into a mechanical brain which can produce interpretations on the basis of a purely intellectual procedure, but to enable him, to sustain the feelings which are stirred in him* . . . Our basic assumption is that the analyst's unconscious understands that of his patient. This rapport on the deep level comes to the surface in the form of feelings which the analyst notices in response to his patient, in his "counter-transference". *This is the most dynamic way in which his patient's voice reaches him.* (Heimann, 1950, pp. 81–82, my italics)

Her use of the words "dynamic way" seems wonderfully apt in relation to my earlier sections on Bergson. The movement here could be characterised as going towards a relational and dynamic understanding and away from advocating the division of roles (in Model 1) where the patient's unconscious communicates in a dynamic way that can be inferred via the transference, and the therapist is relegated to, as Heimann put it, "a mechanical brain", or, in Bergson's terms, a quantitative or static process using only objective analytic functions.

While Heimann's position already highlights the importance of relationship, Winnicott took this further. Winnicott's ideas were already prefiguring the relational turn (Clarke et al., 2008) by positing both the importance of the mother–infant relationship and an intermediate space, a third space that is created by the relationship.

His idea of transitional or potential space (Winnicott, 1971, pp. 98–101) as an intermediate space between the individual and the environment and between inner and outer reality, where there is infinite variability of phenomena, took this into a more social dimension which also included non-human elements. This space was, in his view, where both creative play and cultural experience are located, a place of maximally intense experience of a non-orgiastic kind. This seems to me not only a move away from the drives and libido orientated Freudian formulations to object seeking and object relating, but is one which is also akin to the notion of intensity, which, in turn, applies to a more Bergsonian understanding of affect as both a deeper and more fundamental level of our existence.

Model 3: the relationship as key to the therapeutic encounter, creating a joint third space. While Winnicott prefigures a relational turn in the UK, which did not have much followership, this approach was developed in the USA, and came from ego psychology's emphasis on ego, rather than id. The Freudian notion of "Where Id was, Ego shall be" was played very fully into a more social and political direction. Relationship was key. In White's own words (Jelliffe Papers, 5 November 1919, cited in Schwartz, 1999, p. 166),

> . . . the smallest society conceivable would be composed of two individuals, but there is another element that enters that is of great importance and that is the relationship between the two individuals, and that relationship is a higher state than either one of the individuals alone and contains possibilities which are not resident in either one.

Within this perspective, transference and countertransference are dynamic elements of communication which allow modulation and negotiation of relationship, based on intersubjectivity, within a third space. This brings us to the final part of the theoretical journey of this chapter.

Twoness, thirdness, and intersubjectivity

Benjamin (2004, p. 1) defines "intersubjectivity in terms of a relationship of mutual recognition-a relation in which each person experiences the other as a 'like subject', another mind who can be 'felt with', yet has a distinct, separate center of feeling and perception".

Her paper, "Beyond doer and done to: an intersubjective view of thirdness" (2004), soon to be extended to a book (personal conversation, November 2016), helps us to bring together some of the threads I have sketched so far. The fundamental ideas she articulates and names as "twoness" and "thirdness" have to do with two different modalities that I believe resonate with what has been previously outlined, while adding to them.

Twoness, or complementarity, is characterised by power struggles and doer–done to polarised or split consciousness. In Bergson's terms, it is a static process, it has structure and power relations that can alternate "doer and done to" dynamics, victim–oppressor roles. These roles are complementary, the one cannot be without the other, and projective dynamics tend to be characteristic of it. Model 1 (above), in spite of Freud's best intentions, is a doer–done to model, where one person is the object of the other's well intentioned, yet paternalistic, attention. Object relations has the same tendency, both in Benjamin's view and in my own direct experience of that therapeutic modality. In some ways, it is relatively easier to map this way of relating. To say what you did to me and what I did to you is not so hard to do. What is more difficult is to go behind and/or beyond that, and to co-construct, or allow to emerge, a joint space of thirdness. It might mean going from what we know (Bion's "K" and Bergson's quantity or static processes) and are willing to acknowledge to something that might be other than that (an aspect of "O", or "duration", dynamic, or, in my own terms, an "affective genealogy").

Thirdness is characterised as a quality or experience of intersubjective relatedness that has as its correlate a certain kind of internal mental space. It is closely related to Winnicott's idea of potential or transitional space (Benjamin, 2004, p. 7). Benjamin (p. 7) cites Pizer (1998) as offering the first relational formulation of thirdness and as analysing "transference [phenomena] not in terms of static, projective contents", but in terms of an intersubjective process of negotiation. In her own words, ". . . I consider it crucial not to reify the third, but to consider it primarily a principle, function or relationship, rather than as a 'thing'" (2004, p. 7). In other words, there is difference in kind between twoness and thirdness. Thirdness is not a thing; it is dynamic. The space–experience is shared and co-operative. We surrender to the experience (Benjamin, 2004, p. 8), rather than hold on to it, as we do with concepts, "maxims or ideals" (2004, p. 7). There is something here that seems to chime with Bion's idea of "without memory and desire". Surrendering to the other is not the same as submission, which might describe a compliant attitude, but a letting go to being with the other. "Surrender implies freedom from any intent to control or coerce" (2004, p. 7).

I hope that the reader may be able to glean the parallels between some of the ideas explored so far. What Benjamin is able to do is to track a duality of static and dynamic processes, as different in kind. But, beyond that, she is able to delve into a more complex elaboration of what it takes to be able to facilitate the creation of thirdness. To do this she analyses different aspects of thirdness and links to aspects of neuroscience and the difference between observing analytical and attunement functions. I return to this later.

This analysis gives a picture of how different aspects of our human capacities for different kinds of consciousness are able to come into interrelation and of the complexity of how thirdness is constituted, but also how it might get out of balance. To accomplish this Benjamin distinguishes a duality of process, which I would term as differences in kind, within thirdness and calls them "One in the Third and Third in the One", before going into an exploration of how they might integrate (or not) and what might result from that. "One in the third" (Benjamin, 2004, pp. 16–17) is the part of the third that is constituted by oneness, that is, affective resonance, attunement, oneness of mother and baby in non-verbal rhythmicity or musicality. It is about the non-verbal, gestural, embodied capacity to feel, with the other, empathy and recognition. It is a deep identificatory oneness. "Third in the one" has to do with the ability to hold the tension of difference in relation. It is about holding one's centre and maintaining the capacity to observe, analyse, and think.

For Benjamin, thirdness has its foundation in the early rhythmical adjustment of mother and child, rather than an oedipal triangulation. The primacy of a main carer at an early stage (whoever that might be in the atypical postmodern family make up) and that early relation before and beyond language is what lays the foundations for thirdness. This is, in my view, far more concordant with the primacy of affect in Bergson's and Deleuze's philosophy than with predominant psychoanalytic understandings such as proposed by Kleinian and Lacanian positions, a critique of which can be found in Benjamin's paper (2004, pp. 11–12). Without getting into a major discussion that might distract from the main argument I am slowly building towards, the relative emphasis of such frameworks on language and projective dynamics seems to have somewhat neglected the affective, embodied, non-verbal attunement and focused far more on twoness and third-ness in their more doer–done to modality, as I hope will be evident from the following sections. This, for me, does not mean a total rejection of their views. It means acknowledging their value in being able to map a part of real psychological events, but also their blindness to aspects that do not fit that, in my view, incomplete map. It could also be interesting to note at this point that some of Bion's work not mentioned previously might present a step forward, not only by extending to groups, rather than just intrapsychic life, but by having a concept of work group, in terms of healthy functioning, and not just basic assumption (BA) unconscious and dysfunctional modalities in group behaviour. What is also notable, however, is that he did not leave us much in terms of work group functioning, compared to the work on basic assumptions, yet, here again is a duality within BA dependency and pairing, being based on assumptions of dependency, whether from a leader or a pair, and BA fight/flight being a literal twoness in conflict, offering no accommodation, only kill/be-killed or escape options. The co-operative functioning of the work group is left hanging, much like "O". This is where Bergson and Deleuze have more to say, as does Benjamin.

Thirdness and its vicissitudes: health and pathologies, moral third, and surrender

Work in the neurosciences (Schore, 2003) has associated different predominant functioning to the brain hemispheres, seeing right brain as key in attunement processes and left as key to analytical functions. McGilchrist (2009), while acknowledging the limitations of a neat division of labour between hemispheres, none the less feels able to say that left brain is characterised by a "what" questioning, while the right is about "how". He further points out that science has been so focused on "what" at the expense of "how" that it might have missed the importance of how each hemisphere does what. His basic premise is that there two ways of being in the world, in turn associated to differ-ent brain modalities: one is "to allow things to be present to us in all their embodied particularity" and the other is "to re-present the world in a form that is less truthful, but apparently clearer . . . explicit, abstracted, compartmentalised, fragmented, static. From this world we feel detached, but in relation to it we are powerful" (McGilchrist, 2009, pp. 92–93). But I might add we are only powerful if someone else is powerless, and that someone else could be us, which takes us back to the identificatory "one in the third" and the need for an understanding of these aspects working together, just like the hemispheres must for healthy functioning.

According to Benjamin's scheme, the different aspects constitutive of thirdness have to be related in particular ways. A deep, identificatory "one in the third" is the prerequisite for developing positive aspects of the "observing third", otherwise an asymmetrical relation becomes about twoness and power relations, which might give rise to conflict, submission, or resistance on the part of the less powerful party where the observation of the one who has the upper hand turns to judgement. For Benjamin, these power dynamics are not all there is in the face of asymmetrical power relations; the other possibility is what she terms "moral third". The "moral third" accepts asymmetry, rather than uses it; it accommodates, with the intention to connect to the other, which brings about reflections and self-observation. This acceptance of difference and differentials, of the power to hurt, be hurt, and to make mistakes allows for surrender, a conscious, responsible accommodation aware of both parties' vulnerability, which is not submission. This is in contrast to a static, twoness morality that uses dictates and rules and puts itself in a position of dominance based on sacrifice and duty, rather than empathy and an acceptance of limits in the common interest. A similar contrast is present in Bergson's (1935) last book, *The Two Sources of Morality and Religion*. The observing third, when not in its judgemental guise, is what saves us from falling into the other, from a mindless merging, which can also result in the collapse of thirdness and the doer–done to scenario. We have problems if either function is overwhelmed by the other.

How might all this relate to psycho-social research practice based on creating thirdness from these dualities? I started from dualities in relation to the importance of introspection, intuition, and reflexivity as a way of accessing beneath the surface aspects of reality. I brought together aspects of Bergson and Bion's work to characterise this duality in terms of process and used Bergson's rules of intuition as a method to give us some indications of how this might help us think about framing problems we might wish to research. Part of that was about how to think about differences in kind, which found their expressions also in Bion's ideas on learning as a dynamic process. I then tracked some movements in psychoanalytic work by looking at the basic changes in ideas of transference and countertransference, taking this as a key aspect of psychoanalytic thinking. There, we could see a movement from an objective gaze, which must note yet remain unperturbed by the affective communication in the session, towards an acceptance and valuing of the data produced by affective responses in both parties.

Benjamin's account gives us a more complex set of interconnected elements as necessary for relational practice. I would say this is the proper model for true participant observation, where participation = attunement. Where the participation function takes over the observing function, commonly known problems of "going native" or excessive empathy begin to emerge; however, just as in the therapeutic relation, when observation lacks attunement, it turns to the judgemental and superior attitudes typical of much social science in relation to non-Western cultures and societies. Said's (1978) famous work *Orientalism* seems to map very well the splitting and projective dynamics that Western cultures have unreflexively inflicted on a host of other cultures, abstractly bunched into a category of Orientals, in the name of objectivity.

Relationality = Inter-est = it is between

To conclude: subjectivity is central to psycho-social research, but requires the use of reflexivity. This is the attention of the mind to itself that comes about only in relation to engagement with a third aspect. It is in the attention to the question and external aspects of reality, along with the holding of attention to how we affect and are affected by them, that we might find unexpected answers. Those answers might not come as the abstract rules that the objective third alone might insist on, but a more specific "truth in the moment". This might not give us the answer to everything, yet it could surface far more appropriate answers to the question asked within a contextual time and specific frame.

A relational stance acknowledges the subject(s)-in-relation, both inter- and intrapsychically, but it is not about self-disclosure *per se* (Benjamin, 2004, p. 34). The same is true of research. Within the social sciences, reflexivity has been seen as key, particularly in anthropology. For some time, in the study of "other" cultures, the problem of subjectivity's potential bias has been somewhat amplified by the necessary acknowledgement that we are products of our own culture and it is ultimately impossible to shake that off. Thus, it has become accepted practice to be transparent about one's own background and positioning in anthropological writing (see, for example, Clifford & Marcus, 1986, or Behar, 1996). However, as an explicit example of the importance of the different modalities by which this might be done, it is not unusual to find this is focused on a self-assertive statement of role or status, whether it is in terms of powerful or subservient positioning, or a narcissistic flavour of self-exposure. Less reflexive attention is given to what might really matter in relation to what is being researched (Murphy, 2002, has a critique of this in justifying his own autobiographically based account of fieldwork). This is qualitatively different to what comes across from a narration that really engages with those aspects of subjectivity that might resonate with, or bring about tensions with, what is being researched. A good example of this engagement is Paerregaard's 2002 paper titled "The resonance of fieldwork: ethnographers, informants and the creation of knowledge", which, while not mentioning transference as such, maps how the people of a Peruvian village tried to make sense of who he was by projecting different kinds of identities/labels to him, going from fantasies of him being an exploitative coloniser through progressively less negative ones as they got to know him and accept him. Paerregaard's use of the words "resonance" and "knowledge creation" in the title are not coincidental, as his focus was on intersubjectivity.

Where someone is really interested, they bring about a thirdness in themselves between the "one in the third" and the "third in the one", between attunement and observation. This, in turn, allows for the thirdness of encounter with the truth in the moment. Interest, as a word, gives us a clue. Its etymology tells us it is derived from two roots: *inter*, meaning between, and *est* from the Latin verb *esse*, meaning to be. *Inter est* means "it is between". Thus, language itself gives us an indication of what being interested in something, which is key to learning and research, is about: it is about the space between, in other words, thirdness. Interesting that the word interest has been hijacked (in my view) to indicate the profit one might gain from money and particularly lending, which is essentially about a very asymmetrical arrangement, being indebted to, implying power and mostly doer–done to arrangements.

Interest, as intellectual and emotional curiosity, makes observation keener and attunement stronger. Recognition is then possible in a way that is based on the space between, one that is able to apprehend both quantitative and qualitative aspects of reality in their ever-mingled actuality of lived life. In an ideal world, researcher and researched both partake of these aspects and together create new located understanding. Research, in this way of looking at things, is fundamentally about an encounter; it is about relationship. The resulting data is a co-created shared third element that does not belong to one or the other; in that sense it is truly about participatory research and the ideal we ought to be deploying our subjective and objective capacities in relation to each other, in tension, to put it as French and Simpson (2000) have, and with the intention to learn. Power, in this approach to research, can and should be about creativity, rather than domination.

The problem comes when this shared co-creation does not happen. How can this way of seeing things help us when we come across the fraught problem of disputed findings? When our respondents do not agree with our conclusions? Whose interpretation counts? The word "counts" gives us a clue again of how this problem is usually framed. In terms of "counting", we have an ambiguity of meaning in the word itself: counting is obviously about numbers, counting the "whats", which, in turn, also means what is most important. In this kind of framing, only one can be right, only one can win, whichever one that is. In Benjamin's scheme, this conflictual situation is a clear example of twoness, complementarity, and, obviously, "doer–done-to" dynamics. The problem really comes to light when the researcher's interpretation varies from that of the research subject and the researcher seeks resolution, either by submitting and giving primacy to the respondents' views, or opting to take authority and stick by theirs. I suggest this framework could help us to think about this not as an either/or, but possibly a both–and with a focus on "how" rather than "what". Here, we might be able to reflect that attunement processes might be hard to sustain and that the conflict in findings is itself "the" finding, or a major component of them, that data itself might give a clue to the underlying dynamics. This might have to do with what is being researched in itself, creating what Hollway and Jefferson (2000) refer to as the "defended subject", but it could also be about a "defended researcher", a researcher holding too tightly to "K". Paying attention to transference and countertransference would be appropriate in terms of what this might be communicating, rather than in terms of projection. This would require increased reflexive attention to affective and embodied aspects of both researcher and respondent, carefully held in tension with other aspects of triangulation, be they detailed factual observations, peer supervision, or data analysis processes based on free association. What it might also mean is that the research is not quite done yet, which, of course, is true of any study, which, like this chapter, has to come to an end at some point.

I shall close by surrendering to the limitations of time and space as well as to the limits of knowledge in its written and linear form. I have tried to bend that linearity to characterise the importance not only of using our subjectivity in psycho-social research, but also the importance of the why and how we need to use it. The limited bringing together of different frameworks I hope might have mirrored the relatedness I have advocated and, ideally, elicited a thirdness in their interrelation within the minds of the readers.

References

Abou-Rihan, F. (2008). *Deleuze and Guattari: A Psychoanalytic Itinerary.* London: Continuum.

Behar, R. (1996). *The Vulnerable Observer: Anthropology that Breaks Your Heart.* Boston, MA: Beacon.

Benjamin, J. (2004). Beyond doer and done to: an intersubjective view of thirdness. *Psychoanalytic Quarterly, LXXIII*: 5–46.

Bergson, H. (1913). *Time and Free Will: An Essay on the Immediate Data of Consciousness.* Minneola, NY: Dover [reprinted 2001].

Bergson, H. (1935). *The Two Sources of Morality and Religion.* Notre Dame, IN: Notre Dame University Press [reprinted 1977].

Bion, W. R. (1961). *Experiences in Groups and Other Papers.* London: Tavistock.

Bion, W. R. (1970). *Attention and Interpretation.* London: Tavistock.

Clarke, S., Hahn, H., & Hoggett, P. (2008). *Object Relations and Social Relations: The Implications of the Relational Turn in Psychoanalysis.* London: Karnac.

Clifford, J., & Marcus, G. E. (1986). *Writing Culture: The Poetics and Politics of Ethnography.* Oakland: University of California Press.

Crociani-Windland, L. (2009). How to live and learn: learning, duration and the virtual. In: S. Clarke & P. Hoggett (Eds.), *Researching Beneath the Surface* (pp. 51–79). London: Karnac.

Deleuze, G. (1991). *Bergsonism.* New York: Zone Books.

Eigen, M. (1999). The area of faith in Winnicott, Lacan and Bion. In: S. A. Mitchell & L. Aron (Eds.), *Relational Psychoanalysis, Volume 1: The Emergence of a Tradition* (pp. 1–39). New York: Routledge.

French, R., & Simpson, P. (2000). Learning at the edges between knowing and not-knowing: "translating" Bion. *Organisational and Social Dynamics, 1:* 54–77.

Frosh, S. (2003). Psychosocial studies and psychology: is a critical approach emerging? *Human Relations, 56:* 1547–1567.

Heimann, P. (1950). On counter-transference. *International Journal of Psychoanalysis, 31:* 81–84.

Hinshelwood, R. (1999). Countertransference. *International Journal of Psychoanalysis, 80*(4): 797–818.

Hollway, W., & Jefferson, T. (2000). *Doing Qualitative Research Differently: Free Association, Narrative and the Interview Method.* London: Sage.

Holmes, J. (2014). Countertransference before Heimann—an historical exploration. *Journal of the American Psychoanalytic Association, 62*(4): 603–629.

Joseph, B. (1985). Transference: the total situation. *International Journal of Psychoanalysis, 66*(4): 447–454.

Massumi, B. (2002). *Parables for the Virtual.* Durham, NC: Duke University Press.

McGilchrist, I. (2009). *The Master and his Emissary: The Divided Brain and the Making of the Western World.* New Haven, CT: Yale University Press.

Murphy, P. (2002). The anthropologist's son (or living and learning the field). *Qualitative Inquiry, 8*(2): 246–261.

Paerregaard, K. (2002). The resonance of fieldwork. Ethnographers, informants and the creation of anthropological knowledge. *Social Anthropology, 10*(3): 319–334.

Pizer, S. (1998). *Building Bridges: Negotiation of Paradox in Psychoanalysis.* Hillsdale, NJ: Analytic Press.

Said, E. (1978). *Orientalism.* New York: Pantheon Press.

Schore, A. (2003). *Affect Regulation and the Repair of the Self*. New York: W. W. Norton.

Schwartz, J. (1999). *Cassandra's Daughter: A History of Psychoanalysis*. London: Karnac.

Sperry, R. W. (1968). Hemisphere deconnection and unity in consciousness. *American Psychologist*, 23: 723–733.

White, W. A. (1919). Jelliffe Papers. 5 November 1919. US Library of Congress.

Winnicott, D. W. (1971). *Playing and Reality*. London: Routledge.

CHAPTER THREE

Leaders and their relation to nature

Rembrandt Zegers

Introduction: from nature as outside environment to nature as relating

I felt peaceful in nature, felt connected. I was alone but I did not feel lonely. And that was a revelation for me. At some point a herd of moose came by and in the middle there was like an angel, it was a white moose. That was a magical moment. I tried to make contact with it; step by step I could approach it. I felt they were studying me and I was studying them. I had all the time in the world. (From interview with SMR, whose work involves guiding people into nature. Original interview by the author, 2015)

If the framing of nature is as an environment, as an outside factor that humans are not part of but instead claim to control and steer through the natural sciences, as reflected in rules of law and institutional governance, it is perhaps easier to understand why humans use nature, destroy it, "fix" it, improve it. It would be different if the idea of nature having a value independent of its use for humans, an ethical position known as ecocentric ethics, were more widely explored and discussed. It would also be different if nature could be seen as highly differentiated and with agency. But it is not like that. For instance, as recently as 1987, the UN's World Commission on

Environment and Development prompted widespread adoption of an anthropocentric view of sustainability, which put human needs and wants—or further human expansion and development—above the survival and development needs of other species (Borland & Lindgreen, 2013). As sustainable practices establish themselves, certain concepts are becoming dominant and translated into best practices. Such practices become part of leadership as the sustainability paradigm gains popularity. For instance, elections are held to determine who is most green, sustainability indices are developed, and sustainability reporting is exercised. However, most of the time these activities do not alter an anthropocentric relation to nature. Environmental problems still increase in speed and impact, such as climate change and accelerated loss of species and biodiversity (Curry, 2011; Hailwood, 2015). If this is so, a different understanding of nature altogether is needed that can open up possibilities for different practices and different cultures of relating to nature. In this respect, not only the discourse on sustainability but also that about leaders and their practices need to be looked at. The term "ecological leadership", referring to the leadership that builds on the ecological principle of "everything being related to everything else", has recently been introduced by Western (2013). Contrary to what the term suggests, what Western puts forward as a discourse is not specifically aiming to build leadership that focuses on a sustainability agenda, or an ecocentric ethics, for that matter. At the same time, the literature on leadership and sustainable practice is growing (e.g., Evans et al., 2015; Schein, 2015; Wolfgramm et al., 2015).

Social research shows that knowing based on information from natural sciences does not influence people to act positively to address environmental problems that much. In fact, psychoanalytic research into response to the (natural science informed) knowledge of global warming shows all kinds of forms of denial (Weintrobe, 2013). Although an affective form of engagement with a random group of people in an industrially polluted area shows that, underneath, these people are not in denial, but aware, concerned, and care. Drawing on psychosocial research methods that have their origin in psychoanalytic theory, Lertzman found that taking up a voice and asserting agency in environmental degradation are socially repressed and bring about anxiety (Lertzman, 2015). Where psychoanalysis looks at the unconscious on a psychological and social level, it does not include human's relation to nature. Or it has stopped doing so, despite people such as Searles (1960), who already pointed out quite explicitly the importance of such an exercise. Probably the most impactful thinking in this area comes from Merleau Ponty, who showed that not only the human-to-human relation is largely unconscious, but, equally so, the relation of humans with the body and non-human nature (Merleau Ponty, 1995, Toadvine, 2009).

> I stepped through a doorway out into a big open space, like a garden, a courtyard garden full of trees, I stepped out into it and the sun had just set and it was the point where the temperature changes and the sky was completely clear and it was doing that thing where it was going from blue to a purple colour and it was an instant, instantaneous feeling. I stepped through the door and when my foot hit the floor I said to myself there it is, and that was it there in the moment. It felt as if somebody was pouring beautiful perfect temperature water over me and then it went and something else came in coming back to present reality. And I turned left and carried on my way. (Interview with AKD, whose work involves guiding people into nature. Original interview by the author, 2015)

Eco-centric ethics emerging from a relational perspective

If a relational view of nature is followed, it seems that a different ethic towards nature starts to make sense. In her analysis of her own practice of doing agility training with her dog, Cayenne, Haraway illustrates that, through great effort of practice, observing the relation with her dog, she finally gets it—how to run with her dog without her (the dog) making mistakes.

> The philosophic and literary conceit that all we have is representations, and no access to what animals think and feel, is wrong. Human beings do—or can—know more than we used to know; and the right to make that judgment is rooted in historical, flawed, generative cross species practices. Of course, we are not the "other," and so do not know in that fantastic way. But to claim not to be able to communicate with and to know each other and other critters, however imperfectly, is a denial of mortal entanglements for which we are responsible and in which we respond. Technique, calculation, method—all are indispensable and exacting. But they are not response, which is irreducible

to calculation. Response is getting it that subject-making connection is real. Response is face to face in the contact zone of an entangled relationship. Companion species know this. (Haraway, 2008, p. 445)

Despret (2013) studies the relation between human animals and non-human animals and has made the case for agency of non-human animals.

On the one hand, the "perspective" of another being rests mostly upon "sympathetic projection," and may be difficult to apply to unfamiliar beings, such as bees or even flowers. . . . the very notion of agency still conveys its classic understanding as intentional, rational, and premeditated, and is still embedded in humanist and Christian conceptions of human exceptionalism. (p. 29)

She continues,

Indeed, creatures may appear as "secret agents" as long as we adopt a conventional definition of agency based on subjective experience and autonomous intention. However, when reframed in the terms of "agencement"—an assemblage that produces "agentivity"—agency seems to be much more extensively shared in the living world. (Despret, 2013, p. 29)

She then states that, in situations in which these agencements are manifested, "creatures of different species become, one for another and one with another, companion-agents" (2013, p. 29).

Bauman (2011) describes how global warming can only be meaningfully analysed if going beyond an anthropocentric position. For example: in the Alps, communities are affected because of less snow falling in the winter season. This means that locally a new relation with nature has to be found, as less money can be made from tourism. Skiing places can use artificial snow machines (anthropocentric) or find new ways that are acknowledging that overcrowded skiing facilities are not ecological in the first place. In the UK, communities are affected because of floods from extreme weather. In some places, measures are taken to strengthen "natural" barriers to prevent flooding. Bauman specifically comments on those, calling our current era the Anthropocene, as this continues to put a one-sided, standardised view and ethic on the problem of human planetary influence (Baumann, 2011). The point Bauman is making is not that humans (certain humans that is, more than others) have not influenced the planetary climate, for they have, but it is the wider dominant meaning systems (both religious and scientific) that legitimise certain humans to do so. Changing these meaning systems opens up different responses and develops different kinds of agency in engaging with the environment and environmental problems.

Questions of method

The first question that needed to be answered was to what extent different ways of relating to nature are already acknowledged within (Western) society at large. This was answered through literature study of the different ontologies and epistemologies of relating to nature. Without further extensive discussion, four different ontologies were identified. The dominant ontology is that of the natural sciences that looks for universal knowledge, aiming to produce insights that can be seen as "laws of nature". Another ontology is that of the ethics that study the right ways of being. From there, one takes a range of positions and debates that, roughly, can be distinguished as anthropocentric *vs.* ecocentric ethics. A third ontology is that of spirituality of meaning and meaning making, sometimes described as higher meaning, with reference to religion. Then there is the ontology of perception that Merleau Ponty studied through his phenomenological approach, pointing at the senses and the body playing a decisive role in being part of nature and knowing about nature (Merleau Ponty, 1968, 1995). The research is done using a psycho-social approach to interviewing. The interview technique is based on the principles of the free association narrative interview (FANI) that Hollway and Jefferson (2013) described. The method also used Gendlin's thinking (Gendlin et al., 1968). He, like Ferro and Civitaresse, builds on Merleau Ponty as he provides a protocol to make meaning out of what he calls the bodily "felt sense". A felt sense is the body's sense of a particular problem or situation. His protocol of "focusing" is a way of using "bodily knowing". According to Gendlin, a felt sense is not just there, it must form. "You have to know how to let it form by attending inside your body. When it comes, it is at first unclear, fuzzy" (Gendlin, 2003, p. 10). By following certain steps of creating awareness, a felt sense in the body can come into focus and it can change as it becomes an insight.

In this research, I use Gendlin's concepts as a lens (not as a full therapy protocol) to ask questions in exploring when people refer to using their senses or refer to their bodies.

Another question that needed to be answered was what group of leaders or what practice of leadership to research? Any answer to that question is arbitrary, as illustrated by using an example that Bateson gave in making his point about everything in nature being related to everything else. Bateson shows a picture and asks an audience what it is. Different people give different answers that are all true, although some people in the audience insist that their interpretation is the right one. Nevertheless, to answer the question of who to study, distinctions are made using the very idea of boundary that Bateson pointed out as relative (Bateson, 1979). Through interpreting the relation with nature as "what happens at a boundary level", several boundaries can be identified. For instance, the boundary of self and body, the boundary between a human animal and a non-human animal, the boundary of a human and his/her living conditions, or the political boundary between humans when it concerns nature (in their agency to establish a living or develop human interest and practices). Making this distinction in boundaries is a construct, but a workable one for this research. From there, several leaders can be "defined": leaders who take others into nature, leaders who work with others and non-human animals, leaders directly affected by changes in their living conditions (e.g., food situation, weather), and leaders who work towards objectives of sustainability with or within an organisation of some sort.

The next question that came up in thinking through the method is that of change. If shifts of meaning happen on a pre-reflective level through the body and in a field of interacting with human and non-human (or wider nature) others, then spoken and written language is not the only medium that needs to be looked at. At the same time, it is widely accepted that meaning moves collectively through formal language (to the detriment of ignoring other levels of language). Taking this into account, it is clear that language about nature is not constant. Abram describes how language developed from a very direct relation and connection to nature to the more abstract tool that is known today (Abram, 2010). For instance, Egyptian hieroglyphic language uses pictures of natural phenomena and animals (human and non-human). The meaning and use of language in relating to nature is in no way "linear", as Schouten and others who study the history of humans' relation to nature show. For instance, politics towards nature in the Netherlands has shifted from nature as romantic (sixteenth and seventeenth century landscape painters showing idyllic, friendly landscapes) to conquering land from the sea (making the polders), to conservation of nature reserves as isolated parks all neat and tidy, to allowing these parks to grow wild (Schouten, 2005). As all leaders are part of a culture (or many cultures on many levels) the dynamic of change can be seen as a dynamic of use and shifts in language or shifts of meaning on a larger social scale. Also, as already stated above, this means that language has to be seen as broader than "formal" written or spoken language. It will need to include other forms of expression. Before illustrating data from interviews with several different leaders, some examples of shifts of meaning from literature are discussed.

> The Board of directors had a meeting and we joined after a while. I remember I sat right in the middle. They had had a fierce conversation as I later found out. Before the meeting started (that I joined), I said "You know what? I have to get out a minute because this doesn't feel right". Without being able to see anything tangible, the tension was immense and I felt in the middle of it. And I just noticed, I am not sitting in the right place. (From interview with JSR, whose work involves managing an IT department of a utility company. Original interview by the author, 2015)

How can a shift in meaning come about?

As a different understanding of nature is of such importance, then how can this come about? In psychoanalysis/psycho-social studies, a shift in meaning is currently seen to happen in the field between client and therapist. But psychoanalysis is moving its position to stating that it is not the therapist who individually knows about the client and magically intervenes from that knowing to heal the client. The therapy is a co-creation, as Ferro and Civitarese (2015, p. 153) argue:

> Present-day psychoanalysis is called upon to take account of intermediacy and intersubjectivism, of the (bodily) forms of implicit memory and the inaccessible or fetal and hence unrepressed, unconscious. Not everything can be traced back to perception (as we naively imagine)

and to consciousness, because there is a *fleshy* "perception" that is non-representational—a level of sense that can be described as semiotic but not yet semantic.

It is Merleau Ponty who pointed out the intercorporeal, preverbal, or presymbolic that precedes, and then accompanies, linguistic or symbolic communication. Ferro and Civitarese argue that the unconscious that Merleau Ponty places centrally in his thinking is a different unconscious from Freud's unconscious, for, as they say, Freud's is a "representational repressed and dynamic unconsciousness", whereas Merleau Ponty addresses non- representational unconscious (Ferro & Civitarese, 2015, p. 155). According to them, Merleau Ponty "must take the credit for having been the first to demolish the idea of the isolated subject". The concept of the countertransference, for example, is not genuinely intersubjective because the analyst's subjectivity is seen as the place in which the patient "creates" that phenomenon. The analyst, as a person, remains outside it. For Merleau Ponty, the subject does not arrive, but is "born of inter-subjectivity" (Ferro & Civitarese, 2015, p. 160). Further, they argue that, although the analytic field (as the intersubjective area created by analyst and analysand)

> could be said not to exist outside the minds, that is actually not so. It also includes everything that furnishes the place where the physical persons are situated, as a possible source of stimuli, as well as the more or less subtle actions performed by each in order to force the others to accept projective identifications. (Ferro & Civitarese, 2015, p. 161)

Further on, they state that

> Things too are invested with projections, transferences, and magic thought. One will of course react differently to inanimate objects than to a person, because in the former case one's specific reactivity to a fellow human being is lacking—a reactivity that we now know to be based also on specific neuro-physiological functions" (Ferro & Civitarese, 2015, p. 162)

As a consequence, oscillation between symmetry and asymmetry in the analytic field is a description of the analyst and patient relation, but it can also be a description of relations to non-human others (Ferro & Civitarese, 2015). As they say, "interpretation is no longer directed to the patient, to modifying something in him, but instead to improving the narrative capacity of the field, understood as an un/conscious narration *à deux*" (Ferro & Civitarese, 2015, p. 164). A shift of meaning, therefore, does not happen in an isolated mind, but is the result of what happens in a relation brought to consciousness in a context of already existing personal and cultural history of language and social constructs.

Shifts of meaning: examples from the research

The following data are from interviews with the leaders engaged so far in this study. The focus is on shifts of meaning that interviewees report through the narrative of their biographic experiences. The findings are grouped around accounts of bodily experiences that interviewees talk about, around experiences with non-human animals, and around experiences in a wider context of working with nature. The examples come from transcripts of the interviews leaving out analysis of the interviewee–researcher dynamics. Where fragments of the interview transcripts are given, they are displayed in a different font .

Reference to the body

AKD has developed a professional service taking others into nature. When doing so he does not use information about nature and neither does he provide descriptions or interpretations of what people could or should expect. The process of facilitation that he uses is focusing on containment and helping people to explore what happens in the moment, which makes him suggest during the interview that his leadership would "not go well with corporate culture".

> When we think about dominant culture, it's not very attractive to people, but, for example, in the corporate sector, the private sector, it's not very attractive to do this kind of work, because you become invisible in your leadership. It is very difficult to have power, to make a living, to be seen as credible. All these things that we provide normally in the private sector, I think. These things don't happen, I think, here in what we do.

He has stories of several very powerful experiences he had with being in nature.

I had an experience of merging with a rock. And this didn't fit my world-view at all, so I didn't tell anyone for a long time. That experience changed everything I could think of about my life. So, my politics changed radically, the way I looked changed, my whole perspective on culture changed.

AKD tells how he has no control over calling up the deeper experience of nature; however, he says he recognises it immediately when it happens. He says that it enhances a sense of wellbeing and comes with heightened functioning of the senses (sight, hearing, smell). The experience of merging with a rock while climbing was like something moving, he says (Gendlin, 2003). He phrases it as a shift in his identity and he defines it as an awareness of his ecological self (Diehm, 2006). He studied and reflected on his experiences, interpreting them as being connected to "the web of life".

Other interviewees make reference to similar notions of the lived experience (what it is like) that are difficult to put into words, or being aware that such experience will not fit the culture they operate in as part of their daily activities. One other example of an interviewee meeting critical responses from others when telling about experiences through sensing is ISM. Before the first interview, ISM had already given up her job, being part of the management of a firm, to make a career switch through studying organic farming. She made that switch to be able to work with nature. During the second interview, she was writing her thesis, just back from abroad, where she had done field work in a remote area. ISM describes herself as intuitively sensing the surrounding nature all the time. Different plants, for her, have a different presence. She explains her motivation to go to university to learn in a different way about plants, for she states that she is already familiar with the intuitive sensing way, but now wants to learn more about growing plants in a systematic way.

I have been part of gardening all my life; my grandma had an orchard. Trees and bushes I can feel energy around. I have always worked intuitively and now, through university, I want to learn more systematic knowledge of organic plant growing. So now I have extra signals to understand what is happening. When choosing the faculty, I thought for a moment to do eco-therapy, where you learn to communicate with plants and ecosystems, but I thought, "I already do that."

She describes very strongly how, during her field trip in this remote area, she cannot read the surroundings at first and neither can she read the people. She experiences the native people as having a knowing of her thoughts even before she expresses them. This is all very strange to her, needing her to rely upon her "intuition". She observes and writes down her experiences, expecting to make sense of them some time later when writing her thesis. She refers to a particular event where she is uncomfortable with the location that the locals have pointed out for her and her translator to spend the night. As she handles the situation, she picks another spot that later on appears to be part of the community, whereas sleeping in no-man's-land culturally is seen as not belonging to anybody and, therefore, unprotected and not safe. She refers to sensing and feeling using her body to keep her safe. ISM not only talks about the environment, she clearly talks about people and how she is seeking to understand the relation. In doing so, she has only her bodily feelings and her intuition as sources of information. The different environment provides this opportunity of finding shifts of meaning and looking into how to understand her experiences through her body. ISM says that when she is finally back in the Netherlands, a supervisor does not consider her observations to be scientific. However, she keeps her confidence because another supervisor (someone from the area she visited) recognises and values her stories and experiences. In another interview, ISM says she is thinking of what kind of job or organisation she wants to work with after graduating. Even when one particular idea appeals to her a lot, she decides not to take that job because she has a sense that this organisation will take on sustainability (as it is a start-up) in a way that she cannot subscribe to, as she feels it will be mostly profit driven and, therefore, abusive and out of relation with nature.

A third example of sensing and using his body is JSR. He works in a corporate environment that uses training to support its change objectives. Using state of the art exercises from organisational development (OD) and more recent ideas around "mindfulness" are part of these trainings. JSR is a leader in business and he subscribes to the business investing in the transition to renewable energy and he has a technical background. JSR tells about two incidents of knowing through his body: the first is when, in a training, he is blindfolded and can clearly sense when people come close to him without seeing them.

> So I have done some training in the past using my body. At some point I had to stand opposite somebody else blindfolded and sense what the other was doing. I could sense when the other person began to approach me and I felt ready to defend myself.

The second is when he enters a meeting room to join a directors' meeting where, some minutes before, people were present but not any more. He senses an atmosphere of hostility and feels his body shrinking back as if protecting himself. He later finds out that there has been an argument acted out in the meeting room just before he entered. JSR takes meaning from his experience of knowing through his body.

> In this way maybe intuition could be something people just transmit, conscious or unconscious. Mostly unconscious, I think, when you instinctively know if something works or not. And maybe the question is, if it works in combination with me, you know, that is possible. I am learning to listen to this more and more and then to try if I can argue what it is about. And, even if I cannot, still to accept that something is the matter, or, the other way around, that is also possible.

During the interview, he makes a comment on his peers, including his director, as less inclined to use, or openly refer to, their "intuition". When it comes to ecocentric ethics, JSR expresses many concerns about the environment. He also expresses trust that technical solutions will be found, as he firmly believes they are needed. He is concerned, however, that these might not be in time, as he describes how these technical solutions will take a long time to be implemented. He considers that he would only become an entrepreneur if he were able to scale up a solution different from the work his organisation already does in supporting sustainable solutions, and if that other solution was big enough and quick enough to really make a difference.

Reference to non-human animals and plants

Like AKD, SMR also takes others into nature. He describes his own experience in nature as very impactful and he feels at home in nature even under harsh conditions. On one of his retreats, he meets a moose. SMR tells about this encounter as part of a bigger story of being in wild nature. It is a story of how he discovered that being in nature can enhance his finding out about himself. In this way, he brings others with him into nature for a deliberate experience of building self-confidence, finding out about oneself, as he sees that as powerful help for the people he works with, as they are mostly underprivileged people, or have difficulties sustaining themselves. In the organisation he now works for, he has pushed for this work taking others into nature to be adopted. When asked how his nature experiences have affected him, he is clear about his ethics in seeing any creature as valuable. However, he says his experiences have not made him inflexible in that he defends anything about nature as sacred and not to be touched. He describes how once he was present and helped in the offering (and eating) of a goat when he was on a nature retreat.

The next interviewee also refers to her own development and how a non-human animal was helping her to find out about herself. AJJ works with leadership teams and horses as a profession. AJJ tells how horses have helped her to go through the work of understanding herself. These experiences and this learning made such an impact that she took the opportunity to learn to work with horses and humans, as well as becoming a trainer of horses.

> Horses have been my passion from being a very small child. Then, at some point, I took up my old hobby after twenty years, but it was uncomfortable for myself and the horses at first. I needed to know why. I remember, in the first part of the training, that I was asked to look at myself while getting a horse ready to ride. I found out through the horse that I was stressed and nervous most of the time with other people. I was so used to feeling like that in my body without questioning.

AJJ has learnt to "know" about horses and, because of that, she now keeps her horses in a herd as this is the "natural" way for horses to be. She thinks that "horses in most stables are like factory workers, alienated and not suited to doing the training work with leaders". This reference to keeping horses in a herd is interesting with respect to ecocentric ethics, as it shows an interest and action towards valuing nature beyond its utilitarian value for humans.

NET has been fascinated by nature from a young age but, at some point, chose to join the corporate world and raise a family. He has two homes, an eco-farm that he runs for most of the year and a house in an urban area that is close to his children and grandchildren. As a child, he collected anything out of nature he could get hold of and put it under his microscope. During his corporate career, most weekends were spent with his family and, much of the time, in nature. NET shows elements of ecocentric ethics in his leadership, as he gave an example of how, as a director, he made the decision not to use a certain plant as the source for a product of the company he worked for as it was almost extinct, although the company lost a lot of money on that decision.

Reference to nature at large

WAI's relation to nature is unique in the way she negotiates it with herself, her work, and her organisation. WAI is using a symbolic relation with nature alongside reference to the natural sciences her organisation—one that works on issues of management of natural resources—stands for. WAI switched from working for a multi-national company to an environmental NGO before working in the organisation she was working for during the interview. She stresses several reasons for her career switch to the NGO, most of all wanting her children to have a future. She comments on the ethic of modern technology being a problem, as she presents herself as a person who is inspired by nature. At the same time, she states that she likes to live in the city. For her, the cultural richness of art, theatre, looking at shops, and meeting a variety of people are important. She is regularly asked to give speeches about the changing perspectives of her profession and, in doing so, she emphasises the role of storytelling. WAI expresses experiencing nature in different ways.

> The point is we cannot conquer nature; we have to live with nature. I communicate when I am outside the city, or when I go on my bike through the park, that gives me peace. I can be outside and take up a yoga position and embrace nature. For example, I remember images of light, sun, sea, horses, close to peat from where I came from.

WAI introduced Shamanistic workshops in her current organisation. She expresses shifts using language that describes moods and energies, referring to symbols from Shamanistic practice. In projecting on to these symbolic nature figures, she describes conversations with birds and she describes becoming an animal herself as part of moments of reflection and introspection.

In my Shamanistic experience, my power animal is an eagle. And so I work with my wings. I try to find applications for what I learnt through the Shamanism work with my teacher; sometimes other people criticise me, but I feel right about it and it works for me.

She found an ally in Shamanism as a way of strengthening her intuitive way of thinking and expressing herself, which she sees as important for herself and others.

There is a lot about creating the scientific voice, the voice of authority, but when I am given the space for people, I saw how I created enthusiasm getting people together by addressing what I call the other forces that play a role. Proof of that is that I invited KAN to do the Shamanistic workshop and all who participated at the end were lying on the floor visualising the earth and the sun and then thinking of what symbol they would pick and how that relates to the mission of the organisation. KAN designed it not as pure Shamanism, but, of course, this is rather different work compared to mainstream corporate culture and team building. But all teams that I invited expressed a lot of appreciation.

It is not clear from the interviews what the impact of this has been on WAI's wider organisation, and neither has she expanded on the dilemmas participants from her organisation faced in participating. Nevertheless, what WAI has done is a kind of getting nature "into the organisation" with the potential to enhance people's ways of relating to nature differently from the natural sciences, challenging the organisations dominant meaning system (Bauman, 2011).

Reflection

Psycho-social research uses specific techniques in its research methods, such as drawings, poems, or dreams. That opens the opportunity to use methods based on the senses, using the frame of Gendlin on felt sense and adding this direction of enquiry to interview methods such as FANI. This has been the innovation of the psycho-social methods of research in this project, as questions around bodily sensations and felt sense have been added. A link between psychoanalysis and Merleau Ponty's phenomenology is a link between psychic functioning (representational unconscious) and perception (non-representational unconscious). In doing so, a different object for psycho-social studies is suggested (or an expansion) to "the field". That means the object (of nature) now sits between subjects as they are part of a larger whole and nature becomes part of the meaning making. In the case of non-human animals in their surroundings, sometimes literally through their "agentivity" (Despret, 2013). Both psychoanalysis and phenomenology of perception have influenced each other and both are interested in intersubjectivity. However, as intersubjectivity has the interest of psychoanalytic scholars and practitioners like Ferro and Civitarese, adding non-human aspects to psychoanalytic practice is not widely known or studied yet. Benjamin (2004), for instance, who has studied and written on the intersubjective, has suggested the idea of the third, but she does not go as far as to make a link to the concept of flesh that Merleau Ponty has introduced, where intersubjectivity clearly includes the non-human other. Merleau Ponty was looked at with suspicion by psychoanalysts after Lacan doubted if he (Merleau Ponty) reflected on the unconscious at all (Ferro & Civitarese, 2015, p. 153).

Bringing shifts of meaning—especially when they are based on including the non-human other—into the social and into leadership are not mechanical happenings "just originating from the body". There is a psychic functioning at work as well, bringing the pre-reflective beyond awareness into expression and to a cultural level. From the interview material, it is clear that reference to perception and experiences of intersubjectivity between oneself and non-human nature are expressed and, in some cases, show shifts of meaning (surfacing to the level of cognition and language). It can also be seen from the interviews that perception finds its way into the personal, the group level (see interview with NET or WAI) and the cultural (see ISM) but not always all at the same time. This is clearly because perception is resisted and not only on the level of perception itself (where nature is "the unknown other" relating outside the immediate grasp of human thinking and language), but also because of the very social constructs themselves, originating from historical developments and discourses that have become culturally dominant. As psychoanalysis itself moves up and down in promoting itself against modern cognitive science, the same is true for perception. For instance, Merleau Ponty's investigation into phantom pain clearly is at the boundary of what most humans would consider rational and, therefore, not existing (or mentally not possible and, therefore, incorrect).

So, how could the experience of being one with a rock (see AKD), or a powerful personal meeting with a moose (see SMR) ever be considered psychologically "healthy" and relevant for the future of the planet or be part of conscious strategies and tactics for change?

Merleau Ponty's ontology is not a theory of sustainability, and neither does it directly provide direction for leadership or leaders in their role to enhance sustainability or environmental concern. The implications of his phenomenology and ontology, however, are

to begin the analysis again "from within"—not immanent to a subjectivity, but immanent to the self-organizing configurations of nature within which the perspective of consciousness emerges and from which it can never detach itself. (Toadvine, 2009, p. 48)

If an anthropocentric position in relating to nature is primarily showing itself through the Cartesian "mind–body" split, then the radical suggestion that directly comes from Merleau Ponty is that, actually, nature in this way can never be approached and made sense of. For his ontology points at the necessity of taking a relational position and a position of perception that includes animals, plants, and the wider inanimate nature.

This is how I suggest leadership of the environment should start to orientate itself more, as a position of intersubjectivity with humans and non-human animals, plants, and wider nature included, but also as a position of valuing experience and collective enchantment. What that means and how that works then needs to be discovered over and over again (as the fundamental relation to nature does resist its reification). Following this, then exploring and communicating experience of nature individually and collectively is, by default, a core part of working to be an ecocentric leader. This is more or less overlooked in the sustainability discourse, as most of the time that serves the dominant economic and anthropocentric paradigm, with an interest in stabilising itself by staying with the mind–body split, a social stasis that can no longer be considered responsible or desirable. How easily this can be overlooked—or, rather, how persistent the detached from nature position is—can be seen in the corporate literature on sustainability. For instance, Borland and Lindgreen (2013) make a distinction between transitional (which they call ecoefficient) and transformative (which they call ecocentric) change within corporations, and propose the latter as a framework for strategies to develop ecocentric business. As promising as Borland and Lindgreen's proposed transition into ecocentric business might be, they define ecocentric marketing strategies as:

> Companies that satisfy the needs of industrial and consumer markets remaining within biophysical constraints, only exploiting resources at a rate at which they can be sustainably maintained, recovered or replenished in cradle-to-cradle, closed-loop ecological systems. (Borland & Lindgreen, 2013, p. 183)

They also state,

> The progression toward a transformational strategy is not necessarily smooth and may require a step based change in identity and leap of faith. Just as transformation at an individual level requires a fundamental shift in the depth and level of the individual's learning and understanding, usually precipitated by a negative, life changing experience, (Borland & Lindgreen, 2013, p. 180)

Therefore, they do not seem to escape the anthropocentric position after all by stating that ecocentric marketing strategies should "satisfy the need of markets", missing the point of an intersubjectivity that includes the non-human other. Borland and Lindgreen refer to "a leap of faith" and "a carefully crafted, step by step learning process". This is a perfect way to describe the dilemma of bridging dominant cognitive learning strategies with the space that would allow for shifts of meaning from lived experience of nature.

References

Abram, D. (2010). *Becoming Animal*. Evansville, IN: Vintage.

Bateson, G. (1979). *Mind and Nature: A Necessary Unity (Advances in Systems Theory, Complexity, and the Human Sciences)*. New York: Hampton Press.

Bauman, W. (2011). Religion, science, and nature: shifts in meaning on a changing planet. *Zygon, 46*: 777–792.

Benjamin, J. (2004). Beyond doer and done to: an intersubjective view of thirdness. *Psychoanalytic Quarterly, LXXIII*: 5–46.

Borland, H., & Lindgreen, A. (2013). Sustainability, epistemology, eco-centric business, and marketing strategy: ideology, reality, and vision. *Journal of Business Ethics, 117*: 173–187.

Curry, P. (2011). *Ecological Ethics*. Cambridge, UK: Polity Press.

Despret, V. (2013). From secret agents to interagency. *History and Theory, 52*: 29–44.

Diehm, C. (2006). Arne Naess and the task of gestalt ontology. *Environmental Ethics, 28*(1): 21–35.

Evans, L., Hicks, C., Cohen, P., Case, P., Prideaux, M., & Mills, D. (2015). Understanding leadership in the environmental sciences. *Ecology and Society*, ISSN 1708–3087.

Ferro, A., & Civitarese, G. (2015). *The Analytic Field and Its Transformations*. London: Karnac.

Gendlin, E. (2003). *Focusing*. London: Rider.

Gendlin, E. T., Beebe, III, J., Cassens, J., Klein, M., & Oberlander, M. (1968). Focusing ability in psychotherapy, personality, and creativity. In: M. M. Shlien (Ed.), *Research in Psychotherapy: Vol. III* (pp. 217–241). Washington, DC: American Psychological Association.

Hailwood, S. (2015). Depending on something bigger. *Environmental Values, 24*: 141–144.

Haraway, D. (2008). Training in the contact zone: power, play, and invention in the sport of agility. In: B. da Costa & K. Philip (Eds.), *Tactical Biopolitics* (pp. 445–464). Cambridge, MA: MIT Press.

Hollway, W., & Jefferson, T. (2013). *Doing Qualitative Research Differently*. Los Angeles, CA: Sage.

Lertzman, R. (2015). *Environmental Melancholia, Psychoanalytic Dimensions of Engagement*. Hove: Routledge.

Merleau Ponty, M. (1968). *The Visible and the Invisible*. Evanstone, IL: Northwestern University Press.

Merleau Ponty, M. (1995). *La Nature, notes, cours du College de France*. Paris: Seuil). In: T. Toadvine (2009), *Merleau-Ponty's Philosophy of Nature*. Evanstone, IL: Northwestern University Press.

Schein, S. (2015). *A New Psychology for Sustainable Leadership: The Hidden Power of Ecological Worldviews*. Sheffield: Greenleaf.

Schouten, M. (2005). *Spiegel van de natuur: het natuurbeeld in cultuurhistorisch perspectief* (2e uitgebr. dr.). Uitgeverij: KNNV.

Searles, H. (1960). *The Nonhuman Environment in Normal Development and in Schizophrenia*. New York: International Universities Press.

Toadvine, T. (2009). *Merleau Ponty's Philosophy of Nature*. Evanstone, IL: Northwestern University Press.

Weintrobe, S. (Ed.) (2013). *Engaging with Climate Change: Psychoanalytic and Interdisciplinary Perspectives*. London: Routledge.

Western, S. (2013). *Leadership: A Critical Text*. London: Sage.

Wolfgramm, R., Coleman, S., & Conroy, D. (2015). Dynamic interactions of agency in leadership (DIAL): an integrative framework for analysing agency in sustainability leadership. *Journal of Business Ethics, 126*: 649–662.

PART II
DOING

CHAPTER FOUR

Researching powerful people: the experience of having access to them

Louisa Diana Brunner

Introduction

This chapter is based on my PhD research on "Family business and crisis from a psycho-social perspective". The research was carried out in the qualitative research tradition of psycho-social studies through the collection of primary data obtained by interviewing family members and top management of two medium-sized, family-owned companies with FANI (free association narrative interviews, Hollway & Jefferson, 2013). The respondents were powerful people and part of an elite, upper middle-class/aristocracy.

In this chapter, I present some lessons learnt researching this specific type of powerful people that are the family business owners/leaders/management, or, as Farazmand (1999) defines them, micro-operational elites, or (Pettigrew, 1992, p. 164) managerial elites. Pettigrew (1992, p. 163) also suggests that it "is one of the most important, yet neglected areas of social science research". My focus will be on the direct experience of accessing powerful people which, as Pettigrew (1992, p. 164) argues, has been, and remains, "a source of constraint on studies of elites". There are many other types of powerful people, such as corporate and government leaders, non-profit top management, leaders of trades unions, politicians, heads in academia, and journalists. I suppose that many of the issues I describe also concern other types of powerful people and elites, but I concentrate on what I have been able to understand from my direct research data and experience privileging the depth of the micro intraorganisational level instead of the breadth of macro-organisational systems or broad society.

Initially, I present a short overview on how powerful people/elites traditionally have been, and are, designated and researched. A vignette from my PhD reflexive research diary on accessing powerful research subjects is illustrated and discussed. Later, the issue of identification with the research subject's values is addressed. Finally, I conclude with a few ideas on some dilemmas and tensions researchers need to be aware of when working psycho-socially with powerful people.

A brief overview on researching powerful people

The theme of powerful people and elites is extensive, studied by many disciplines, debated and controversial, but the purpose of this chapter is to understand what psycho-social studies can contribute specifically in researching them. In examining literature on different approaches mainly (although not exclusively) from a qualitative research perspective where my research is located, two methodological aspects are taken into consideration. On the one hand, how powerful people and/or elites have traditionally been designated or interpreted from a conceptual point of view in terms of the research subjects. On the other hand, how they have been, and are, actually researched in terms of method.

From a historical perspective, early–mid twentieth century sociology and political sciences (e.g., Meisel, 1958; Mills, 1956; Mosca, 1939; Pareto, 1916) have a track record of studying elites and powerful or privileged groups. Most of these studies are theoretical descriptions of wide general societal dynamics and are based on secondary data. I understand there are two basic streams of thought in sociology and political sciences dealing with elites and powerful people: "Elite theory and the concept of power elite, as opposed to the Marxist notion of ruling class . . ." (Farazmand, 1999, p. 324). I do not want to follow this path here, but I want to acknowledge that these two ways of thinking about elites are deeply different and have an impact on the researcher's views. A Marxist or post-Marxist approach to elite or powerful people always comprises an element of conflict in terms of class dynamics, while the elite theory seems more descriptive of inner elite and powerful people dynamics. Since the second part of the twentieth century, in the transition from modern to postmodern in social sciences, other influential schools of thought about power dynamics in society have emerged and influenced qualitative research and also psycho-social studies: for example, feminist theories (Olesen, 2011), postcolonial critique, or race studies (Denzin & Lincoln, 2005). These latter theories, led by broad political and antagonistic agendas towards established elites, aim fundamentally to study and give "a voice" to and empower women and people in less dominant countries or from less powerful ethnic groups. For example, feminist literature and research in this millennium is very diversified in terms of conceptual and pragmatic perspectives and is mainly interested in "emergent questions of gendered social justice...that reflect national contexts where feminist agendas differ widely" (Olesen, 2011, p. 129).

A controversial debate is also if the term elite implies a class element or has to do mainly with social stratification. For example Odendahl and Shaw (2002, p. 301) argue that "the ability to evoke images of 'specifiable groups of persons' is what differentiates elite from other concepts such as class". Furthermore, as Mikecz (2012, p. 483) suggests, generally

> Studies using elites—business, political, or social—are quite rare; most research in social sciences involve "ordinary" individuals leading to an asymmetry in the distribution of knowledge. . . . Elite-oriented studies aim to lessen this asymmetry by providing a flow of knowledge the other way.

The editors of this volume of *Researching Beneath the Surface*, in reviewing an earlier draft of this chapter, have suggested a hypothesis about this. "There's not much by comparison written about investigating 'above'—if anything, sociologists and feminists are not keen to give up the position of privilege that goes along with being a researcher!" Although theories such as feminist ones, postcolonial critiques, or other types of social sciences are important as part of the psycho-social conceptual apparatus, I did not feel them specifically relevant for my research.

More recently, qualitative research authors in social sciences have investigated elites through the collection of primary data. Their work is mainly based on an elite theory approach (Mikecz, 2012; Odendahl & Shaw, 2002; Petkov & Kaoullas, 2016). Odendahl and Shaw (2002, p. 299) suggest that "Elite individuals and groups occupy the top echelons of society . . . Elites generally have more knowledge, money and status and assume a higher position than others in the population". Bergman Blix and Wettergren (2015, p. 692) say that, according to Mills (1999[1956]), "The elite differ from ordinary people in being 'in command' of things beyond the control of ordinary people . . ." Mills (1956, p. 3) calls them "higher circles". A characteristic of elites, as Tittenbrun (2013, p. 135) points out, is that

> elites need to have few bonds of interaction or association . . . Such solidarity occurs only if social mobility, leisure time, socialization, education, intermarriage and other social relations are such that the members of an elite are tied together in regular and recurrent patters of association . . .

Considering the conceptual complexities briefly described above, I prefer the definition of powerful people instead of elites. I feel the word elite is restrictive and encapsulates the concept in a category and limits it. The idea of powerful people or a powerful person feels more dynamic, less broadly sociological, more psycho-social because it better relates to the "here and now" experience of the research activity itself and bridges theory and practice better, as I show in the unfolding of this chapter.

How powerful people have been, and are, researched

For the purpose of this chapter and relevant to the type of powerful people addressed, I have identified four main approaches.

1. Sociological studies, which are based on secondary data and mainly theoretical, as already suggested above. Such theories are important methodologically for psycho-social studies and generally for my conceptual background and ideas, but my research, in its practice about organisational and managerial elites/powerful people at a micro level with all "the nitty and gritty" organisational issues, has not been much influenced by them.

2. "The studies of managerial and organisational elites also include sort of heads of private, public trade unions, educational, cultural, and religious institutions, and voluntary associations" (Pettigrew, 1992, p. 164). Many of these research are conceptualised within the positivist tradition and focus, for example, on the links "between demographic characteristics of top management teams to a variety of organisational outcomes such as performance, innovativeness and strategic change" (Pettigrew, 1992, p. 164) or study of boards, strategic leadership, leadership selection, and succession or other managerial themes.

3. The psycho-dynamic, systemic, and group relations traditions are mainly concerned with methods of working (both professionally and academically) with leadership, authority, and role dynamics of the top leaders of institutions; they do not specifically research elites/powerful people as a social entity. On the one hand, some authors, for example Hirschhorn and Gilmore (2004) on an academic medical centre, Stein (2004) in some of his pivotal papers on the dynamics of catastrophes, Long (2008) on perverse organisations, Lucey (2015) on corporate culture, present ideas, vignettes, and explanatory cases on organisational elites based on secondary sources and/or from the experience working with leaders in their own professions.

4. In recent times, the research carried out in the qualitative research tradition is the most relevant for my research (although the powerful people are different), because it is based on direct field data collection. For example, Petkov and Kaoullas (2016) interviewed policy-making elites, Thuesen (2011) representatives of ministries, trades unions, employers, Mikecz (2012) political and economic elites, and Odendahl and Shaw (2002) philanthropic elites. Two main challenges have been encountered by most of the authors in researching elites and that has been my experience, too: accessibility and "being in the presence" (Erlich et al., 2009) of powerful people.

On the one hand, Odendahl and Shaw (2002, p. 304) suggest that "Interviewing elites calls into question issues of control, power and accessibility" and is "a source of constraint on studies of elite" (Pettigrew, 1992, p. 164). Most of the research (Mikecz, 2012; Odendahl & Shaw, 2002; Petkov & Kaoullas, 2016; Plesner, 2011; Thuesen, 2011) has shown that accessibility is the main challenge with this type of research subjects. Different strategies have been adopted, such as the use of intermediaries (Pektov & Kaoullas, 2016) or gatekeepers who "surround these people and control access to them" (Mikecz, 2012, p. 486). As is shown in the vignette in the next section Odendahl and Shaw (2002, p. 307) suggest "gaining permission to interview an elite subject requires extensive preparation, homework and creativity on the part of the researcher, as well as the right credentials and contacts". Furthermore, Odendahl and Shaw (2002, p. 306) say that a good result can be "predicted upon the researcher's overall knowledge of the elite culture under study, in combination with the personal status and institutional affiliation". It emerges that without getting through an intermediary or a gatekeeper or attending powerful people's events/circle through direct contact with them, it is very difficult to have access to them.

On the other hand, most of the authors who have studied elites agree upon the complexity of the experience of "being in the presence" of powerful people or in a powerful location. This challenges the researcher's own power and cannot be denied (Hunter, 1995). This has a personal inner dimension in terms of the researcher's age, identity, class, and status (Odendahl & Shaw, 2002), and how he exercises his authority and power. There is also an external dimension in terms of personal connections and affiliations, as described above and in the next sections, which are so important for powerful people. This has all sorts of implications in the relationship within the research: for example, Odendahl and Shaw (2002, p. 311) say that a "flattering approach doubtless led to more forthcoming responses". There is no doubt that powerful people are used to having their power recognised and often have many "dignitaries". As they (Odendahl & Shaw, 2002, p. 310) also suggest, "Customs of courtesy, friendliness and professional demeanour are much appreciated . . . In the social upper class these attributes are even more valued and expected than in wider society . . ."

Having all this in mind, the interviewing part does not seem the most difficult phase for most of the authors (Mikecz, 2012; Odendahl & Shaw, 2002; Petkov & Kaoullas, 2016; Plesner, 2011; Thuesen, 2011) and in my experience. However, the preparation and negotiations, prior to the interview, in terms of the location and the time allocated by the interviewee, is the most complicated phase and is quite time-consuming, as is described in the next section.

A vignette: getting to know God

I present a vignette from my reflexive research diary, which I kept throughout my PhD journey. I used it mostly as a countertransference account in which I wrote my feelings and emotions, my intellectual questions and puzzlement, almost immediately after any research encounter. I felt it was instrumental in containing them and, I hoped, in understanding what was going on within me emotionally and intellectually in relation to the interviewee and the examined system. This vignette comes from an encounter with a company in the earlier stages of my research journey. I was not able to include it as a case study in my research project; nevertheless, I think that the vignette tells a lot about the first steps in the encounters with powerful people. All names have been changed and some parts of my diary omitted to protect confidentiality in publication.

A colleague asked me, as a favour for a project of hers, to meet with Mr Laiten, a board member of the Lopez Group, a large well-known multi-national company. When I met him, I realised that the Lopez Group is a family business and I thought it would be a good case study. Mr Laiten seemed a nice and open person and so, after talking it over with my colleague for ethical reasons, I asked Mr Laiten if I could interview the Lopez family. He told me that he would try to talk to them. So I suggested meeting him again to tell him more about my PhD. He invited me to the Lopez group site.

This time, I felt very intimidated at meeting a board member of a large multi-national company, I felt very small in my PhD student role. As the previous time, I was welcomed by the receptionist, who asked me my details and told me that the secretary would come to take me upstairs. I was taken to the top floor and left in a room to wait. Then Mr Laiten arrived. He has had a long career on many international boards. He is a good-looking man in his seventies, elegant, a typical international manager, one of those men you meet on the planes in business class and who are part of an exclusive group of board members worldwide. In the interview, he had pointed out that board members of multi-national corporations are a very exclusive group; it is a much closed circle. This was very evident. I had already written to him about my research ("Family business and crisis: a psycho-social perspective"), but he wanted to hear the whole story again. At a certain point, he told me that it seemed that the Lopez Group had never had a crisis and it was doing

well. He also started to ask what Mr Lopez would gain from the interview. What was the added value for him? I must say that I was very
surprised. I had thought that such a sophisticated man would know the
value of research. I told him that it would be a contribution to research
and a space for reflection and thinking in the presence of a researcher.
Suddenly, he said that it would be interesting for Mr Lopez, the President
[of the company], the only male in the family and the charismatic leader,
to be interviewed, since he does not have children. His next younger
sister has two girls and the youngest sister has a girl. There could be a
crisis about the continuation of the family since the new generation are
all girls. He said that Mr Lopez did not seem to want to think about this.
I said that it would be very interesting for me.

Then Mr Laiten got into a complicated conversation on how to
present me to Mr Lopez. So I asked him if he thought that Mr Lopez
would accept contributing to the research and being interviewed. Mr
Laiten said that it would depend on how he presented it. He started to
ask if I knew the two most famous people on the Board, who I had read
about since they are public figures; they are often interviewed in the
press, but not personally. He said it would make it easier for him when
asking Mr Lopez to participate. I said that I did not know them personally, but if he wanted to be reassured, I would send the link from the
University of the West of England website where they talk about my
PhD. It did not seem enough; he wanted the public figure as a guarantee.
I told him that if I had been there as a consultant it would have been
different, but in this case it was a research, and if somebody did not want
to participate I could understand.

I thought this was wonderful data about interviewing the top-of-the-
ladder powerful people.

But then he said, again, that it would be interesting for me to interview Mr Lopez and he would talk to him this time or next time when he
came to a Board meeting.

I had the feeling that Mr Laiten did not totally understand what I am
doing and the way I am doing it. It was beyond his *Weltanschauung*. It
seemed so strange to him that I did not use my relations with powerful
people to push my research. I had a very different image of him when I
met him previously. He had seemed very open-minded and I liked him.
This was why I had this idea of asking for his help in the research. He
seemed much more defended during this second meeting, as if I wanted
to penetrate the family secrets. Who was I? As a Board member he
seemed to be part of a collective collusion to build a certain image or
"told story", a public image of Mr Lopez, where they are aware of the

problems or secrets, but they must be very firmly kept inside. Who was I, wanting to know more of the real story or experience? I was an outsider, and not part of the "lobby" or of the family.

I sent him the link to the Centre for Psycho-Social studies website. In the end, he suggested that I call Mr Lopez on the phone. When I called Mr Lopez, he said that they did not have a crisis luckily, so there was no reason to be researched, but he agreed to meet me.

Going to meet Mr Lopez, I was very nervous, I got lost and arrived ten minutes late. I was taken by his personal secretary to the top floor of a big building, to the Board room, a wonderful room, lovely view; it looked like being in heaven waiting for God. The secretaries were very nice and helpful. Mr Lopez arrived as if he was God directly. He is in his mid-sixties. I told him again about my research and he did not seem convinced. Since, in the phone call, he had said that luckily they did not have any crisis, as a tactic I thought that I could use the phrase turning points instead of crisis in the conversation there. But he said that perhaps the only difficulty he had was looking for managers for the subsidiaries abroad. I explained to him that I was interested in the connection between the company and the family and that I wanted to interview the family members (him, his younger sisters) in the board and the top management. He said that there had been problems about generation transition at the time of his father but at present there was no problem. At a certain point, I said that I would be interested to understand more about how they decided the roles of the three siblings, and he said that he is the eldest so he was his father's heir and he decides everything. He almost seemed angry and was very authoritarian. He said "I do not have children", but then he asked me if I wanted the book his father wrote, since he thought it talked of the issues I am looking at. Obviously, I said yes. He went out, shouting to his secretary to find the book and gave it to me. He thanked me for the visit and I said that he should not participate in the research if he did not feel like it. As mentioned above, the latter was what happened.

Reflections on the vignette

I now present some issues that this vignette raises for a psycho-social researcher. The vignette is the most extreme case I encountered in my research; nevertheless, the dynamics of accessing and researching powerful people was, in some way, quite similar to other cases mentioned in the section, "A brief overview on researching powerful people", above (Mikecz, 2012; Odendahl & Shaw, 2002; Petkov & Kaoullas, 2016).

Acessibility and the intermediaries/gatekeepers

The vignette shows quite clearly how many barriers, both physical (the meetings on the top floor) and emotional, there are in meeting a powerful company leader. The path to direct contact with this power-ful potential "research subject" (Hollway & Jefferson, 2000) was very tortuous and it was about entering a closed "higher circle" (Mills, 1956) and negotiating with the intermediary. My colleague who intro-duced me to the Lopez Group is a well-established professional, Mr Laiten was a filter and part of the powerful elite clan, but they needed further guarantees from some famous Board members. This confirms what was suggested by Mills (1956, p. 281) that "members of higher circles know one another as personal friends . . . they mingle with one another on the golf club, in gentleman's clubs, on transcontinental airplanes, and on ocean liners" Mills (1956, p. 283) also says that their interests (political and social ideas, leisure time activities, and affini-ties, origins, education, careers) "make it possible for them to say, about one another: He is, of course, 'one of us'". I felt that I was not perceived as one of them socially, it was quite clear that they did not consider me part of their "higher circles" (Mills, 1956). They wanted me to show my pedigree and to mobilise contacts to reach those famous people as a guarantee for them to trust me. Furthermore, I was also a woman in what sounded like a very male orientated culture. As suggested above, a neutral, straightforward approach in contacting the research participants, such as writing a letter asking them to participate in the research, cannot work. For example, I have worked most of my life with family businesses and with their leaders, who are, in different degrees, all powerful people in their companies and domains.

When I started my PhD research wanting to interview the leaders of the company, I could foresee some of the issues described in the vignette. I decided to find and approach the companies to be researched through my professional network. Nevertheless, what I thought would be a smooth path turned out to be full of complications and obstacles. Full of enthusiasm for my research project, confident in my skills in approaching entrepreneurs, and trusting my network, I contacted different parties. As with Mr Laiten in the case of the Lopez group, the main dynamic was that nearly every person I contacted seemed very interested in helping me find the companies during our first conversation but, in practice, in most cases nothing ensued. For example, in two cases I contacted a colleague and that person perceived me as a competitor and an invader/intruder in her/his space. In the transition from expressing an interest in putting me in touch with a company, something would block the process. But nobody asked me for a guarantee from famous Board members, except in the Lopez case. It could be due to the fact that most of the other contacts were with less prominent companies. It took almost a year of "false starts" (as in the Lopez group) to find the two companies that are part of my research.

From these disappointments and frustrations, I learnt that in order to have access to a family business and to a company for research, both directly with the owners, who are powerful people in their organisation and through intermediaries or gatekeepers, negotiations are long and complicated.

Gatekeepers are commonly used in ethnographic research to access the field (O'Reilly, 2009). Qualitative researchers (e.g., Mikecz, 2012; Petkov & Kaoullas, 2016) agree upon the important role of intermediaries and gatekeepers. They are "the key people who let us in, give us permission, or grant access" (O'Reilly, 2009, p. 1). Morrill and colleagues (2009) argue that "identifying gatekeepers provides useful analytic devices for learning about the vocabularies of structure in an organization". Intermediaries can have both formal and informal roles in the organisation and they can shed light on "the various boundaries of an organization, the existence of particular organizational components, how legitimate authority is organized . . ." (Morrill et al., 2009, p. 68). Furthermore, the person through whom access is gained will have an important impact on the research itself (O'Reilly, 2009).

As described in the vignette, in my case my initial contact with Mr Laiten was as an interviewee of another research, then he became an intermediary who put me in touch with Mr Lopez, and, later, a gatekeeper. At the time, I did not take into account these transitions and his new role of gatekeeper. So, as mentioned above, I wrote in my research diary that I was surprised that he had started to ask me what Mr Lopez would gain from the interview. I also wrote that I had thought that such a sophisticated man would know the value of research. This transition confused me, but it is also evidence how roles can change and be fluid and how they have an impact on the research process.

Privacy and trust

Confidentiality is an essential feature in my experience of researching powerful people; it is the first thing one needs to state and guarantee in the encounter. But it is not enough: privacy and confidentiality are *over the surface*, and this type of interviewees also need *under the surface* trust in you.

The theme of trust is very broad, too, so I focus only on my research experience and just highlight a few definitions of trust to frame this idea. Rousseau and colleagues (1998, p. 395) define trust as "a psychological state comprising the intention to accept vulnerability based upon positive expectations of the intentions or behaviour of another". With regard to trust, Sundaramurthy (2008, p. 89) also suggests "individuals engaged in exchanges will make sincere efforts to uphold their commitments and will not take advantage of the given opportunity". From a psychoanalytical perspective, Fonagy and Allison (2014) talk about

> trust in the authenticity and personal relevance of interpersonally transmitted information; (Sperber et al., 2010; Wilson & Sperber, 2012) between the patient and the therapist in a way that helps the patient to relinquish the rigidity that characterizes individuals with enduring personality pathology.

Fonagy and Allison (2014, p. 373) also suggest that "secure attachment experiences . . . are also key to the formation of epistemic trust—that is, an individual's willingness to consider new knowledge from another person as trustworthy, generalizable, and relevant to the self". As a psycho-social researcher, I think it is fundamental to have these definitions in mind as a conceptual framework, but, in a brief encounter, especially in the initial phases of a research in recruiting the interviewees, it would have been too complicated to check issues such as the attachment history of potential participants, although it might come up in the narrative material.

In my research, it involved also entering family life, its intimacy and its secrets. Psycho-socially, this type of trust can be framed as a "rapport". It is something warm, a primitive, affective, instinctive, and emotional dimension a bit like the baby's need to trust the mother. It is a challenge for the researcher because of the personal and professional boundary management involved. With regard to the external context, it is quite obvious that powerful people are afraid of being used and/or abused due to their position, power, assets, and wealth. In my experience, usually they are quite aware both of the seduction of their authority and power and of the envious feelings they can evoke in others and the destructiveness that can be induced by their power and/or wealth. They never know why people contact them and what they want from them. Therefore, this is one of the many reasons for having intermediaries and gatekeepers and it is easier for them to stay in their closed, well-known circles (Mills, 1956) where they know the cultural norms and codes and they feel they can share such experience.

In my research experience, the issue of gaining the trust of the interviewees oscillated in two opposite directions. On the one hand, there has been the extreme case of Mr Lopez, described above, where conquering his trust was impossible. On the other hand, in the two case studies of my PhD research, trust was not an issue with the interviewee. A powerful example was signing the informed consent, a document containing consent to participate in the project that requires a signature, which was presented to each interviewee before the interview process began. For most of them, it was the first moment of the encounter with me. After seeing me for only fifteen minutes, the first interviewee in the first case study signed the informed consent without reading it. I had suggested that he should read it, but he said, "I trust you." It was quite unexpected and shocking, I was ready for all sorts of negotiations. Most of the others signed the informed consent more or less in the same way, hardly reading it. In my experience, entrepreneurs do not believe in these sorts of obligations or, at least, less than other types of professionals.

Furthermore, they are often quite quick because time is very precious and they mainly follow their own intuition more than rational or legal criteria. So, my interviewees' reactions were consistent with their community cultural behaviour and traits. I also wondered if my interviewees understood the overall research project and, therefore, could trust me, since they signed it unhesitatingly. Did they trust me because I had been referred by a reliable person, intermediary, or gatekeeper, or due to the way I presented myself and my professional background, or because of the university where I was doing my PhD? Although I will never have a complete answer to these questions, in the interviewing phase, in reading the transcripts, listening to the tapes, and during the data analysis, it never occurred to me that they had not understood what I was doing. Perhaps they did not understand the nuances or the sophistication or technicalities of a psychosocial approach, and perhaps they gained some sort of narcissistic reward in terms of the prestige of being researched for a foreign university. However, my feeling was that intuitively they knew and adhered to my research in search of something they hoped could benefit them personally, although they did not know consciously what it could be, and, therefore, they trusted me. I hypothesise that this type of behaviour could occur also with other types of powerful people, although personally I have not researched them directly.

The power allure of the environment

In the Lopez case, more than in any other one in my research, the physical environment and the very deferent behaviour of the people around Mr Lopez (his employees) contributed to create the power allure. They depend on him and on his authority and power for their jobs. The fact that Mr Lopez's office was on the top floor, the view over the town, the type of furniture, all had a strong impact. The secretaries treated me with deference. Although this could all be my own projection, I felt that they also perceived me as a lucky and important person because I had access to Mr Lopez, therefore they empowered me. But as mentioned above, nevertheless I felt very small in my student role when I was in the presence of Mr Lopez or Mr Laiten. When I realised that there were some difficulties in carrying out the research, I immediately said to Mr Lopez that he should not participate in the research if he did not feel like it. I colluded, and, defensively, my attitude was take it or leave it. I was so scared and overwhelmed by that power.

While I was reviewing the first draft of this chapter, I read in the newspapers that Mr Lopez had died. It shocked and saddened me; he was my age. Suddenly, I remembered that Mr Laiten had told me that Mr Lopez had been seriously ill. I read the obituaries carefully and the image that emerged was different from my experience with him. He was presented as a caring, thoughtful, and sensible man. Obviously, I am aware that obituaries, as memorials, usually present the best of the deceased person. But, in the case of Mr Lopez, there was something authentic, loving, and real in those writings. So I asked myself, who was Mr Lopez really, beyond his power mask and role? I asked myself what I had really understood of him and what I had projected on him. What a pity I could not carry out the interviews in his company.

So, the power allure depends also on the position of the researcher and her projections. When I was referred to Mr Laiten by my colleague from a well-known university, he recognised my authority. When I was welcomed by the Lopez Group staff as a guest entering the system, I was greeted as powerful; when I was researching as a PhD student, it was much more difficult to retain my authority. The image and power of Mr Lopez that I had introjected was different from that portrayed in the obituaries. What emerges from all this is that power is not static, but fluid, it changes depending of the position of those involved, the projections and projective identifications that affect the dynamics. Furthermore, it is evidence that it is not only about individual authority and power, but it is the whole system: that recognising a person's authority and power contributes to making people powerful (Obholzer & Roberts, 1994).

Resistance to change

There was also another dimension involved in my encounter with Mr Lopez's resistance to participating in the research which needs to be mentioned and taken into account in the research process, although perhaps it is not specific to powerful people. As we know, any encounter of a consultant or a researcher with a system can lead, *per se*, to a change in the system. In my case, the PhD researcher role and my consultant background consciously or unconsciously could convey the idea of me as an agent of potential change that was not necessarily desired or requested. In the Lopez Group case, this could be one of the reasons for not participating in the research. In my encounter with Mr Laiten, I had the feeling that, although he was slightly ambivalent, he thought that Mr Lopez could benefit from being interviewed. I undervalued that Mr Laiten could have had his own agenda. This small potential possibility contributed to my decision to contact Mr Lopez, who instead gave me the feeling of a strong resistance to change. But reflecting about it now, years later, at the time I was a bit naïve and I colluded with my desire and ambition to have them on board with my research and I forgot my consultant background. Probably, Mr Lopez could not gain anything, because he did not want to change, he could not change. He resisted defensively and unconsciously because being researched meant being confronted with the problem of succession and his death (he was ill) and this had just to be acknowledged.

Identification with the researched subjects' values

I want to deal with an issue that I was confronted with during my research journey with regard to powerful people, which needs to be addressed in a psycho-social project. I feel that psycho-social studies, as described in most of the literature I was able to review, have a socio-political agenda. As suggested earlier, it developed at a specific historical moment of the emergence of the need for change in society (Frosh, 2014; Hoggett, 2014) and is inspired by disciplines that challenge the social and political *status quo*, for example, critical theory, feminist theory, postcolonial critique, etc. They inform psycho-social studies and constantly remind the researcher of the social, political, and specific cultural national dimension involved. As Williams (2012, p. 19) argues, "the familiar focus for studying social problems is the down-system people who are poor, oppressed and powerless". However, having researched family business, I also had to take into account the business dimension, although family business is a bit in the middle because profit is certainly an aim for the survival of the firm, care and wellbeing of the family is also pursued. So, it is obvious that such a type of organisation, as all businesses and their leaders, pursues a set of primary tasks based on performance and profit margins, a task which is different from a "non-profit" one which pursues, for example, care or the health of the community. I feel that there is sort of tension and ambiguity (in the sense of different interpretations) in terms of values between psycho-social studies, the methodology used, and the research object in terms of the business aims involved in family business or in any other type of business. In my research experience, it is not an insurmountable one, but it is something to be aware of when researching businesses and powerful people psycho-socially.

Furthermore, when I started my PhD research journey, my main concern or interest was about family businesses as organisations, their leadership and management structure, and dynamics in respect to crisis. I did not immediately make the link to the fact that I was going to interview powerful people or elites. It was only in progress that I realised the importance of this dimension and how this topic had not been much explored in psycho-social studies. One of my major learnings from psycho-social studies is the issue of the "subject's position". Frosh (2003, p. 1564) conceptualises the psycho-social subject "as a meeting point of inner and outer forces, something constructed and yet constructing, a power-using subject which is also subject to power". Clarke and Hoggett (2009, p. 13) suggest that positioning "refers to the positions a subject can adopt in relation to a discourse such as class . . .". Positioning is fundamental for locating both researcher and the researched subject, identifying where they came from, where they are "put" in reality, and/or in the mental and unconscious map (Clarke & Hoggett, 2009). It is as in geography, where you need to know where things are on the map to understand them and make sense. In this respect, I was aware that my biography was an important part of my motivation to research family business and powerful people.

On my father's side, I came from a Jewish family that owned a business, but, unfortunately, the family business had to be closed during the depression in 1929. My mother came from a German–Jewish intellectual family. Both my parents and their families deeply suffered the consequences of the Holocaust. I was brought up in a bourgeois family. But the powerful people and elite dimension was not immediately consciously easy to position and acknowledge in my internal map with respect to my PhD research. It has probably to do with the fact that I was quite ambivalent about the privileged world in which I lived. In the past, this has played out in a sort of rebellion to it, in a denial of such belonging, and a strong need to make my way alone. In any case, when I was able to recognise and connect all this, despite all the contradictions, my personal "position" and experience were important when researching and "interviewing up", because I could understand and identify with some of the social and cultural dynamics of powerful people.

All this, my personal experience about positioning and the tensions and ambivalence between methodology and researched object described above, has led me to think that a certain degree of emphatic identification with the researched subject's values is necessary to be able to carry out a psycho-social research, and in research in general. On the more psychological side, in psychotherapy Bordin (1979) introduced the concept of a working alliance between the therapist and the patient. Unlike transference, it is about "a reality-oriented relation-ship" (Johnson & Wright, 2002, p. 260). According to Bordin (1979, p. 252) "The working therapeutic alliance between the person who seeks change and the one who offers to be the change agent is one of the keys, if not the key, to the change process". In family business consultancy, a "chemistry meeting" is suggested before deciding to work with the client to explore whether one is able to work with her/him (Hilburt-Davis & Dyer, 2003, p. 36). As Johnson and Wright (2002, p. 260) suggest, "the strength of the alliance is determined by the compatibility of the demands of a particular therapeutic alliance and the characteristics of the client and therapist".

On the other hand, on a more societal side, as addressed above, the positionality of the researcher is a key element. For example, I could not have worked with my interviewees had I been too shocked by their wealth, seduced or envious of it, or had I felt the need to ques-tion it for some ideological reason. The job of the researcher is to understand the emotional logic behind certain phenomena, in spite of any ideological challenge or position. Nevertheless, this is fraught with problems, depending on where the researcher comes from and what ideas he has, for example, about society and how he relates polit-ically and ideologically to the profit and not-for-profit dimension and, therefore, in my research into the family business. In my case, my family background proved to be helpful. I was brought up in a family business culture, so I can understand the logic behind the desire to have and run a company that pursues profits. But, as stated above, I am ambivalent about this matter, in the sense that, at the same time, I can understand and identify with the more socially and politically orientated values of psycho-social studies. As with any other subjec-tive dimension of the researcher, it inevitably has an impact in the research encounter and it is important for the researcher to be aware of her own assumptions, value base, ambiguities, and also internal contradictions. In this sense, I have specifically found psycho-social reflexive practices helpful in being alerted that, for example, the trans-ference–countertransference dynamics tell us something not just about the researched subject, but also about ourselves. As Beedell (2009, p. 117) suggests,

the reflexive interviewer needs to be more than just an emotional labourer, s/he needs to be a kind of psychological athlete: conscious of their own strengths and weaknesses or injuries, imbued with courage and stamina, and able to acknowledge and use the characteristics of the "psychological equipment" with which they work.

For example, as presented in the vignette, initially I was irritated with Mr Laiten when he enquired (I felt it almost as an inquisition) about who I knew among the famous Board members. I am quite allergic to that type of "connections" approach, due also to my ambivalence to powerful people described above. I felt the whole location overwhelming and "too powerful" for my taste and for who I am and where I come from. The way Mr Lopez treated his secretaries was unbearable, as also his chauvinist culture about women. My ambition to have such a prominent company to present to my dissertation panel had led me to pursue the meetings with them. All this made me more vulnerable to the possibility of being caught in a "projective identification" dynamic. In psychoanalysis, "the concept of 'projective identification' has illuminated the subtle but powerful ways in which a subject can be nudged, seduced, or coerced into occupying a particular position in relation to the other" (Clarke & Hoggett, 2009, p. 13). Probably, I colluded with the system which had pushed me also to have the fantasy that if I had been allowed to research them, I would have had to manage the feeling of being "too small" and excluded as a woman the whole time and work could not take place.

Therefore, I believe that some degree of empathic identification with the values and beliefs of the research participants plays an important role. Such identification also means that the researched subject can feel the empathy and care of the researcher and, thereby, feel contained. As in the vignette, if the researcher is too ambivalent about the values of the researched subject a good working alliance, although limited temporarily as a research encounter, cannot happen and this has implications for the ethical dimension of the encounter in terms of the researcher's projections and countertransference management.

Concluding thoughts

Personally, I am pleased that I was able to open this new and original path in psycho-social studies by researching powerful people, although, as described in this chapter, many are the challenges for the researcher, who needs to be continuously attentive and alert. Some issues are specific to powerful people, as I have tried to highlight, and need to be recognised as such. These are, for example, accessibility and the participation in the research itself (which I have addressed extensively in this chapter), their values, the power dynamic, resistances, and the need for some degree of emphatic identification with the researched subject. In terms of lessons learnt from a methods point of view about the dilemmas and tensions that the psycho-social researcher is confronted with, I would like to outline a few aspects.

The need of coherence in the research design between the method and the researched subject

In designing my research as a psycho-social research project on powerful people, at its outset some ideas were drawn from the qualitative research tradition. Research shows that researching elites needs some adjustments to these types of participants (Mikecz, 2012; Plesner, 2011; Thuesen 2011). For example, Bergman Blix & Wettergren (2015, p. 692) suggest that "in building trust when conducting elite interviews", or researchers' "styles in the process of negotiating status" are important. It is helpful to use an approach based on "practical rationality . . . often translated as 'practical reasoning'" (Thuesen, 2011, p. 613). Therefore, ". . . one should act according to experience and contextual circumstances rather than seeking universal rules for guidance (Flyvbjerg, 2001, pp. 55–60)" (Thuesen, 2011, p. 613). It is about "emotional sensitivity in developing a qualitative methodology relevant for studying tension-rife social situations" (Thuesen, 2011, p. 620).

As stated throughout this chapter, the powerful people I have researched are a specific type of powerful people, family business owners and managers. So, I had to carefully take into account who my research subjects were and adopt a qualitative method which could facilitate access during the interview and the work, by giving them the stage and not openly challenging their power directly. This was also true when asking for access, as in the Lopez case, in presenting the research project and type of methods. The choice of the methods played a fundamental role. Besides all the other aspects suggested in this chapter, some degree of coherence between the method used and the research subjects is necessary. For example, in my PhD cases (unfortunately, I did not carry out the interviews in the Lopez case),

FANI (Hollway & Jefferson, 2000, 2013), as a psycho-social narrative and associative methodology and method, proved helpful with powerful people such as organisational owners and managers of family businesses.

Successful entrepreneurs or top managers usually feel they are the "sovereign in their kingdom" and have the full stage in their company, as described in the vignette. They enjoy telling their success story, which enhances their public image, they are used to talking to journalists, and they often seem to have some sort of prepared story ready. I was aware that there could be a tension and some risks between the FANI method aiming to uncover the hidden narratives and the desire of the successful person to tell a success story. Nevertheless, my idea was that asking them their story could be something they could appreciate and would facilitate them, as "defended subjects", to cope with the anxiety inherent in any research encounter; thus, this method could be less threatening initially for them and a good entry point. My assumption was that having established a relationship by means of FANI (Hollway & Jefferson, 2000, 2013), I could hope that the "life history" *and beneath the surface* material would emerge from the "told story". This proved to be true, but some alerts were necessary. On the one hand, during the interview narrative, I kept in my mind the potential tension between the "told story" and the "life experience". Furthermore, I used reflexive practices such as a research diary, supervision, meetings with colleagues, and, in the data analysis phase, working through the researched material and my emotional experience.

The position and subjectivity of the researcher

As already stated, as for every psycho-social researcher researching powerful people, the researcher's positioning and subjectivity awareness and management, as well as that of the researched, is a fundamental tool. But, in researching powerful people, this needs to be stretched a bit more. I have argued that some degree of emphatic identification with the researched subject is necessary, which is an emotional dimension or asset of the researcher. Yet, it can also become part of a technique, skill, or competence in the pursuit of an intersubjective "relationship of mutual recognition—a relation in which each person experiences the other as a 'like subject', another mind who can be 'felt with', yet has a distinct, separate center of feeling and perception" (Benjamin, 2004, p. 5). This can help to create a space and time, an ". . . intersubjective process . . ." (Benjamin, 2004, p. 19) in search of a co-production of meaning by the researcher and the researched subject together.

Beneath the surface

But what makes a difference in a psycho-social approach in researching powerful people, as in any other type of psycho-social research, is the possibility of going beyond a descriptive picture and reaching a deeper level of understanding on the specificity of these "researched subjects" in the "here and now". A psycho-social method and its reflexive practices, also just getting access to powerful people, allows one to recognise their particular anxieties and to explore dynamics individually and socially, as I have tried to outline in this chapter by presenting my dilemmas, tensions, ambivalences, emotional reactions, and questions. Obviously, all this is fraught with problems and needs openness, flexibility, and adaptation on behalf of the researcher. A psycho-social approach has a vast toolbox for exploring the unconscious: I have used FANI, but there are many others, such as social dreaming, visual techniques, and observation, which also could be experimented with to investigate powerful people *beneath the surface*.

In this chapter, I mainly, although not exclusively, focused on having access to powerful people and I have also introduced some ideas about accessing them during the interviews. In terms of practice, I would argue that a psycho-social researcher studying powerful people also needs specific skills and competence in handling all the complicated processes described in this chapter. Sharing a social background "in terms of age, class, gender, ethnicity . . ." (Bergman Blix & Wettergren, 2015, p. 693) with the research subject could perhaps facilitate the job and the empathic identification with the researched subject. Nevertheless, in any case, a constant awareness is necessary through reflexive practices of the seductions, problems, and challenges that being in the presence of powerful people stirs up in ourselves, confronts us in terms of our values, and makes us more vulnerable to projections and projective identification mechanisms.

Conclusion

To conclude, I want to suggest that my research and this chapter shows once more that psycho-social studies, as an interdisciplinary and transdisciplinary methodology and method (Hoggett, 2014), are not a monolithic field and the flexibility this method provides can be helpful in designing research on specific research subjects, such as powerful people. The fluidity and multi-disciplines dimension makes this a "transdisciplinary space"

> an open and contested and hence democratic space; there can be freedom of thought without policing by orthodoxies and entrenched interests; and we can trawl back in time and across in space for the ideas and approaches that might enrich our work. (Frosh, 2014, p. 159)

Although it is fraught with complexities and some limitation, and caution is necessary, this allows the researcher, as in my case, with powerful people to pragmatically pick among the disciplines of psycho-social studies and use the conceptual framework which best fits to understand a specific research subject.

References

Beedell, P. (2009). Charting the clear waters and murky depth. In: S. Clarke & P. Hoggett (Eds.), *Researching Beneath the Surface. Pyscho-Social Research Methods in Practice* (pp. 101–119). London: Karnac.

Benjamin, J. (2004). Beyond doer and done to: an intersubjective view of thirdness. *Psychoanalytic Quarterly, 73*: 5–46.

Bergman Blix, S., & Wettergren, A. (2015). The emotional labour of gaining and maintaining access to the field. *Qualitative Research, 15*(6): 688–704.

Bordin, E. S. (1979). The generalizability of the psychoanalytic concept of the working alliance. *Psychotherapy: Theory, Research and Practice, 16*(3): 252–260.

Clarke, S., & Hoggett, P. (2009). *Researching Beneath the Surface. Pyscho-Social Research Methods in Practice.* London: Karnac.

Denzin, N. K., & Lincoln, Y. S. (2005). *The Sage Handbook of Qualitative Research* (3rd edn). London: Sage.

Erlich, S., Erlich-Ginor, M., & Beland, H. (Eds.) (2009). *"Fed with Tears – Poisoned with Milk". The Nazareth Group-Relations-Conferences, Germans and Israelis—The Past in the Present.* Giessen: Psychosocial.

Farazmand, A. (1999). The elite question. Towards a normative elite theory of organisation. *Administration and Society, 31*(3): 321–360.

Fonagy, P., & Allison, E. (2014). The role of mentalizing and epistemic trust in the therapeutic relationship. *Psychotherapy, 51*(3): 372–380.

Frosh, S. (2003). Psychosocial studies and psychology: is a critical approach emerging? *Human Relations, 56*(12): 1545–1567.

Frosh, S. (2014). The nature of the psychosocial: debates from studies in the psychosocial. *Journal of Psycho-Social Studies, 8*(1): 159–169.

Hilburt-Davis, J., & Dyer, W. G. (2003). *Consulting to Family Businesses: A Practical Guide to Contracting, Assessment, and Implementation.* New York: John Wiley.

Hirschhorn, L., & Gilmore, T. (2004). Working in retreats: learning from the group relations tradition. In: L. Gould, L. F. Stapley, & M. Stein (Eds.), *Experiential Learning in Organisations. Applications of the Tavistock Group Relations Approach* (pp. 85–101). London: Karnac.

Hoggett, P. (2014). Learning from three practices. *Journal of Psycho-Social Studies, 8*(1): 179–196.

Hollway, W., & Jefferson, T. (2000). *Doing Qualitative Research Differently. Free Association, Narrative and the Interview Method.* London: Sage.

Hollway, W., & Jefferson, T. (2013). *Doing Qualitative Research Differently: A Psycho-social Approach* (2nd edn). London: Sage.

Hunter, A. (1995). Local knowledge and local power: notes on the ethnography of local community elites. In: R. Hertz & J. B. Imber (Eds.), *Studying Elites Using Qualitative Methods* (pp. 151–170). Thousand Oaks, CA: Sage.

Johnson, L. N., & Wright, D. W. (2002). Revisiting Bordin's theory on the therapeutic alliance: implications for family therapy. *Contemporary Family Therapy, 24*(2): 257–269.

Long, S. (2008). *The Perverse Organisation and Its Deadly Sins.* London: Karnac.

Lucey, A. (2015). Corporate cultures and inner conflicts. In: D. Armstrong & M. Rustin (Eds.), *Social Defences Against Anxiety: Explorations in a Paradigm* (pp. 213–222). London: Karnac.

Meisel, J. H. (1958). *The Myth of the Ruling Class: Gaetano Mosca and the "Elite".* Ann Arbor, MI: University of Michigan Press.

Mikecz, R. (2012). Interviewing elites: addressing methodological issues. *Qualitative Inquiry, 18*: 424–493.

Mills, C. W. (1956). *The Power Elite.* New York: Oxford University Press [reprinted Oxford: Oxford University Press, 1999].

Morrill, C., Buller, D. B., Klein Buller, M., & Larkey, L. L. (2009). Toward an organizational perspective on identifying and managing formal gatekeepers. *Qualitative Sociology, 22*(1): 51–72.

Mosca, G. (1939). *The Ruling Class,* H. D. Kahn (Trans.). New York: McGraw-Hill.

Obholzer, A., & Roberts, V. (Eds.) (1994). *The Unconscious at Work: Individual and Organisational Stress in Human Services.* London: Routledge.

Odendahl, T., & Shaw, A. M. (2002). Interviewing elites. In: J. E. Gubrium & J. A. Holstein (Eds.), *Handbook of Interview Research: Context and Method* (pp. 229–317). Thousand Oaks, CA: Sage.

Olesen, V. (2011). Feminist qualitative research in the millennium's first decade: developments, challenges, prospects. In: N. K. Denzin & Y. S. Lincoln (Eds.), *Handbook of Qualitative Research* (4th edn) (pp. 129–146). Thousand Oaks, CA: Sage.

O'Reilly, K. (2009). *Key Concepts in Ethnography.* London: Sage.

Pareto, V. (2016). *Trattato di Sociologiia Generale.* Florence: G. Barbera.

Petkov, M., & Kaoullas, L. G. (2016). Overcoming respondent resistance at elite interviews using an intermediary. *Qualitative Research, 16*(4): 411–429.

Pettigrew, A. M. (1992). On studying managerial elites. *Strategic Management Journal, 13*(Special Issue), "Fundamental Themes in Strategy Process Research": 163–182.

Plesner, U. (2011). Studying sideways: displacing the problem of power in research interviews with sociologists and journalists. *Qualitative Inquiry, 17*: 471–482.

Rousseau, D., Sitkin, S., Burt, R., & Camerer, C. (1998). Not so different after all: a cross discipline view of trust. *Academy of Management Review, 23*: 405–421.

Sperber, D., Clement, F., Heintz, C., Mascaro, O., Mercier, H., Origgi, G., & Wilson, D. (2010). Epistemic vigilance. *Mind & Language, 25*: 359–393.

Stein, M. (2004). The critical period of disasters: insights from sensemaking and psychoanalytic theory. *Human Relations, 57*(10): 1243–1261.

Sundaramurthy, C. (2008). Sustaining trust within family businesses. *Family Business Review, 22*(1): 91–102.

Thuesen, F. (2011). Navigating between dialogue and confrontation: phronesis and emotions in interviewing elites on ethnic discrimination. *Qualitative Inquiry, 7*(7): 613–622.

Tittenbrun, J. (2013). Ralph Daharendorf's conflict theory of social differ-
    entiation and elite theory. *Innovative Issues and Approaches in Social
    Sciences*, 6(3): 117–140.
Williams, C. (2012). *Researching Power, Elites and Leadership*. London: Sage.
Wilson, D., & Sperber, D. (2012). *Meaning and Relevance*. Cambridge:
    Cambridge University Press.

CHAPTER FIVE

"Every human being is an artist": from social representation to creative experiences of self

Julian Manley

Introduction

In a chapter I wrote for the first *Researching Beneath the Surface* book (Clarke & Hoggett, 2009), I suggested that there was room within the panoply of psycho-social methods for a method focused on visual imagery and affect rather than words (Manley, 2009). In that chapter, titled "Words are not enough", I concluded that psycho-social studies should work towards an understanding of how unconscious images are intimately linked to affect, an inclusion of this understanding in our research, and the creation of new methodologies that allow for the assessment and evaluation of affect in psycho-social research (2009, p. 96). The reason for needing to do this was, I suggested, to reach the "beneath the surface" understandings of complex situations that defied discursive explanations. At the time of writing, 2009, it was only social dreaming (Lawrence, 2005; Manley, 2014), with its emphasis on dream images and free association, which went some way towards satisfying these demands. However, at the time, social dreaming was largely practice-based rather than research-orientated. Work using social dreaming in research is now under way (Berman & Manley, in press; Karolia & Manley, in press; Manley & Trustram,

2016); however, until recently, the practice-based orientation of social dreaming had stymied its development as a psycho-social research method (Manley, 2009). Furthermore, the use of dreams is itself problematical, since they are perhaps our most abstract and incomprehensible expressions of thought, undoubtedly emerging from our unconscious and difficult to interpret with any degree of certainty. This is partly a philosophical and epistemological question. In other words, it depends on your point of view. In 2009, I went on to say that it would be easier to accept the use of social dreaming and related methods in research by approaching them through a Deleuzian lens. It was through Deleuzian ideas of "affect", "difference", and "becoming" that I tried to make sense of aspects of working with the visual imagination (Manley, 2009).

The method discussed in the present chapter—the visual matrix—is the result of the development of these thoughts. In the visual matrix, we do away with social dreaming's emphasis on dreams but continue with the use of imagery in the mind and free association. As in social dreaming, we are primarily concerned with how the expression of affect through shared unconscious images and visualisations can help us to discover and understand complexities that would otherwise remain hidden and unexpressed. In developing the visual matrix with colleagues at the Psychosocial Research Unit at the University of Central Lancashire, the focus has been on developing it as a method for research by locating the visual matrix within the framework of a research topic or question and developing a rigorous analytical method for the interpretation of data (Froggett et al., 2015; Manley & Roy, 2017; Manley et al., 2016).

In the present chapter, I aim to further explore the usefulness of taking on a Deleuzian approach to the visual matrix. Previous work on the visual matrix has combined various approaches to understanding the method: via Deleuzian concepts of affect and a rhizomatic understanding of how the images make meaning through being interlinked in web-like patterns, instead of sequences of words in sentences; through Alfred Lorenzer's concept of "scenic understanding", which suggests that a "scene" such as that created in the associated images of the visual matrix can be used to describe the moment when the individual in the visual matrix shares with others a symbolic world in images or words; by references to the world of object relations and psychoanalytically informed thinking, which is more familiar to psycho-social studies, such as Bion's theory of thinking, containment, and reverie, and Winnicott's potential space (Froggett et al., 2015, p. 5). The present chapter tries to see how far the visual matrix can be perceived as a truly Deleuzian method, by bringing in further Deleuzian ideas and theories and testing them against a case study that used the visual matrix as the primary research method. In doing so, I will also attempt to situate Deleuze within the possibilities of psycho-social research methods.

The case study: an artwork in the archive

The context of the research is an artwork and exhibition titled "Demolition Street", which ran from 5th May to 5th June 2015 at the Lancashire County Archive. "Demolition Street" is at once a record and an aesthetic expression of the artist William Titley's engagement with the enforced eviction of a community from their homes in Bright Street in a small town in the North West of England.

The artwork consisted of photography, found objects, and videos of the remaining residents talking about their immanent eviction. The videos were located inside and outside a wooden triangular structure. Inside this structure, the videos depicted the pictures of the interviewees but the audio consisted of only the breaths and gaps in between the spoken words. The videos on the outside showed the opposite, the spoken words with the pauses, sighs, and intakes of breath cut out. The effect was that of emphasising the emotional information expressed in the sighs and pauses of the interviewees on the one hand, and, on the other hand, the relative sterility of the spoken word without these natural interjections. By manipulating the sound of the videos, the artist is pointing out that the exhibition experience is appealing to all the senses, not just the visual. This reminds us of the complexity of talking about "visual" as if it were somehow possible to separate it from the other senses. It also speaks to the experience of the visual matrix, which is an embodied, felt experience and not just a process of visual codification or simple symbolisation. Other videos were located inside the archive lockers, creating a claustrophobic sense of confined and private space for the viewer. The found objects included door handles, forgotten mail, and an iconic ironing board (see Image 2, on p. 114) that was used as an image to represent the exhibition. One of the archive's computers displayed a continuous list of names of people who had lived in Bright Street, to a sound of "tick-tock" in headphones, repeated over and over. The central theme of the exhibition was described by the artist as "issues of displacement in the face of adversity and legislation of regeneration and the renewal of place" (artist's information leaflet).

Place, space, and territory

The exhibition in 2015 brought the reality of a regeneration scheme from the past—the "Housing Market Renewal Initiative" in Bright Street, Colne, Lancashire, 2005—to a new territory where past is archived and stored for present and future, the Lancashire County Archives in Preston. The archive exists to "collect and preserve Lancashire's unique and irreplaceable archives and make them available for exploring personal, family or community history and heritage" (www.lancashire.gov.uk/libraries-and-archives.aspx). The exhibition, with its collection of found objects, photographs, and videos, can be seen as a temporary contribution to the archive, which brings the artwork close to a historical record. At the same time, the exhibition was an intrusion into the space of the archive, and put a strain on the more usual use of the lecture room, for example, as noted in the internal evaluation document produced by the archive.

The arts project and the visual matrix process begin, therefore, with challenges to "territories" in space and time, a Deleuzian prerequisite for creative thinking, *"like a passage from the finite to the infinite, but also from territory to deterritorialization"* (Deleuze & Guattari, 1994, p. 180, original emphasis). According to Deleuze and Guattari, it is deterritorialisation that rids us of the familiar and routine and creates new "territories" where creativity is released. This is simply explained in the following extract from *A Thousand Plateaus*:

> The orchid deterritorializes by forming an image, a tracing of a wasp: but the wasp reterritorializes on that image. The wasp is nevertheless deterritorialized, becoming a piece in the orchid's reproductive apparatus. But it reterritorializes the orchid by transporting its pollen the orchid by transporting its pollen. (Deleuze & Guattari, 1988, p. 10)

The extract refers to the ability of the orchid to mimic the female wasp, thus attracting the male wasp, that then inadvertently picks up the orchid's pollen, which is finally transported away for pollination elsewhere (www.youtube.com/watch?v=-h8I3cqpgnA). Orchid and wasp exist in a mutual and creative relationship where two different territories are shared, belonging either to the orchid or the wasp and, in a relational creativity, to both. Similarly, once Bright Street has been deterritorialised from its physical origins in place and time—its territory—and made into a collection of pieces that together form an artwork titled "Demolition Street", which is subsequently reterritorialised into the Lancashire County Archive, we are engaged in a creative process that creates new territories that are populated by creative "others"—the visitors to the exhibition. The creation of yet another territory, that of the visual matrix, is an extension of the process, where the contributions of the visitors become a collective social testament and creative act that can be at once individual and collective. Through the visual matrix, the creative experiences of the visitors in contact with the exhibition were developed into something more than feedback or assessment of the experience of seeing the artwork. Armstrong, in discussing the relationship between exterior (outer world) and interior (inner world) images, describes the embodied, emotional, and "becoming" nature of this process:

> When I look at a great painting, say one of Cezanne's still lives, I do not see the emotional experience that was the origin of Cezanne's transforming work as an artist. Rather, I have an emotional experience myself . . . I do not just understand or see something new, I become something new. (Armstrong, 2005, p. 16)

It is in this inner process of "becoming", which Deleuze and Guattari (1994, p. 179) directly linked to "sensation" as part of the artistic experience, that the spectator is no longer what he or she was, but "becomes" a new or different being.

The visual matrix in the archive

In "Demolition Street", I conducted four visual matrices over the period of the exhibition. Each visual matrix consisted of between ten and fifteen participants, some of whom assisted in more than one and others who were only present for a single matrix, making for a different mix of people every time. The participants were recruited via the distribution of flyers, email lists, radio interviews, and a press release. A condition of participation was to have viewed the exhibition at least once, and each visual matrix was preceded by an unguided viewing of the exhibition. Each session was two hours long and consisted of the visual matrix itself (sixty minutes); a break (fifteen minutes); and a post-matrix discussion (forty-five minutes). Additionally, the participants were invited to leave the post-matrix discussion for a few minutes at a time, in order to personally video-record a personal thought or feeling in a separate room, if they wanted to. In this way, participants could get a sense of the way their individual image-affects could be simultaneously both individual and shared. This individual recording was then incorporated into the exhibition the next day, thus becoming part of the collective process once more.

The main challenge for a psycho-social researcher new to the method is the gathering together of a group of people who are clear about, and committed to, the task and to ensure that the session proceeds in a contained and undisturbed manner. If the task is properly explained to the participants and time is given over to the answering of questions, if everyone is committed to staying the full two hours, and if the room is quiet and undisturbed, then, more often than not, the visual matrix "runs itself".

In the matrix, participants were encouraged to offer images and feelings that they had had while visiting the exhibition or were spontaneously arising during the matrix itself. These images/affect were not necessarily direct reactions to the artwork as object(s) but, in the way described by Armstrong, above, expressions of the embodied experiences of each individual shared and interconnected with those of others in the matrix.

Rhizomes, intensities of affect, and time(lessness)

Deleuze conceived of affect as being the expression of multi-layered intensities of emotion distributed in what he called a "rhizome". That is to say, in an indefinite, directionless, interconnected tangle, where meaning arises through temporary and heterogeneous connections of intensity of affect, which are constantly fluctuating. Deleuze and Guattari's example of the wasp and the orchid (1988, p. 10) is further developed by calling this unlikely partnership a "rhizome". The emergence of meaning in the visual matrix through these expressions occurs in this rhizomatic fashion, where each visual and affective fragment (which I have previously called "image-affect" (Manley, 2009)) creates unstable relationships with other fragments. Temporary meanings are constantly emerging and submerging through these interconnected intensities of image-affects. The relationships between the images are subject to constant potential change during the course of the matrix. They are not fixed meanings. With the introduction of new image-affects, meanings emerge through a resonance with other, previously expressed, images, but not in an immediately sequential fashion. An image expressed towards the end of the matrix might well "ignite" an image that had been expressed at the beginning. A new image could trigger the intensity, value, and relevance of an image that had, until then, been dormant.

This process is highly suggestive of a Deleuzian understanding of "intensities" of affect. The rhizome of image-affects behaves like Deleuze's description of "intensive multiplicities", consisting of "particles" whose "relations are distances; their movements are Brownian [JM's note: Brownian movement describes the random movement of microscopic particles suspended in a liquid or gas]; their quantities are intensities, differences in intensity" (Deleuze & Guattari, 1988, p. 33). Importantly, although this rhizome in the visual matrix might have emerged into being in the time span of the matrix, this visual matrix time is that of Bergson's "duration" rather than clock time: "uninterrupted transition, multiplicity without divisibility and succession without interruption" (Bergson, 2002, p. 205). Its meanings are not dependent on logical, linear clock time sequences, but are emergent according to intensities within a multiplicity of potential meanings that might occur at any time and in any order. This is why the rhizome in the matrix corresponds to a truly Deleuzian "rhizomatic multiplicities", as opposed to linear branching out, what Deleuze and Guattari called "aborescent multiplicities" (1988, p. 33). By "aborescent", they are referring to the multiple branchings out of a plant or a tree, which—unlike the rhizome—follow clear lines of direction.

The participant sensation in the matrix, then, is one of being immersed in a present space of timelessness, Bergson's "duration", during which expression emerges through a state of "reverie", in the sense that Bion described (Froggett et al., 2015, n. 15). Within the containing space of the visual matrix, a new temporary space–time is established, a new territory. In these conditions, the participants in the matrix are able to enter into creative, visual, and deeply affective relationships with each other, leading to profoundly new ways of feeling and thinking that they would not otherwise have had access to:

> [I was] tearful and emotional, the lights were going out for Bright Street. I was wary of workshop and enjoyed it. I liked the open approach ... Don't get that opportunity often. So often in life you are not able to express about how you feel about what you have seen, I am more likely to think more deeply about things I see and I want to react to. (Participant A, individual recording)

The individual subsumed in the social

The visual matrix brings up important questions of the role of the personal in the (social) collective. Due to its innate creative expressivity, fostered by the instruction to think and feel in visual images, to describe not explain, and to allow meaning to emerge in intensities of affect that are ignited within a rhizomatic structure of shared thinking, the visual matrix touches on the "language" of artistic creation. When used in conjunction with an artwork, in this case "Demolition Street", this effect may be further enhanced. According to Fuglsang and Sørensen, when discussing the mapping of the "social field" from a Deleuzian perspective, "aesthetic expressivity has always been about life as it is actualised in affects that move beyond the self-conscious subject" (2006, p. 11). The visual matrix does, indeed, move beyond the self-conscious subject. This is emphasised first by the way the gaze of each of the participants is diverted from engaging with another person as a result of being asked to sit in a "snowflake" pattern seating arrangement, and, second, by offering images that "float" in the space of the matrix, that are not directed at any other participant in the matrix. In this way, each participant in the matrix achieves a degree of anonymity. This is reflected in the way meaning is allowed to emerge in the course of the matrix. The visual matrix is not focused on individual meanings but, rather, with whatever sense that can be made through a piecing together of the various contributions that have been offered to the space. This visual matrix space, or territory, is more like a Deleuzian "zone of indetermination" (Deleuze & Guatarri, 1994, p. 173) than a space of definition and cognition. In the matrix we experience what Deleuze called "nonorganic life of things", meaning that the creative expression of the matrix creates a vital intensity of affect which is connected together by images in the matrix and unattached to individuals. The "non-organic life" Deleuze refers to is also that of his concept of the "Body without Organs" (BwO). What he meant by this was that by giving our individual bodies that encase our individual organs an especial importance and value, we hinder ourselves from seeing other, rhizomatically connected, systems beyond our immediate knowledge. The visual matrix creates a BwO by removing the importance of the individual in the matrix and replacing this with the "body" of the shared space, the new-found territory.

Thoughts and feelings from the visual matrix

Images such as Image 1 encouraged the expression of a series of image-affects that exposed the gross indignity and inappropriateness of people's personal, private, inner lives being exposed to the public, seemingly without care or concern about the personal, the biological reality of each of the affected people who were evicted:

> Exposure, buildings where the wall has come down, you've got the inside outside, that inside is very personal, a home exposed. And the house is almost "alive", infused with human experience. (VM1)

In this extract, the affective intensity of the image is highlighted through the near personification of the house, resonating with a similar image taken from VM2:

> Individual personalities embodied in the fronts of the individual flats, each flat has a personality in the little black and white images.

Therefore, the tearing down of the walls in the demolition process turns the houses into something that is no longer associated with the people, as we see in VM4:

> I couldn't associate the buildings with the people, I thought they were totally divorced from each other because of what had happened

Image 1.   Photograph from "Demolition Street".

In an example of how experiencing the artwork and the visual matrix brought out the intensity of this dismay at the exposure and powerlessness of the individual, several participants in the fourth visual matrix associated to the sense of the inside being exposed to the outside:

I lived in Dalston in the late 60s and there was a half-demolished build-ing and pink floral wallpaper exposed to the whole of Dalston Junction and they didn't clear away [the] building very fast in those days and it was just there for months, if not years, and something painfully intimate being exposed.

My flat was demolished and my interior walls were exposed to the world and I walked past them every day and that hurt. Your house is supposed to be your sanctuary, then it's not . . . Somebody else can take it.

One of the pictures of the interior walls, I took picture of a demolition site in Bolton, it's almost exactly the same colours as well. (VM4)

In these extracts, the Deleuzian sense of intensity of affect is clearly displayed. Through description, the affect is allowed to emerge without the mediation of cognitive explanation. The visual matrix specifically demands that no explanations or interpretations be given to people's contributions. It is through the accumulation of the descriptions and the subtle differences between each one, rather than their similarities, that the intensity of affect is intensified. The general feel of "something painfully intimate being exposed" of the first contribution is combined with the second's very personal "my flat" and "my interior walls" being "exposed to the world" and the feeling of "hurt" that this generated; this is then connected to the power of an other, "someone else can take it". Finally, the third extract suggests the reach of this power by saying that he or she took a picture of another demolition site, which resonated with the demolition pictures of Bright Street. Each communication has been similar but significantly different, thus contributing to an accumulation of affect experienced as intensity.

Difference was expressly connected to intensity by Deleuze, "intensity, understood as pure difference in itself . . . that which can be perceived only from the point of view of a transcendental sensibility . . ." (Deleuze, 2004, p. 181). For Deleuze, this transcendental sensibility is specifically differentiated from "empirical sensibility" (2004, p. 181). In the context of "Demolition Street" and the visual matrices, I understand the "transcendental" to reside in the lived experience of the visitors to the exhibition, later shared in the creative space of the visual matrix. This shows how the visual matrix can be used to allow for the emergence of profoundly affective responses to our (social) "collective" domain.

This affective understanding of the nature of the communication in the matrix was developed in different ways. For example, it was compared to what might be lying beneath the rubble:

I wonder what's buried underneath?

What lies beneath the surface, urban archaeology?

What people call a home. (VM2)

In this example, what is "beneath the surface" seems to echo the idea that this language of affects is, indeed, unconscious and this is identified with the "home" that defines the self and the value of each person, rather than the houses that are demolished as valueless.

It is within the potential space of the visual matrix that the participants in the matrices are able to delve into questions of the nature and meaning of time. This joins together the sense of disjointed time, or time standing still produced by the images of "Demolition Street" and the actual thinking process of the visual matrix itself. In VM2, this is introduced through an image of Dr Who that is a good example of the way creative space of the visual matrix works in making connections between the value of people and the passing of time in the conjuring of a succinct or "condensed" (in Freud's sense of the word) image:

> Dr Who
>
> Who, being an operative word, who had lived there? Who do the doors belong to? And then what, what had happened to them? Where had they gone? Where were they now? Who are their descendants? How have they all changed?
>
> Timelord.
>
> Image of one of the old Dr Whos coming down in his Tardis in the middle of Bright Street and getting people into it and going back in time. (VM2)

Through the exhibition and the visual matrix, the participants have, so to speak, been transformed into "Timelords", enabling them to go back in time, not only the actual time of "Demolition Street" before and after demolition, but to the undefined time of childhood past and nostalgia, where people ask themselves about their own identities, "who" they are as much as "who" the residents of Bright Street were. "Demolition Street" evoked for many the loss of a spirit of community past, and with it an important sense of community warmth, despite the rational knowledge that by moving on living standards have risen. Once again, the visual matrix enables a perspective of affect that challenges the rational:

> A sense of who's been there, thinking of people in different eras, different styles, different dress, different outlook, different interests, different music, feeling that it was all there in the past, almost like ghost voices,

wondering what it meant to those people. And also a sense that I prob-ably wouldn't have liked to live there, and people might have moved on to something that might have been a better standard, so, in some cases it's already positive, but a sense that warmth of the community and togetherness and sharing might have been progressively lost. (VM2)

VM2 continues to connect the past warmth of community, person-ally felt, with the complex affect of pride:

Reminds me of the mill towns of my childhood in New England, the steep hills, poverty, and remembering the pride, very proud . . .

My grandma was proud of her front step and used to clean it as a point of pride.

You could eat your dinner off those steps couldn't you?

Sparkling . . .

She did and the neighbours did as well.

Point of pride . . . (VM2)

Furthermore, the locus of pride returns once again to the houses as representative of the feelings of the people within them, and, therefore, with an understated comment on the effects of faceless demolition:

Cleanliness and pride: but the houses were completely clean and kept with pride. The house meant everything. (VM2)

The creative experiences of exhibition and visual matrix led the third visual matrix to conclude that maybe art itself could reinstate community pride by citing the intervention of Turner Prize winners, Assemble. In this, there is a hope that art can, indeed, through an aesthetic sensibility that is otherwise lost, be the hope for the future of these homes. Rather than being demolished, maybe they could have been rebuilt like the renovated houses of Assemble. The creative thinking of the matrix makes such a dream possible:

The young people, artists, I don't think it's Toxteth, who are candidates for the Turner Prize [Assemble]—I have a visual image that was in the paper, but also a real sense of hope in using houses differently, reminded me of Chicago? [Detroit], because the houses are not going to be used, people are not interested in them, we can be interested in completely different things, floors can come down, you can just have a double height room. We can do what we like, just that sense of possibility, and creating something that looked so beautiful and different. (VM3)

The alternative to this was found in a resilient humour, and was introduced through regular reference to a particular sense of British humour—the Carry On films, Morecombe and Wise, Monty Python—that never seems to die.

The ultimate humorous connection between resilience in the face of falling houses comes in the image of Buster Keaton standing firm while the façade of a house literally falls through him:

The best one is Buster Keaton where the front of the house falls down and he's standing still standing there, millimetre perfect. He's standing just in the window space. (VM4)

The complex example of *Dr Who*, discussed above, is also echoed in a link made between comedy, science fiction, and time in a reference to *Red Dwarf*:

A re-run of *Red Dwarf*, never seen this one before, a photographic developing solution got contaminated and whenever it produced a photograph, it comes alive and you go back to the moment as long as you don't step out of the frame. (VM4)

In this case, the participants in the matrix are given a similar opportunity to go back to the past, but the comedy acts as a buffer to disappointment and a further indication of resilience.

The "social" and the use of the visual matrix as a psycho-social method

Where psycho-social studies diverges from other psychoanalytically informed practice is in its marriage with the "social". The visual matrix is truly a psycho-social method in the way it merges psyche and society. The use of the method in the context of a socially engaged artist makes this particularly illustrative of the value of the visual matrix as a psycho-social method.

Latour—influenced by Gabriel Tarde's view of the social as distinct from Durkheim's—goes to great lengths to redefine "social" as being similar to an interconnectedness between all things, not just people, emphasising description rather than explanation as a primary aim of social investigation, and difference rather than similitude as the key to meaning-making. For Latour, "the factors gathered in the past under the label of a 'social domain' are simply some of the elements to be assembled in the future in what I will call not a society but a *collective*" (Latour, 2005, p. 14, original emphasis). Adopting this approach frees us to discuss process, association, movement, and exploration, rather than (social) objects in themselves. The viewing of such potential objects—the artwork as object for example, or a "social problem" such as urban regeneration—is instead viewed as a participation in a network of connections through associations and relational intersubjectivities. This "collectivity" emerges as an indistinguishable web of relationships between things and people as subjects in relationship with a creative process that makes the whole network available for experience. This interconnected network thus redefines the object of the "problem" as a human and not-so-human process of contemplation, where many inconclusive avenues of meaning can co-exist in an undeniable complexity.

I have used Latour in this context to bring up questions of the definition of the "social" because this is crucial in approaching "Demolition Street" as a work of art that may be connected to a "social" problem or issue and yet retains its status as something that exists in itself, a non-fixed, ephemeral body of interconnectedness which is indeterminate in its relationship to the "social". In the visual matrix, we are able to maintain an idea of "social" that is at once societal, personal and shared within the context of the visual matrix. This is what Deleuze and Guattari called a "bloc of sensations, that is to say, a compound of percepts and affects" (Deleuze & Guattari, 1994, p. 164). Just as "affect" is more than "affection", "percept" is more than "perception" (p. 164). According to Deleuze, both affect and percept refer to an inwardly embodied movement that combine mind and body and are powerful enough to produce the sensation that they exist beyond the self. Perception and affection are simple acts of seeing and feeling, whereas percept and affect are active movements of intensity: "Percepts are not perceptions, they are packets of sensations and relations that outlive those who experience them. Affects are not feelings, they are becomings that go beyond those who live through them (they become other)" (Deleuze, quoted in Thrift, 2008, p. 116).

Similarly, Deleuze's view of a work of art was that it was a "being of sensation and nothing else: it exists in itself" (Deleuze & Guatarri, 1994, p. 164). In these ways, we are able to interconnect the participants in the visual matrix within a "bloc of sensations" that includes the participants themselves, the artwork, and the actual street in ways that blur the distinction between reality and imagination.

A Deleuzian method

Although a recent publication has been dedicated to *Deleuze and Research Methodologies* (Coleman & Ringrose, 2013), these studies have largely been focused on using a Deleuzian approach within existing methodologies ("ethnography, group and individual interviewing, film-making and online research") (Coleman & Ringrose, 2013, p. 3). In the present chapter, I am suggesting that the method itself can be viewed from a Deleuzian perspective.

This will also give meaning to Beuy's famous dictum "Every human being is an artist" (Beuys, quoted in Harrison & Wood, 2003, p. 929), because the visual matrix, I contend, encourages a space of creativity for the participants in association with the artwork and each other, putting each participant in the role of artist for the duration of the visual matrix. This is where Deleuze and Beuys can be seen to resonate: in Beuys, art is the democratic and creative space, where each person is in creative conjunction with the other: "The most important thing to me is that man, by virtue of his products, has experience of how he can contribute to the whole and not only produce articles but become a sculptor or architect of the whole social organism" (Beuys, quoted in Harrison & Wood, 2003, p. 904). And for Deleuze, "Art begins not with the flesh but with the house. That is why architecture is the first of the arts" (Deleuze & Guatarri, 1994, p. 186). Both conceive of an architecture as a "territory" (Deleuze), or "whole social organism" (Beuys), which will lead to different creations outside this territory or organism: Deleuze's "Universe" and "deterritorialization" (Deleuze & Guatarri, 1994, p. 186); and Beuy's "organization of society" (Beuys, quoted in Harrison & Wood, 2003, p. 904). Beuys echoes Deleuze's "bloc of sensations" when he states that "art looks more towards a field where sensitivity is developed into an organ of cognition and hence explores areas quite different from formal logic"

(Beuys, quoted in Harrison & Wood, 2003, p. 905). Whatever is created in the territory has to expand out into something beyond, "from endosensation to exosensation" (Deleuze & Guattari, 1994, p. 185). Deleuze's metaphorical use of "House" is particularly apt to this study, where the artwork and the visual matrix are engaged with demolition of houses, where what was inside the house is exposed to the outside and where, in the visual matrix, the deterritorialisation of the artwork produces a new creative "territory" in the space of visual matrix.

The essential difference, according to Deleuze in his book on Francis Bacon and art, is between a form of representation and a more ineffable experience of affect. Just as Deleuze believes Bacon's art is non-representational and, therefore, more closely aligned to affective experience, so is the experience of the visual matrix. For Deleuze, the BwO is "flesh and nerve" and experience runs through the whole like a "wave" of affective intensities which become "sensation . . . linked to the body", whereupon "it ceases to be representative and becomes real" (Deleuze, 2005, p. 33). Take, for example, the image of the ironing board, which was one of the iconic images from the exhibition (Image 2) and led to various expressions of affect in the visual matrices.

The following passage from the second visual matrix engages and develops the affective resonance of the image of the ironing board:

> My ironing board is wooden, and my mum's neighbour who came from Jamaica gave it to me as a wedding present, and even though it's the most rickety-rackety thing . . . it's had lots of covers . . . I've still got it, I still use it, rarely because I rarely iron, but I do still use it . . .
>
> One doesn't think of an ironing board having a history usually . . .
>
> Remember my mother with her wooden ironing board, and she did iron lots, ironing in front of the telly.
>
> Yep, watching Coronation Street . . . that's what mine did, and I used to have to learn how to iron by practising ironing my dad's hankies.
>
> Tea towels . . .
>
> Ironing sheets . . .
>
> Sheets, tea towels, socks, pants . . .
>
> Me dad's socks . . .
>
> Quite right! (VM2)

Image 2.   The image of the ironing board on the exhibition poster.

As revealed in the bemused comment "One doesn't think of an ironing board having a history usually", the ironing board's lowly status, especially this cited old-fashioned wooden one, is an unlikely candidate for any form of representation. Instead, what we have is experience and affect. In its use, it encourages a process of care and attention that links to the memory of a wedding present that is not representative of the love in the marriage, but of the experienced reality of ageing and preservation, care and reflection, and renewal. It has a value in experience despite being "rickety-rackety". It has a deeper connection with community, since it was the mother's neighbour who gave it to her. It does not represent community, but it expresses some of the affect of that community that endures in the speaker. The experience of everyday care, shared by others in the matrix, is important precisely because of its everydayness. The list of especially ordinary clothing that has been ironed, ends up with "Me dad's socks", which brings in a sense of humour which itself is an expression of affect, the humour mentioned above connected to resilience. The wave of affect thus expressed is that of the BwO of the matrix. It does not belong to any particular individual. The multiplicity of meanings therein exists as a systemic whole, the collage of image-affects.

Smooth space and becomings in the visual matrix

This BwO of the matrix is only made possible by the containing space of the matrix being made openly available for free association, by being, in Deleuzian terms, a "smooth space", not "striated". The "smooth space" is that of the "nomad", where travel, like process, is an end in itself rather than destination. In the visual matrix, we have a smooth space where images, thoughts, and affect can arise, connect, disappear, and reappear without any set order or destination. "Smooth space . . . is a space of affects, more than one of properties" (Deleuze & Guatarri, 1988, p. 479). In the visual matrix, this leads to a sense of "becoming", as we have already noted in the fusion of house and person, "becoming house". It is through the free flowing associations of the matrix, unbound by thought conventions, that unexpected couplings can occur and merge as becomings. Another important example of becoming in the matrices include becoming a resident of Bright Street through the process of experiencing the "smooth space" of affect in the matrix where such a journey is made possible through the futuring "magic" of *Dr Who* or *Red Dwarf*. The smooth space of the visual matrix, then, is far removed from "striated" space, where thinking moves in specific lines and directions that are predetermined by an already conceived outcome.

The future time implied in *Dr Who* and *Red Dwarf* seems at first to belie the archival nature of the exhibition and its location in the Lancashire County Archives. At first sight, it would seem that "Demolition Street" should be about a lost past, and, indeed, many of the matrices evoked a sense of lost childhood and nostalgia for a community spirit that has disappeared. However, what the visual matrix shows is that the aesthetic experience of the visitors to the exhibition is such that past, present, and future can be combined into a single experience that resonates with Bergson's concept of time and reality, where what counts in the reality of the experience is the intensity of particular points and levels of affects as held together by the aesthetic experience of the matrix. This experienced reality is unlike the archived reality. In that sense, it is virtual. However, in the moment of shared creative affect, the virtual becomes real and the future is just as tangible as the past. This is the process of duration that Bergson described in his treatises on time, as adopted by Deleuze:

> All these levels or degrees and all these points are themselves virtual. They belong to a single Time; they coexist in a Unity; they are enclosed in a Simplicity; they form the potential parts of a Whole that is itself virtual. They are *the reality of this virtual*. (Deleuze, 1991, p. 100, original emphasis)

This is why the experience of the visual matrix is a creative experience. Since an "objective" reality cannot function in this new space (the space of the archive is invaded, so to speak, by the new territory of the artwork and then the visual matrix), a new, created/creative/creating reality has emerged. In these conditions, as Zepke points out, art "is an experience of becoming, an experiential body of becoming, an experimentation producing new realities" (Zepke, 2005, p. 4), and the aesthetic experience of the artwork is inseparable from ontology: "Aesthetics then, is inseparable from ontology, because experience is, for Deleuze & Guattari, irreducibly real" (Zepke, 2005, p. 3).

The way Deleuze himself puts it, in his discussion of Bacon, again strongly resonates with the experience of the artwork and the free associative experience of the visual matrix:

> It is like the emergence of another world. For these marks, these traits, are irrational, involuntary, accidental, free, random. They are nonrepresentative, nonillustrative, nonnarrative. They are no longer either significant or signifiers: they are asignifying traits. They are traits of sensation . . . (Deleuze 2005, p. 71)

"Every human being is an artist"

One of the participants who recorded a personal feedback video commented, "Don't know the people but I feel I do. I am those people" (Participant B, personal video recording).

This clear statement of becoming is one of the keys to the sense of creative process undergone by the participants in the visual matrices following the experience of engagement with "Demolition Street". In this process, it is clear how each participant in the visual matrices can be considered an artist, creating new realities out of the virtual; it is in this virtual that an experience of intensity of affect is created that makes the virtual real. In this way, the dual experience of the visual matrix in conjunction with the artwork has created a new virtual/real "territory" out of the deterritorialisation of Bright Street and its relocation into a new assemblage of "Demolition Street", the archive, and, finally, the visual matrix. Along with the shifting territory or locus, time is redefined in a Bergsonian and Deleuzian sense, so that past, present, and future can be experienced in a new moment. Such a new moment within a new space creates the Deleuzian "plateau", an idea that Deleuze acknowledged was suggested by Bateson (2000). Each "plateau" is a "smooth space" of free flowing association that occurs in the visual matrix. A new "body" of interconnected, rhizomatic intensities of affect is created: a Body without Organs. Art, according to Bateson, is a primary process, therefore an unconscious process, where "there are no markers to indicate to the conscious mind that the message material is metaphoric" (Bateson, 2000, p. 140). This well describes the process of the visual matrix, almost an artwork in itself, and the participants almost artists too, becoming artists.

Conclusion: from self to "no self"

The visual matrix method presents the psycho-social researcher with a means of gathering complex, nuanced data that is shared and rooted in affect. The theoretical siting of this work within the philosophical Deleuzian paradigm clarifies the method as a whole and identifies the visual matrix as an epistemic tool for an ontological position that goes beyond the assumptions behind the psychoanalytically informed methods that are more usual in psycho-social studies. Conceptually, I believe that the visual matrix provides a method that brings together many strands from the broad domains of psychology and philosophy, which, somewhat reluctantly, seem to flow together and apart in a "love–hate" or "approach–avoidance" fashion (O'Donohue & Kitchener. 1996, p. xiii). It also speaks to Latour's "associology" and his attempts to reconfigure sociology. We have, therefore, the beginnings of a new ontology that is "holistic" in its embracing of what might otherwise have been viewed as separate ways of understanding the world. The bringing together of the "psycho" and the "social" is certainly part of this new vision.

Previous publications have indicated some of the specific advantages of using the visual matrix in research, in particular where complex issues which are difficult to express are part of the research project, where understanding affect is especially important, and where the researcher is seeking shared data rather than individual feedback (Froggett et al., 2015; Manley & Roy, 2017; Manley et al., 2016). We can add to these the suggestion that the visual matrix is an inherently creative method that can be used to bring the past to present experience: each participant in the visual matrix temporarily becomes an artist and a "time lord" of the visual matrix. In analysing the data, the psycho-social researcher places herself in an ontological position that reassesses history and fact. The data might not be empirical "fact", but it is still "true" as felt experience. Deleuze believed that philosophy was the act of creating ideas. The visual matrix provides the shared created ideas of the participants, with their roots in affect. There is often a joy in the creative act—even if the material is negative or troublesome—that gives value to the process itself. When the research subjects are participating in this process of creation, there is a predisposition to "say what you really feel". This is supported by the sensation in the visual matrix that each individual is somehow saying what everyone else feels, what the space itself "feels". The self, which is often so important in psychoanalytically informed research, here becomes a "non-self", where group dynamic processes, such as Bion's basic assumptions, are largely attenuated due to this sense of "non-self" of the visual matrix. The visual matrix is, therefore, useful in its application to an understanding of what might be termed a "shared unconscious", where the matrix becomes something like a BwO. The visual matrix is, therefore, particularly effective where the research is focused on shared affect rather than individual knowledge.

We might ask ourselves how self relates to non-self and what kind of paradox is usefully being evinced here. The nexus that links self and non-self is creativity. It is only through the creative imagination, the suspension of disbelief, that the self within each individual can also be the non-self that belongs to the whole in the visual matrix. This process of the creative imagination is an experiential one, therefore not representative of social "fact". It is, instead, a process experienced as social reality. The visual matrix is a research method that encourages every human being to be an artist, including the researcher.

References

Armstrong, D. (2005). *Organization in the Mind*. London: Karnac

Bateson, G. (2000). *Steps to An Ecology of Mind*. London: University of Chicago Press.

Berman, H., & Manley, J. (In press). Social dreaming and creativity in South Africa: imag(in)ing the unthought known. In: J. Adlam, J. Gilligan, T. Kluttig, B. Lee, B. Young, & J. L. Young (Eds.), *Creative States: Overcoming Violence*. London: Jessica Kingsley.

Clarke, S., & Hoggett, P. (Eds.) (2009). *Researching Beneath the Surface: Psycho-social Research Methods in Practice*. London: Karnac.

Coleman, R., & Ringrose, J. (2013). *Deleuze and Research Methodologies*. Edinburgh: Edinburgh University Press.

Deleuze, G. (1991). *Bergsonism*. New York: Zone Books.

Deleuze, G. (2004). *Difference and Repetition*. London: Continuum.

Deleuze, G. (2005). *Francis Bacon*. London: Bloomsbury.

Deleuze, G., & Guatarri, F. (1988). *A Thousand Plateaus*. London: Continuum.

Deleuze, G., & Guatarri, F. (1994). *What is Philosophy?* London: Verso.

Froggett, L., Manley, J., & Roy, A. (2015). The visual matrix method: imagery and affect in a group-based research setting. *Forum: Qualitative Social Research*, 16(3): www.qualitative-research.net/index.php/fqs/article/view/2308.

Fuglsang, M., & Sørensen, B. M. (2006). *Deleuze and the Social*. Edinburgh: Edinburgh University Press.

Harrison, C., & Wood, P. (2003). *Art in Theory 1900–2000*. London: Blackwell.

Karolia, I., & Manley, J. (In press). "1 in 5 Brit Muslims sympathy for Jihadi": the lived experience of UK Muslims following the terror attacks in Paris. In: J. Adlam, J. Gilligan, T. Kluttig, B. Lee, B. Young, & J. L. Young (Eds.), *Creative States: Overcoming Violence*. London: Jessica Kingsley (in press).

Latour, B. (2005). *Reassembling the Social*. Oxford: Oxford University Press.

Lawrence, W. G. (2005). *An Introduction to Social Dreaming: Transforming Thinking*. London: Karnac.

O'Donohue, W., & Kitchener, R. F. (Eds.) (1996). *The Philosophy of Psychology*. London: Sage.

Manley, J. (2009). When words are not enough. In: S. Clarke & P. Hoggett (Eds.), *Researching Beneath the Surface: Psycho-social Research Methods in Practice* (pp. 79–99). London: Karnac.

Manley, J. (2014). Gordon Lawrence's social dreaming matrix: background, origins, history and development. *Organisational and Social Dynamics*, 14(2): 322–342.

Manley, J., & Roy, A. (2017). The visual matrix: a psycho-social method for discovering unspoken complexities in social care practice. *Psychoanalysis, Culture and Society*, 22(2): 132–153.

Manley, J., & Trustram, M. (2016). Such endings that are not over: the slave trade, social dreaming and affect in a museum. *Psychoanalysis, Culture and Society*, On-line first, doi:10.1057/s41282–016–0032-x .

Manley, J., Roy, A., & Froggett, L. (2015). Researching recovery from substance misuse using visual methods. In: L. Hardwick, R. Smith, & A. Worsley (Eds.), *Innovation in Social Work Research* (pp. 191–212). London: Jessica Kingsley.

Thrift, N. (2008). *Non-Representational Theory*. London: Routledge.

Zepke, S. (2005). *Art as Abstract Machine. Ontology and Aesthetics in Deleuze and Guatarri*. London: Routledge.

CHAPTER SIX

Prospects for the Listening Post as a psycho-social methodology

Anne-Marie Cummins

An introduction to Listening Posts

As a form of enquiry into social life, the idea of the Listening Post is centrally associated with OPUS (Organisation to Promote Understanding in Society), a UK charity founded in 1975. More fundamentally, perhaps, for those unfamiliar with the method, its origins, along with OPUS itself, lie with the traditions of applied psychology and psychoanalysis instituted by the Tavistock Institute of Human Relations in the post Second World War era. Problematically, given what we know about the sheer intractability of unconscious processes, OPUS describes itself as committed to understanding conscious and unconscious processes in society with a view to promoting rationality, authority, and responsibility in decision-making. The method was first trialled in 1975 and was in development until 2000. Since 1981, OPUS has been running a programme of annual, national, and, since 2004, international Listening Posts. The version currently in operation was finalised in 2000. A recent mailshot describes them thus:

> Listening Posts are regular meetings that take a "snapshot" of society at a particular moment in time. They explore the idea that a small

group, when studying the behaviour of the wider social system that is society, will unconsciously express some of the characteristics of society and that these are discernible from the themes and patterns emerging from the discussion. (OPUS Mailshot, 2017)

By running Listening Posts on the same day in locations throughout the UK and once a year in locations world-wide, it is thought possible to collect a series of "emotional snapshots" of the preoccupations and anxieties of citizens though time and space. A group of ten to twelve people meet and, in a free-associative way, draw on their citizen roles to try to understand better what might be going on *under the surface* in society. Listening Posts, it is thought, stand to the social unconscious as the analytic hour stands to the individual unconscious. The written reports from these Listening Posts are collated and published on the OPUS website (www.users.globalnet.co.uk/ ~opusuk/) and, just as the mass observation studies of the 1930s served as an archive of everyday life, so Listening Posts can be seen an archives of social anxiety, public sentiment, and the unconscious dynamics of the social. According to Lionel Stapley (personal communication, May 2005), the recently retired Director of OPUS, the preoccupations of citizens as collected at Listening Posts turn up in the National Press in leader articles, features, and essays some six months later.

In one sense, we can liken the Listening Post to a focus group. Like its older (and ugly?) sister, the Listening Post collects free associations, but from subjects in their citizen role as opposed to their consumer role (interestingly, both have a common Freudian pedigree in that Freud's nephew, Edward Bernays, a pioneer of the focus group, drew on psychoanalytic ideas about unconscious desire in order to market products). In the 1980s, focus groups were rediscovered in the social sciences under the title of "group interviews". They also became a routine tool for party political research into voter habits and desires. Putting all of this together, it seems that the 1980s marked a social and psychic "moment" where there was recognition of the potential of researching groups and group dynamics to reveal what was otherwise unseen or occult. One thing to note is that, unlike focus groups (in their various political, commercial, and social science formations), Listening Posts to this day remain relatively unknown outside a narrow circle of initiates and fellow travellers.

The Listening Post as method

Listening Posts, along with group relations conferences and consultancy, are, first and foremost, examples of applied psychoanalysis. They were envisaged as a way of promoting understanding of self and society, not as a form of political praxis, and not as a form of social research, or even psycho-social research. However, for psycho-socially orientated social scientists, their findings are potentially rich sources of data, and the Listening Post method itself promises an innovative and radical way of investigating the social unconscious. The first proposition one must accept in undertaking such a project is the idea that society and the wider group is *in* the individual-as-citizen, that disturbances in society (and the group) are *in* the individual citizen, and, finally, that emotions and phantasies can insert themselves into the citizen role. Just as a fractal demonstrates recursive self-similarity, so the group of eight to twelve—the ideal size of a Listening Post group—is said to resemble society as a whole.

Then there is the event itself—a precise set of procedures with precise timings. Listening Posts have three distinct "stages"—four if we count the production of a report for the OPUS Archives. Their overall aim, according to Stapley, is "to enable participants as individual citizens to reflect on their own relatedness to society and to try and develop an understanding of what is happening in society at the moment" (2003, p. 1). For this to happen, what is needed is the active presence of a carefully trained convener whose adherence to, and understanding of, the method allows for expert management of the event, its planning, and its aftermath. The presence of trained conveners also allegedly allows for a degree of confidence in interconvener reliability in the way in which the method is administered over time and territory. The "results", we can be assured, are discovered or uncovered directly from the proper management of the process, rather than being a reflection of the convener's own preoccupations.

The stages of a Listening Post move quite deliberately from the level of the "social" to the level of the "psycho": free associations from everyday concerns are generated (Stage 1); they are then ordered and themed (Stage 2) and analysed in the group under the supervision and guidance of the convener (Stage 3) to see what hypotheses might be built from the group's associations and what these hypotheses reveal about group (unconscious) preoccupations and formations as they apply to society. High value is given to synthesising interpretations of the group's thoughts and free associations, that is, to the convener-guided construction of hypotheses at Stage 3 about what might be going on under the surface of society. Conveners, in their training, are advised that hypotheses should take the form "because of A, members of society do or feel B, resulting in C". The convener role is, therefore, a complex one: she is at times a participant (Stage 1), at times a manager, a consultant, and/or a facilitator (Stages 2 and 3). Finally, she is an author, submitting a report to OPUS. Participants are invited to comment on, or add to, a draft of this report before it is centrally logged, but the convener has authorial and editorial control of the final product.

To anyone trained in the research methods of the social sciences (which includes this author), there is an immediate set of problems about the representativeness of the assembled individuals to speak for "society" and an even bigger problem about what is *meant* by "society". These reservations will be returned to, but, for the moment, let us consider what it might be possible for this method to yield in terms of the production of psycho-social data and ask the question, in what way, if at all, do the products of Listening Posts reveal the social unconscious as manifested in groups?

I now present some findings for a Listening Post held in the UK in June 2007 at which I was the convener. Eleven other Listening Posts were taking place simultaneously across the UK. My particular group was smaller than ideal and consisted of only seven members, three of whom had previously contributed to Listening Posts and all of whom had been recruited via email networks for people interested in psycho-social studies. Here is a summary of the findings or "prod-ucts" of this Listening Post. What is presented below is not the raw data from Stage 1, but themes that emerged at Stage 2 and the hypotheses that were formed in Stage 3. They are also, it is worth pointing out, very typical of the tone and linguistic repertoires that the method produces.

Themes

1.   Existing in tension between the personal and the global, the macro and the micro.

2.   Not trusting media representation of political reality/facts *vs.* interpretation of facts.
3.   The "sick society" and whether to belong to it.

Hypotheses

Hypothesis 1: Because of the simultaneous desire to know and not know about the complexity of national and global problems, the media are thought of as sources of persecution, darkness, and pollution. However, we are caught in a dilemma: we need to have the "mess" out there framed and ordered, yet we also see the framing as coercive. We both want and do not want a picture of what is going on in the world because to have the picture faces us with uncomfortable and insoluble questions about the levels of our basic social responsibility as citizens. This results in a split in we citizens, as though we, too, have a tabloid, paranoid–schizoid self and a thoughtful, depressive self (who is in some despair). Here, too, there could be grounds for both optimism and pessimism.

Hypotheses 2: Such is the anxiety provoked by the task of coming to know what might be under the surface of one's mind as a citizen, the space for thoughtfulness is colonised by depressive anxiety. Citizens feel that, somehow, they ought to know and ought to be better at the task. Premature answers and overly conceptual forms of knowing predominate. As a result, a paradoxical or perverse situation is produced whereby recognition of "failure" to achieve the task (of collectively searching our minds for underlying intelligence about what might be happening in society) becomes a hard-won achievement.

Such findings are not untypical. Reading the reports of UK Listening Posts over the past thirty-five years, one finds the same stories, the same lamentations, over and over again. They are stories of failed dependency, decline, disillusionment with authority, lack of trust in institutions, the impossibility of managing risk, and a withdrawal into nostalgia and the private domain. These reports are rich sources of data about the flow of sentiment in public life, describing what Frosh (2003, p. 1551) calls "eruptions of subjectivity" and the ways in which the "excesses" of psychic functioning leak into the social. They are also, to use an earlier phrase, "an intelligible field of study" describing the preoccupations of *some* citizens and describing *a* version of the social unconscious as experienced by an educated liberal-left who are committed to the public sector and to social justice. The impacts of neo-liberalism or "globalisation"—to use the language more typical of Listening Post Reports—are felt keenly by those in this milieu, whether they be participants, conveners, or architects of the OPUS tradition.

To give some examples of this tradition and way of thinking, the following from Khaleelee and Miller (1985) is typical of the version of political history held by key players.

> We can see Chamberlain's flight leadership of 1938–9 succeeded by Churchill's fight leadership and then in 1945 by an abrupt transition to dependency culture . . . continued till the 1970's by governments of both complexions. (pp. 379–380)

Dartington (2000, p. 9) puts it slightly differently:

> there is a subversion of old forms of power, but we are aware also that the old ways remain potent, faced with the disruption of old bound- aries, of dependency needs no longer met by the disintegration and fragmentation of institutions, people have felt a sense of abandonment where they are unable to challenge or fight back – but take flight into privatisation of the public self.

In defence of Listening Posts, perhaps none of this should be a surprise. After all, members of Listening Posts, by definition, are not representative of society as a whole and, although "ordinary" citizens are thin on the ground, it can be said that the method's utility is in the space it makes for concerned citizens' sustained reflection and think- ing. Furthermore, the archives of Listening Posts at national and inter- national level represent a rich research resource, tracing the less conscious political preoccupations of the liberal left and, in this sense, track the democratic deficit that has governed centre-right politics since the 1980s.

The Listening Post: some methodological questions

This still leaves questions regarding the products and provenance of Listening Posts: are we *really* listening here to the unconscious in groups? One possibility is that yes, we are, but what we are hearing is a very one-sided version of the unconscious. It is perhaps already obvious from the example above that the dynamics discovered (or even created) by the Listening Post in its current formation tend to reveal an unconscious covered with anxiety. Given the origins of the parent traditions of group relations, open systems theory and Kleinian and post-Kleinian theory, this is perhaps not unexpected. The unconscious, in so far as it can be known in these communities of knowledge and practice, is taken to be a place of repressed and painful thoughts, wishes, and knowledge dominated by splitting, envy, projection, paranoid and depressive anxiety, and so on. These default Kleinian and post-Kleinian frameworks, which accompany the method and inform its interpretive repertoires, translate easily into the language of unconscious phantasy at the level of the group. A more Lacanian approach might want to explore the disjuncture, at the level of the social, between the registers of symbolic, the imaginary, and the real. A more relational approach might want to look at the intersubjective relationships between participants as evidenced in the Listening Post group dynamics and their connection to Listening Post products. A more generous reading of the unconscious might want to point to an exploration of psychic genera, in other words, more than just repressed material, and to the more creative metaphors, patterns, and associations which we know to be typical of the unconscious thinking revealed by free associative method when we are not focusing on trauma or anxiety (Bollas, 2002). These approaches to the construction and interpretation of data are ruled out by the method as it currently stands.

Were these frameworks to be included, even potentially, it would still leave another question: what convincing justification can there be for saying that the products of the Listening Post, based, after all, on very limited and self-chosen samples of citizens, can tell us something about society as a whole? Drawing on the work of those centrally associated with the development of the Listening Post, can any good arguments be offered for accepting the proposition that Listening Posts do, indeed, tap the social unconscious beyond the immediate group?

Much of the intellectual inspiration for accepting this position comes from Bion's 1962 book *Experiences in Groups*, where, echoing Freud (1921c), he claims that there is no meaningful division between individual and group psychology and, further, that the *small* group of ten to twelve is "an intelligible field of study" reflecting dynamics outside and beyond it. Trist comments,

> it became apparent that [he] was using the word group interchangeably for the face to face group and the wider society. For him there was one "socio" and all "socio" had a "psycho" dimension and all "psycho" a social dimension. (Trist, 1985, p. 33, quoted in Shapiro & Carr, 2006)

Taking this up, Khaleelee and Miller claim that one can sometimes see

> The appearance in lower level systems of dynamics that belong to a higher level. Our tentative hypothesis is that number as such is not the determining factor. In other words, groups that are small in size may express phenomena that do not belong to the small group itself but are manifestations of the larger group or even society. (1985, p. 367)

They go on to cite Rioch's 1975 observation that the dynamics one could expect to come up at group relations conferences were not only the local and organisational concerns of members, but also "the tone and preoccupation of a nation" (Rioch, 1975, p. 56, cited in Khaleelee & Miller, 1985). For a more recent take on this claim, we can look to Shapiro and Carr (2006) on the phenomenon of the general replicating itself in the specific. They say,

> Each of us takes up membership in a number of groups. Their ideals and values permeate our thinking. . . . Our commitment to group membership is both a behavioural interpretation of an aspect of society and an enactment of our relatedness to it. The relationship is reciprocal: groups shape our understanding of society. Our various groups are significant contexts – often unconscious and covert – that form our interpretations of the world. (2006, p. 245)

It is as though committing oneself to the idea that group and individual psychology are inseparable also commits one to the idea that the small group "stands for" society. The interpretative constraints that hold in group relations working conferences, which set up temporary learning organisations or organisations in miniature in order to study them, are here much expanded; one is not just consulting to, and interpreting, the dynamics of the working conference and its role-holders, one claims be consulting to society-as-a-whole, as it is manifested in Listening Post members.

This raises a profound question: is it possible to locate, let alone consult to, the social unconscious? On the basis of the material amassed by Listening Posts since the 1980s, we have evidence aplenty to support the claim that they repeatedly register *something* of the affective undercurrents operating in pockets of social life. Hoggett (2006) makes a useful link here with Raymond Williams' ideas about structures of feeling. What Williams means by this is

> Characteristic elements of impulse, restraint and tone: specifically affective of consciousness and relationships; not feelings against thought, but thoughts as felt and feelings as thought ... yet we are also defining a social experience which is still in process, often indeed not recognised as social but taken to be private, idiosyncratic, and even isolating but which in analysis (though rarely otherwise) has its emergent, connecting and dominant characteristics. (1977, p. 132)

This seems to capture something about the Listening Post that accurately describes its "products". They can tell us something, at least in Stages 1 and 2 (see above), about affective undercurrents operating in daily life, about the emotions and phantasies that insert themselves into what it means to be a particular type of citizen and about how the social penetrates the psychic and *vice versa*. However, this is not to say we are in the presence of *the* social unconscious, rather that we are in the presence of *a* social unconscious or structure of feeling typical of a certain social (liberal) milieu. One might even say that Listening Posts, rather than revealing the social unconscious, are ritual enactments of a set of social anxieties and preoccupations typical of left and liberal-leaning, educated, and reasonably affluent social groups, all of whom tend to be in middle age or later life. In this sense, and, perhaps, only in this sense, they are an "intelligible field of study" revealing the paranoid and depressive anxieties of such populations in relation to citizenship.

Because of their propensity to attract a like-minded and socially non-diverse membership, there is some justification for the claim that there is an in-built tendency for Listening Posts to enact the disenchantment and anxiety of the generally like-minded; they can be seen more as objects of identification than objects of use, a criticism also levelled at the tradition of group relations conferences, but not, interestingly, focus groups (which seem to attract far less psychic investment from their participants). There is something about the intensity of experiences in Listening Posts and the level of identification with the method itself that is both a strength and a weakness, whatever the claims about recursive self-similarity and the dynamics of higher level systems being present in lower level systems. Even the ex-Director of OPUS has expressed reservations:

> There was some feeling that in a global context the caffè latte set of liberal intellectuals was a minority under threat – and this was where some of the fear came in. There was a sense of the irrelevance of this group, first because they were not listened to in the political process, but secondly because they are such a small group . . . yet it is this group which is most represented in the Listening Post process. (Stapley & Collie, 2005, p. 113)

The Listening Post: a psycho-social methodology?

If the sampling frame is less than adequate, what of the other intellectual psycho-social credentials of the Listening Post? Are these enough to balance the weaknesses explored above? Drawing on the extant literature (e.g., Alvesson & Sköldberg, 2000; Hoggett & Clarke, 2009; Hollway & Froggett, 2012; Hollway & Jefferson, 2013; Walkerdine et al., 2001), the development of psycho-social methods of research might be expected to display awareness of some or all of the following.

1.   A critical grasp of the epistemological implications of the existence of the social unconscious in its dynamic and relational forms.
2.   A critical grasp of the complex connections between ways of knowing and methods of enquiry, and an understanding of the impact of the emotional construction of the research environment.
3.   An understanding of what we might call the psycho-politics of interpretation and data analysis, a double reflexivity which reflects on the subjectivity and emotional responses of the researcher *and* her authority in constructing and colouring processes of data collection and data analysis. Linked to this we might add, as does Clarke (2006), the ability of the research to give voice to the research subjects as opposed to giving voice to a theoretical paradigm.

How do Listening Posts measure up? On the first criterion (critical grasp of the epistemological implications of the existence of the unconscious in its dynamic and relational forms) Listening Posts do well. The "pedigree", which goes back to group relations and psycho-analytically informed consultancy, is saturated with experience and understanding at this level. There is now an influential corpus of literature based on Kleinian and post-Kleinian understandings of the destructive unconscious forces which operate beneath the surface of group and organisational life, some of which have entered business schools and management education (e.g., Huffington et al., 2004).

On the second criterion (connecting ways of knowing and methods of enquiry), the verdict is mixed: on the one hand, there is an obvious and thought-through connection between the way of knowing and the method of enquiry, crucially regarding the importance given to the play of free association in a group context. Where Listening Post methodology does less well is in grasping the obscure connections between the frame itself (the method, with its various stages) and the products of enquiry (the published report). By this, I mean the very obvious point that the method "makes" the finding, that the phenomena observed are also, as in all research methods, a by-product of the measuring instrument. In relation to group relations conferences, this has sometimes been a disputed assumption. Barham, for instance, noted that

> Bion and his colleagues believed that the sorts of dramatic actions generated within the frame of the method were to be viewed as essential and permanent truths about human relationships, as manifestation of a universal problematic of "the group". (Barham, 1984, p. 42)

when, in fact, it is equally possible to see them as (distorted) products of the frame itself with its non-naturalistic recreation of organisational and work environments. The same could be said of Listening Posts: perhaps there is something about their structure and procedures that produces the same dramas and variations on a theme (fearful and anxious responses to late modernity, globalisation, and neo-liberalism) over and over again. Even sympathetic exponents of the method, such as Shapiro and Carr, also have pointed out,

> it is possible to extrapolate from the individual to the group and from the group to society . . . but it is worth questioning whether there is an

intellectual activity beyond which speculation becomes ungrounded, so filled with projection without reality testing that it can become both stimulating and nonsense. (2006, p. 242)

To take this further, because the interpretative frame proceeds from what we might call a Kleinian realist perspective, there is also a belief that Listening Posts give relatively unproblematic expression to the inner world of participants, that the method "releases" inner preoccupations, internal anxieties, and structures of feeling which are pre-existing but unformulated, unthought, but essentially knowable, psychic facts. Is this true? Can one access affective experience in any unmediated way? The sentiments produced in Listening Posts—and, indeed, any other research method—are at least partially created by the very particular sets of discursive practices embedded in the training of conveners, but also in the context of a deliberately excluded set of here-and-now group dynamics (the training of conveners makes it clear that minimal attention is to be given to here-and-now group dynamics). Neither is there anything in the intellectual or practice roots of Listening Posts to suggest that there is something ontologically problematic about either their processes or products. What I am suggesting is that a more emotionally and theoretically complex reading of the Listening Post environment is possible and desirable.

On the third criterion (an understanding of the psycho-politics of interpretation and data analysis), Listening Posts have some way to go. Who decides what things mean, whose "voice" predominates in interpretation and whose tends not to be heard? Perhaps this is not problematised because the Tavistock tradition has always had a preoccupation with authority, and, in particular, the authority of the consultant. The reasons for this are complex. As part of post-war institutional reform, the Tavistock paradigm was part of a set of assumptions about hierarchy, authority, and leadership and it did not seek to challenge these terms of reference—if for no other reason than that this would have jeopardised its privileged place within networks of referral (Boxer, 2000). The tradition has subsequently had difficulty in fully conceptualising the social and relations of *power* because, to use Boxer's words, to do so would "call into question its hierarchical place within the referral networks" (2000, p. 157). This has meant that the two realms—power relations and the unconscious processes—have become unfastened. "This separation, inherent in the circumstances surrounding the origins of the paradigm, was installed within the paradigm itself" (Boxer, 2000, p. 165).

However, to bring Listening Posts into a more thoroughly psycho-social frame, the questions of "voice" and authority can no longer be evaded. As Frost (2015) has said,

> the psycho-social approach overall highlights the relationship between the knower with the known. In other words how one studies a/the subject and perhaps even why we are looking at it, is also a product of what is in our heads, hearts and lives as people constructing knowledge. The researchers and theorists who are building the psycho-social knowledge base here are also implicated. They are not pretending to be objective or all- knowing, but accepting that personal experiences and leanings, class backgrounds and psychic worlds, impact on perceptions and discussions, the choices as to what counts and how it is written about it. (2015, p. 18, online version)

There is little awareness of, or engagement with, these questions in current iterations of Listening Post methodology.

It is true that there is thinking about (political) power and authority in the concerns and preoccupations of participants and conveners, but this does not extend to a preoccupation with, or theorisation of, the power and authority of the convener. The training of conveners and their background in group relations reinforces the idea of "expert" authority in a way that lacks the reflexivity one would expect in a robust version of psycho-social method. The tremendous and unacknowledged authority given to the convener, both in the compilation of the report and in the authority taken to name hypotheses on behalf of the group, is the proverbial elephant in the room.

As a psycho-socially informed methodology, Listening Posts are not yet in what Burman and Frosh (2005) would call a "post-foundationalist" stage and are somewhere stuck in the adaptationist and structuralist paradigms typical of post-Second World War social science. One of the key features of the post-foundational turn is the challenge to received authority "and an understanding of knowledge as perspectival, that is, as structured according to particular historical and cultural contexts which make it more difficult to privilege one perspective over another" (Burman & Frosh, 2005, p. 9). The voices of participants in Listening Posts are heard, and recorded in the written up report, but much is squeezed out in an attempt to give voice to the method and the theoretical paradigm behind it.

The listening matrix?

At the time of writing, and under the aegis of a new Director at OPUS, a steering group of experienced Listening Post conveners is considering ways of experimenting with the method, which, to remind us, has not changed since 2000. Within this group, there is recognition of several of the issues mentioned in this chapter: the narrowness in social background of participants, the way in which the pursuit of linear hypotheses (the "gold standard" of the Listening Post) means the more "wordless", affective, embodied aspects of social experience are not captured, and the over-determined and over-determining role of the convener. What will emerge from this initiative remains to be seen—including the question of whether any resultant method will resemble a Listening Post or a listening matrix. In the spirit of this exploration, the final part of this paper suggests ways of refreshing Listening Post methodology to take on board one of the major developments in psycho-social research methods.

One very obvious way forward is to work much more closely with the idea of the matrix, as has been done with the development of social dreaming and social photo matrices (Lawrence, 2005; Sievers, 2008). By matrix, what is meant is a protected space in which thoughts, feelings, images, and affect can gestate until they are ready to be born. In the earlier part of the twenty-first century, such methods were more likely to be used in the world of psychoanalytically informed organisational consultancy but, along with the use of the visual matrix (Froggett et al., 2015), they are becoming typical psycho-social methods in what we might call the post-FANI (Hollway & Jefferson, 2013) stage of psycho-social research. Matrices, as discussed elsewhere in this volume, are ways of exploring and researching experiences which are affective, embodied, unarticulated, and hard-to-think, such as transitions to old age, dementia, death, and dying (see Liveng et al., 2017).

Unlike the group, which is governed by an ostensibly articulable set of group dynamics, and unlike the idea of there being a metaphorical "post" or collection point for citizen's psychic contributions, the use of a matrix methodology allows for the kind of free associative thinking typical of classical Freudian dream theory. Processes of condensation and displacement, mobile cathexes, and primary process thinking will produce "collages", or fretwork, of image, metaphors, symbolisation, and unbidden links not normally accessible by other discursive methods. The collages, or sets of affective meanings and links, which emerge in the matrix tell us something about subjective *and* trans-subjective affective structures. They are both psycho and social, but to be created and born they require (a) a different type of containing structure from the conventional Listening Post (often the seating arrangements will be in a "snowflake" pattern, which allows the emergence of reverie and a "day-dreaming" state of mind); (b) a different relationship to the authority of the convener, whose role is containing and facilitative rather than directing and authoritative; (c) a commitment to the contingency and provisionality of the "product" of such free associative reverie. There is to be no master-reading of the results, there is no preset interpretive model into which results must be slotted.

In matrix-driven research, the discursive "products" of the matrix are recorded, mapped, and discussed by the participants in a first stage of sense making, immediately following the matrix itself. They are, at a later, second stage, discussed and further analysed by the participant–researchers who were in the original matrix. These discussions can form the basis of published research findings. It is important to iterate here that, unlike Listening Posts with their all-powerful conveners, there is no one overall authoritative or dominant voice. Polysemy replaces authority. The idea that one can have (scientific or pseudoscientific) knowledge about hidden processes in society through the construction of hypotheses is replaced by more open-textured, changing, and changeable readings of data. Matrix-focused work acknowledges that while contributions are, in a very obvious sense, individual in origin, they are also impersonal and belong to a shared socio-cultural realm which is, in its own right, a rich source of meaning, open to many readings, including ones that are political, critical, and socio-cultural, as well as post-Kleinian.

To return for a moment to Listening Posts and their stages: the first stage is the free association to the everyday concerns of participants, the second is the ordering of these into themes, and the third is the production of overarching hypotheses about what might be going on under the surface of society. These hypotheses, normally constructed within a post-Kleinian theoretical framework, are more concerned with showing how society is "in" the individual than exploring the creative or playful side of primary process thinking or exploring the relationship between modes of subjectivity and wider-socio-cultural forces. Listening Posts and their hypotheses tend to produce a form of knowledge in which rich and deep connections between ideas, images, and affect are closed down or pinned down, rather than being boundless sources of potential meaning. This, I have argued, is, at least in part, a product of the veiled authority relations in the method. So, is it possible to work with the Listening Post stages in a more matrix-like way? Is it possible to be less formalistic about data collection, for free associations to be free-er, for participants to have more ownership of the production and interpretation of Listening Post products?

One method currently being trialled (by me) is the development of a variation of the Listening-Post using a more matrix-type format to produce what we might call "social poetry". As in the Listening Post, in Stage 1 participants are invited to share their internal and external, personal and political, preoccupations, but making special note of the images, symbols, and metaphors that come up in these exchanges. The kind of practical containment required here is one that provides maximum opportunities for intersubjective reverie, so, a quiet, uninterrupted space, the "snowflake" pattern of chairs, and a willingness by the facilitator(s) to model the associative process. The real innovation, however, comes in Stage 2: instead of the convener taking authority to collect and collate themes from Stage 1, we have a variation on the poetry game invented by the surrealists, "exquisite corpse" (Adamowicz, 1998), which is conducted in sub-groups of four to six people.

Each participant writes, at the top of the page, a single line or short phrase based on an image, metaphor, symbol, or phrase that has resonated with them from the previous discussion (e.g., "let loose balloons over the hills across Europe").

The piece of paper is then folded over, hiding the written sentence or phrase (so the next participant cannot see the original line) and passed on. However, *one word* of the first phrase (e.g., "balloons") is written at the beginning of the new line by the originator of the phrase.

The piece of paper is then passed to the person on the right. She constructs *another*, a second, sentence in response to the single word she has received. She is free to draw on her own associative links to the word, and/or make links with the material in Stage 1. The point is to work with resonances and evocations rather than to summarise, analyse, or hypothesise.

Having written this second phrase, she selects a single evocative word from it and writes it on the next line for the next person to see and associate to.

And so on, until all in the small group have contributed to the final "poem".

What we have in these pieces of "social poetry" is an emotionally, visually, and affectively complex account of under-the-surface preoccupations, a conjunction of personal and social experience, which then forms the basis of a discussion and sense-making phase or stage (Stage 3). Rather than the production of a set of single and binding hypotheses about what is going on in society, or a claim that these products "speak for" society, the point is for the post-matrix group to decide themselves on the interpretative frames of reference, with the convener taking a facilitative, rather than a leading, role. At a later, research-only phase, more work can be done on the products of the "listening matrix" scanning the poems for recurrent themes and images, or puzzles and mysteries, or other resonances of interest to the researchers.

This is a much less ambitious project than Listening Posts. In return for giving up the claims to be able to tell what is going on, at a psychic level, in "society", one is offered the opportunity to look at non-subjectivist subjectivity (Krüeger, 2017), at intersubjective meaning making and socio-cultural sources of meaning which might, or may not, have purchase and relevance beyond the assembled people making up the matrix. The ego of the convener (and, behind that, the sharp voice of the authoritative superego function of convener training) is replaced by a matrix with its own mind that supersedes the individual egos of its members

Overall, this chapter has argued that Listening Posts are products what we might call a mid-twentieth century, foundationalist paradigm, one whose version of social science and applied psychoanalytic thinking is relatively untouched by the more reflexive approaches attuned to power and difference. In order for Listening Posts to overcome some of their current methodological limitations, some features that currently define the method might have to be mourned and given up. These include: the idea that the method reveals, relatively unproblematically, psychic truths about what is going on in "society", that society as a whole can be studied via the small group, and that the authority of the convener, and strict adherence to the method of hypothesis production, are unquestionable givens.

Some of these limitations can be overcome by replacing the metaphor of "post" with that of a "matrix", by replacing the idea of single and final interpretation with that of more open interpretations, and by replacing the aim of understanding one's relatedness to society as a citizen with that of exploring intersubjective and socio-cultural sources of meaning making. For some adherents of the Listening Post method as it stands, this will be a step too far. For others it will be a relief.

References

Adamowicz, E. (1998). *Surrealist Collage in Text and Image: Dissecting the Exquisite Corpse.* Cambridge: Cambridge University Press.

Alvesson, M., & Sköldberg, K. (2000). *Reflexive Methodology: New Vistas for Qualitative Research.* London: Sage.

Barham, P. (1984). Cultural forms and psychoanalysis: some problems. In: B. Richards (Ed.), *Capitalism and Infancy: Essays on Psychoanalysis and Politics* (pp. 38–54). London: Free Association Books.

Bion, W. (1962). *Experiences in Groups.* London: Tavistock.

Bollas, C. (2002). *Free Association.* Cambridge: Ikon Books.

Boxer, P. (2000). The dilemmas of ignorance. In: C. Oakley (Ed.), *What Is A Group? A New Look at Theory in Practice* (pp. 147–168). London: Rebus.

Burman, E., & Frosh, S. (2005). New currents in contemporary social theory and implications for group-analytic theory and practice (Special Issue). *Group Analysis, 38*(1): 7–15.

Clarke, S. (2006). Theory and practice: psychoanalytic sociology and psycho-social studies. *Sociology, 40*(6); 1153–1169.

Dartington, T. (2000). The pre-occupation of the citizen – reflections from the OPUS Listening Posts. *Organisational and Social Dynamics, 1*(1): 94–112.

Freud, S. (1921c). *Group Psychology and the Analysis of the Ego. S. E., 18*: 67–143. London: Hogarth.

Froggett, L., Manley, J., & Roy, A. (2015).The visual matrix method: imagery and affect in a group-based research setting. *FQS: Forum:*

Qualitative Social Research Socialforschung, 16(3) (available at: www.qualitative-research.net/index.php/fqs/article/view/2308). DOI: 4.6.16.

Frosh, S. (2003). Psychosocial studies and psychology: is a critical approach emerging? *Human Relations, 56*(12): 1545–1567.

Frost, E. (2015). Why social work and sociology need psychosocial studies. *Nordic Social Work Research, 5*(Special 1ssue): 85–97 (available at http://eprints.uwe.ac.uk/27381/).

Hoggett, P. (2006). Connecting, arguing and fighting. *Psychoanalysis, Culture and Society, 11*: 1–16.

Hoggett, P., & Clarke, S. (2009). *Researching Beneath the Surface*. London: Karnac.

Hollway, H., & Froggett, L. (2012). Researching in-between subjective experience and reality. *FQS – Forum: Qualitative Social Research, 13*(3) (available at: www.qualitative-research.net/index.php/fqs/article/view/1899) DOI: 3.4.17.

Hollway, W., & Jefferson, T. (2013). *Doing Qualitative Research Differently: A Psychosocial Approach* (2nd edn). London: Sage.

Huffington, C., Halton, W., Armstrong, D., & Pooley, J. (Eds.) (2004). *Working Below the Surface: The Emotional Life of Contemporary Organizations*. London: Karnac.

Khaleelee, O., & Miller, E. (1985). Beyond the small group: society as an intelligible field of study. In: M. Pines (Ed.), *Bion and Group Psychotherapy* (pp. 334–385). London: Tavistock/Routledge.

Krüeger, S. (2017). Dropping depth hermeneutics into psychosocial studies – a Lorenzerian perspective. *Journal of Psychosocial Studies, 10*(1) (available at: www.psychosocial-studies-association.org/wp-content/uploads/2017/05/Steffen-Krueger-Dropping-Depth-Hermeneutics-into-Psychosocial-Studies-a-Lorenzerian-perspective.pdf accessed 6 June 2017).

Lawrence, W. G. (2005). *Introduction to Social Dreaming: Transforming Thinking*. London: Karnac.

Liveng, A., Ramvi, E., Froggett, L., Manley, J., Lading, Å., & Haga-Gribsrud, B. (2017). Imagining transitions in old age through the Visual Matrix method: thinking about what is hard to bear. *Journal of Social Work Practice, 31*(2): 155–170 DOI:10.1080/02650533.2017.1305342: http://www.tandfonline.com/doi/full/10.1080/02650533.2017.1305342

OPUS (2017). events@opus.org.uk to anne-marie.cummins@uwe.ac.uk. Summer Listening Post, 28th June. Sent 12th June 2017.

Shapiro, E., & Carr, W. (2006). These people were some kind of solution: can society in any sense be understood? *Organisational and Social Dynamics, 6*(2): 41–258.

Sievers, B. (2008). Perhaps it is the role of pictures to get in contact with the uncanny: the social photo matrix as a method to promote the understanding of the unconscious in organisations. *Organisational and Social Dynamics*, 8(2): 234–254.

Stapley, L. (2003). Britain and the world at the dawn of 2003 – report of a New Year's Listening Post. *Organisational and Social Dynamics*, 3(1): 165–169.

Stapley, L., & Collie, A. (2005). Global dynamics at the dawn of 2005. *Organisational and Social Dynamics*, 5(1): 111–134.

Walkerdine, V., Lucey, H., & Melody, J. (2001). *Growing Up Girl: Psychosocial Explorations of Gender and Class*. London: Palgrave.

Williams, R. (1977). *Marxism and Literature*. Cambridge: Cambridge University Press.

PART III
EXPERIENCING

CHAPTER SEVEN

The challenges of being a mature doctoral student: the supportive role of vertical and lateral third spaces

Rose Redding Mersky

Introduction

Between the ages of sixty-four and seventy-one, I undertook my doctoral studies at the University of the West of England in Bristol, where I was closely affiliated with the Centre for Psycho-social Studies (now called the Psycho-social Research Theme group of the University of the West of England). Although I was already an experienced organisational consultant and a published writer, I had to start from scratch in the student role and learn to do research. I naturally sought out the support of various others, with whom I have openly shared my work and my ongoing journey. These others include a German supervisor, my husband (a colleague), various organisational development colleagues who functioned as my process consultants, and a fellow UWE doctoral student. Other sources of support were provided by the university: my two supervisors (one of whom was my Director of Studies), the role analysis group that met during the bi-annual seminars, and my doctoral colleagues. I also add my reflexive journal to this list, as it was my ongoing thinking companion.

As I have reflected on these support systems, I realise that they were not just accidental formations. In each a certain kind of work took place. In fact, each has had its own particular function in my learning. Together, they helped to contain my experience as a learner and researcher.

When I began my studies in 2009, I did not realise how truly difficult it would be to take on this new identity, to be a student, especially at my age and stage professionally. On the one hand, I had many, many resources to draw upon. I was an experienced writer, and I had published extensively. I was married to a German "doctor father", who had himself supervised countless numbers of doctoral students, knew how to construct bibliographies, and, in general, was always there to support me. I had colleagues who took on valuable roles as process consultants. And I was undertaking this study, not because I wanted to make a career move, but because I was passionately interested in the drawing of dreams, and this interest was so intense that I decided I wanted support for doing the research. The praxis that is the topic of my dissertation is called "social dream-drawing".

I see all of these various relationships, in one way or another, as third spaces. As theorised by Benjamin (2004), the concept of the third characterises the co-created space between patient and analysand. This space serves as a creative holding space between the two role holders that binds them together in a collective joint task, that of learning. It is a "shared third" (Benjamin, 2004, p. 19) that stands outside each of them as individuals and yet links them together in the service of the task of psychoanalysis. It not only holds the work over time, but holds the connection between the two when they are separated, so that the insights and working through connected to it can take place in the absence of the physical other.

This construct moves us beyond the technical focus on the transferential and countertransferential dynamics between the two. While these processes certainly take place and can be said to characterise the interaction, they do not completely capture what is actually created and how learning is made of them. Even Hirsch's (1996) notion of the transferential–countertransferential matrix, in which the patient's early issues are enacted and illuminated, is not so much a third space, but a deeply enmeshed and tangled space between them.

The concept of the third has been applied to the psycho-social perspective by Clarke and Hoggett (2009, p. 17), who refer to "the perspective of the 'third'" as central to undertaking psycho-social research. They emphasise that having "different perspectives regarding the data" (p. 19) or having one's data "perceived from different vantage points" (p. 19) provides a kind of external check on the rigours of undertaking psycho-social research. In addition, the supervision and support of third figures allow the researcher to "see" what is strikingly present to others but was in the blind spot of the researcher. They also have a very important function in mitigating the potential pitfalls of psycho-social research. As Hollway and Jefferson (2013, p. 154) put it, "If psychoanalytic concepts are congruent and subordinated to a holistic treatment of data, they can be safeguarded against 'wild analysis'".

While I heartily endorse this perspective, I also see the idea of the third as relevant to the internal experience of the doctoral journey, as well as the content of one's dissertation. In my case, in particular, I was undergoing a major change in professional identity, which is probably not too unusual for an older doctoral student. Fortunately, the psycho-social approach recognises that such a transition exists and provides support for this process.

Some specific vignettes of third spaces

I have thought of these spaces as vertical and horizontal (lateral) third spaces, and in order to give a flavour of what I am talking about, I will offer some vignettes. On the vertical axis, I will describe an example from the third space created between myself and my UWE Director of Studies, and then between myself and my German supervisor. On the horizontal axis, I will describe an example from the third space between myself and a close fellow student, and then between myself and the doctoral organisational role analysis group.

Vertical 1. My Director of Studies: "Do I deserve to be a doctor? Will I make it?"

In the vertical third space, I was being guided by professionals who made a commitment to help me specifically with the course of my study. Some (UWE supervisors, progression examiners, progress reviewer, course instructors) took on this role and this commitment as part of their professional obligations to students. As such, in their work with me, they were representing the demands of the university and also ensuring to the university that this student would fulfil its expectations. They either chose or were asked to work with me. I did not choose them. Being authorised in these roles by the university and by my agreement to participate as a student meant that I agreed to follow their guidance and, in a sense, surrender my own authority to their judgements. This made the transferential processes very difficult, especially relating to criticism of my work. At the same time, however, it assured me that whenever I might be making a wrong step, I would be properly guided.

Without doubt, and I think most people will agree, the working relationship in the dyad between a doctoral student and one's Director of Studies, is a complicated and fraught one. In a certain way, it is very difficult to create one's own third space here, due to the major demands on both parties from outside sources ultimately to produce a successful product. Not much can be held truly within the dyad that is not deeply influenced by external reality.

I have come to realise that the Director of Studies must stand on a very insecure boundary between, on the one hand, the pressures of the university and, on the other hand, the immense insecurity and dependency of her student. Given this difficult role, I think my Director of Studies took quite a risk in supporting the direction I wanted to take, because I was, on the one hand, developing a way of working in organisations (in an organisational role), which I then intended to research (from the researcher role). I needed the support for both roles, which I received.

From my perspective, as an older student, I found myself very much regressing in my relationship to my Director of Studies, who was much younger than I. One cannot ignore one's Director of Studies. She holds you together and keeps you on track. She tells you what to do next. She guides you and judges you and prepares you for other examiners. In this role, she cannot love everything you do, even if you wish her to.

The Director of Studies must somehow remain a good object to the student while, at the same time, containing the demands of the other (i.e., the university). This role is not unlike the mother, tasting the hot food for the baby and blowing on it, so that it can be palatable and digestible. At times, my transferences have been overwhelmingly positive and, at one particular juncture, overwhelmingly negative. It has been a major effort for me to contain these unconscious processes in order to stay in role, preserve the relationships, and achieve the tasks at hand.

What brought on an overwhelming negative transferential reaction on my part was related to two emails sent to me by my Director of Studies, outlining the problems with two chapters that I was actually quite proud of and tremendously relieved to have finished. In defending myself against what I experienced as a narcissistic wound and very deep feelings of failure, I found myself feeling extremely critical of my two supervisors for what I saw as their failure to provide me with the proper guidance on what should be included in such chapters. I experienced the tone of the two emails as "cold" and attacking. Suddenly, I felt abandoned by my up to then "we are totally with you in this process" supervisors. My Director of Studies, particularly, had gone over to the dark side.

Upon much reflection, I realised that this intense feeling of disappointment with my supervisors (an echo of an earlier negative reaction to a female progression examiner) and an almost baffling contempt regarding their failure, was actually not new. In 1990, as an adult student in a professional training programme for psychoanalytic consulting, this same affect was expressed by a number of my fellow students, who were permanently angry with the directors of the programme because of the poor quality of the copies of the articles we were assigned to read. The supplies were defective and so were the suppliers.

Being captured by this same extreme feeling towards my supervisors has made me realise how extremely difficult it is to be an adult learner and to be the teachers of an adult learner. The transferential dynamic between the child learner and the teacher is completely different. The vulnerable, professional, insecure adult learner requires perfection from the adults. As my Director of Studies noted in her feedback to another chapter, supervisors are those who are: "the 'subject supposed to know', the one who has all the answers and all the 'supplies'". It seems, as well, as if this dynamic especially occurs when the student feels vulnerable to his or her own failure in the new learning process. As Phillips has written (2012, p. 65): "In this familiar division of labour there is a plenitude – the one who, because he is supposed to know, is in the know – and there is an inadequacy:

parents and children, teachers and students . . .". This connects also to Ogden's (1999) notion of the asymmetricality in the relationship between the power and status of the analyst and the patient.

This experience, which I fortunately realised was an overreaction and related to some primitive experiences with my unpredictable mother, consumed my therapy sessions for months, until I was able to locate the early experience, connect it to this overreaction, and internally return to work. Both my supervisors, sensing the distance, gave me the space to work this through, without prodding me for explanations or better chapters, which I very much appreciate. I credit them for truly being, in Winnicott's terms, "good enough mothers" (1971).

Vertical 2: my German supervisor: "Can I develop SDD and also honour and grieve my lost colleague?"

Even before I began my studies at UWE, I asked a German colleague, Ellen, to supervise me in developing the praxis of social dream drawing (SDD). Because she was not in any way affiliated with UWE, this dyad was not vulnerable to the external pressures so present in my first example. In fact, she was a good colleague who was interested in my professional development and also interested in the work I was doing. Between us, we developed a role relationship of supervisor and supervisee that built on our joint needs and wishes. I would say that we both held this third space as very important, but also very much as a luxury for both of us. No money changed hands, and, during the course of my studies, we met six times, either at her office or mine. We lived an hour apart by car.

As opposed to the monitoring role of my UWE supervisors, Ellen was not in a position to evaluate or guide me. She had no "stake", so to say, in my doctorate, although she certainly wanted me to be successful professionally. She and I were free to share, associate, and think together. In many ways, our work held many aspects of myself, that is, the creativity of developing something new and my "Germanness", having moved to Germany just four years earlier.

I would say that this third space held the territory between my beginnings of SDD and the university. The important example is the work we did on my mourning of a key colleague, who sponsored my first social dream drawing group in the Netherlands. Her death, after the group's third session, not only brought our group work to an end, but our identity as well, as some were unwilling to meet again. This loss of a dear colleague influenced my feelings towards continuing with social dream drawing, especially since our last session together failed in many ways, and she expressed her disapproval of my work. We had only just begun to talk this over when she suddenly died. It was my work with my German supervisor that helped me to separate the mourning process of my colleague from the desire to continue to work on SDD. Ironically, my lost colleague was also a colleague of my German supervisor. We attended her funeral together. So, it could be said that this third space was one of co-mourning. Eventually, as my UWE supervisors took over the role of the development of social dream drawing, my German supervisor and I were freer to work on the loss, which then had a place to be worked through.

Lateral/horizontal 1. My doctoral colleague: "Am I competent enough to cope with this unbelievably challenging work?"

In the horizontal third space, I was so very fortunate to have a fellow doctoral student who was in the same general professional field. Although we did not know one another previously, we immediately spoke the same language, so to say. She was a year ahead of me in the programme, and was an invaluable help in orientating me to where to find information and who to ask about what. However, over time, through the various hurdles and failures we both experienced, the relationship grew to be a much deeper one. I felt that this third space is where I held all of my struggling efforts and insecurities.

While the conversation was sometimes about the specifics of our respective dissertation topics, we mostly talked about the experiences of doing a doctorate and the many difficulties it entails. Skyping regularly and meeting up in Bristol and other venues, we have engaged in a deep ongoing process of peer review (Creswell & Miller, 2000), not only by supporting one another's research processes, but also reflecting deeply on our experiences as researchers.

Although I had achieved a certain status as a published organisational thinker in relation to consultation, I was starting from the beginning as a graduate student learning to be a researcher. This was not very easy to do at my stage of life. Here, it was a great advantage to have close contact with my fellow doctoral student, who is near to my age and going through the same transition. Both of us, established in one field, were, and still are, struggling to establish our identities as psycho-social researchers. Both of us were driven to undertake doctoral studies by a passionate interest in a particular topic. As I noted in my reflexive journal (26 May 2012): our relationship "mobilizes our professional selves, and very much helps us integrate our professional selves with the student identity. We can be our professional selves in how we think about our work and how we plan together. That is very self-affirming."

At the same time, we were both able to help one another using our existing professional expertise. For example, during the course of my studies, I had the tendency, especially once I had finished a major step (such as doing my first data analysis scan), to want to dig deeper rather than go on to the next step. My doctoral colleague, who could identify with this tendency, was a great help. As I noted in my reflexive journal on 12 April 2012 regarding a recent Skype conversation with her: "I wanted to talk about being stuck, in a no man's land, about my impressions of [the] data analysis phase. After catching her up with everything, she made a very important comment. Sounds like, in a sense, I am just avoiding getting on to the next step! That was a bit of a shock, but, you know, I think she was right. It is a kind of resistance to go on ahead and get going. We talked for quite a while. . . . We began to realise that both of us are somehow stuck just before we actually create our product that will reveal all our thinking and also reveal us as the thinkers that we are. And both of us are anxious about this next stage. We prefer to stay in our heads or in our experiences. Not to move ahead. For both of us this is a breakthrough."

This collegial third space was not just a place to play or gossip (although, being human, we did a bit of both, of course). It was not a defensive or pairing space. Instead, we created for ourselves over time a trusting and open space to bring up whatever was spilling over from the experiences of our respective doctoral journeys. By coincidence (or not), we had the same two female supervisors and the same Director of Studies.

Sometimes, our experiences were similar, and sometimes they were not. In any case, we each had our own struggles with the demands of the task of the doctorate, and each of us had our own separate relationship with our supervisors and the university. Thus, this could be seen as an example of a triangulation: myself, my colleague, and the system. In describing triangular spaces in organisations, Tietel (2002) makes the point that, in order to sustain a healthy working relationship, one must accept that the other two members of the triangle have a relationship with one another that excludes one. Thus, my colleague in the programme had her own relationship with the supervisory pair that I was excluded from and *vice versa*. As Tietel puts it, ". . . this step is tied to a fundamental act of acknowledgement: the recognition of the fact that not only I entertain a relationship with the two actors but that they also have a relationship with each other" (2002, p. 43) and with other third parties.

In our case, we did not conceive of ourselves as a coalition against others. We wanted very much to be valued and successful students of the university and, at the same time, to maintain our own separateness. As such, we were constantly struggling to hold and utilise our expert identities in one field, while fumbling and stumbling into a new identity in another. It was, in other words, a very demanding process of "separation and attachment" (Tietel, 2002, p. 43), as opposed to one of coalition, where you are either in or out, for or against.

This avoidance of splitting ("we are the poor, persecuted, but really good students. Where is the caring, appreciative university?") meant that, for the full length of our studies, we had to carry the uncertainty of our capacity and ability to actually succeed at the overwhelming task that we had taken on. It was not that our previous experience was invalid, but we soon grew to realise that it was not sufficient to achieve a successful result.

In retrospect, I think we were very much helped by our own personal strengths, particularly our ability to stay mostly in the depressive position. Tietel (2002, p. 36) notes that such a position helps one to manage the triangular reality and "bearing ambivalence". Therefore, neither of us had an interest in winning over the other to a particular point of view. Instead, we helped one another to cope. Although there were clear frustrations with university demands, we did not primarily focus on these problems in order to comfort or soothe ourselves. In retrospect, I give myself and my colleague a lot of credit for somehow realising this, although we had never articulated it.

Lateral 2. Role analysis group: "Can I dare to go beyond my colleagues and be on an intellectual par with my mentors?"

The ongoing doctoral role analysis group, which meets during the doctoral seminars, has as its aim "to provide participants with the resources and conditions for examining their experiences of research and framing them systematically" (programme handout). As such, it has been a major support and source of insight, especially with regard to my status and my identity in relation to my family and to my professional field, socio-analysis. It provided a vital space to bring to mind an issue that might otherwise exist but not be consciously thought about and worked on.

This group meets for a few hours during each bi-annual doctoral seminar and is facilitated by a member of the faculty, but not one's direct supervisors. Each group consists of four or five student participants, each of whom has the opportunity to share with the group an issue of concern relating to the role as researcher or the research itself. Group members then offer their thoughts and associations for the presenter to consider and integrate. For the first few years of my study, I was blessed to have been in a stable group with the same participants and the same facilitator.

In the first few sessions, it was an amazing experience to be, in one way or another, busy with issues around my father (my success being used by him to enhance his reputation) and then with issues with my mother (prone to envious attacks). Not least, this made me realise how strongly these introjections continued to influence me. However, after I had settled into the research role and into my studies, what began to emerge were the issues relating to an organisation that had been my professional home for over thirty years. The feeling of belonging to such an organisation, the sense of security and identity that it gave me, began to be challenged by the sense that I could no longer develop intellectually or professionally by staying completely loyal to it. And, in a sense, my development as a theorist would, in many ways, conflict with the familiar role I had in this system. As I noted in my reflexive journal on 9th July 2012: "One extremely important new point is what I realised in the Role Group. It is one thing to help others develop new thinking, quite another for me to develop new theory! And that is what I am doing and I am needing the support of the University to do that, the imprimatur, so to say. One could say there are three levels: Theory, Thinking, Knowledge. I am aiming for the top level . . . But also developing a new theory is an act of separation . . ."

While the role analysis group was very much a collegial group, the fact that it was housed in the university in the context of doctoral studies meant that I could do a certain kind of work only in this setting and with others going through perhaps similar identity changes. Outside the university experience, this would have felt much too arrogant to share with others.

Underlying theory regarding vertical and horizontal (lateral) axes

This section discusses recent formulations regarding the importance of the horizontal axis, both in organisations and in family therapy. I connect these formulations to my experience as a doctoral student and present an argument for the importance of both axes to contain and support the doctoral journey.

Increasingly, organisational theorists are noting the growing relevance and prevalence of lateral organisational formations in contemporary organisations. Armstrong (2007, p. 194) defines them as "a relation between collaborating persons, role holders, groups or teams that is unmediated by any actual or assumed hierarchical authority". He notes the growing frequency of teams working laterally in organisations, even teams that have no apparent authorisation or leadership. I take this definition to apply directly to the work both with my colleague and with the doctoral role analysis group described above. It also applies to many other third spaces that I had with colleagues. Interestingly, although the doctoral role analysis group at UWE was facilitated by the ex-Director of the Centre for Psycho-social Studies, in his role as group facilitator, I experienced it as a lateral group.

Armstrong notes that lateral relationships have tended to be ignored in psychoanalysis, in favour of those regarding the vertical axis of parent and child. Particularly, the so-called latency period is seen to be a more or less empty period between the oedipal conflict and the beginning of sexual identity. Mitchell (2014), in her exploration of sibling relationships, takes this idea much further in proposing that this middle period is actually a very rich time of experimentation, friendship forming and storming, skill development, and curiosity. From Mitchell's perspective, latency is a period of great "richness, a time of best friends, bullies, playing with peers, inventing, reflecting and learning . . . far from a gap, it is full." (2014, p. 9).

From Mitchell's viewpoint, the movement to the social explosion begins when the next sibling is expected and then arrives on the scene. The first child is no longer the "only" one and faces annihilation. The mother, instinctively knowing this, begins to direct the child outwardly to the social arena, and, as she notes, "when the toddler separates from the mother it is destined to form a lateral group of peers" (2014, p. 1).This "explosion" (p. 10) is an intense response to the trauma of being displaced by the new child. As Mitchell puts it,

> The "sibling trauma" equates to the toddler's experience of annihilation or death on someone else taking its place and all which that place and its emerging sense of individual identity signified. It is always horizontal. At its centre is kill or be killed. Prohibited, this must be socialized. (2014, p. 8)

Upon the entrance of the new sibling, the soon to be displaced child faces the enormous challenge of how to relate to this sibling *and* relate to the reality of no longer being the special one, being emphatically prohibited either from killing the intruder or engaging in incestuous loving. Thus, as Mitchell notes (2014, p. 7), "The trauma of separation and the sibling trauma are the same event from two perspectives". The child, in a sense, "solves" this dilemma, both for the family and for himself, by diving into the social realm and developing and enjoying "a range of lateral relations along a horizontal axis" (2014, p. 2). The child, while staying in the family, is, at the same time, separating from it, and undertakes

> a second route to latency, a movement direct from the dual relation of mother-and-baby/infant to the multi-person relations of the social group. Along this horizontal axis, the trauma is processed as a rite of passage from infancy to childhood. (Mitchell, 2014, p. 9)

Here, I would like to return to my theme of the double axes of third spaces. I see my pursuit of, and deep involvement with, various horizontal (lateral) support systems as an example of how I stayed in the family (i.e., the university) and separated from it as well. From my perspective, the vertical (or family) relationships have to do with getting on with the task and the various external and internal challenges to this goal (standards, measures, testing, evaluating, performance, success, achievement). On the other hand, the horizontal axes (social) provided the "playground" for the explosion of feeling and thinking. Together, they helped me to create a whole, balanced, and integrated system, even though the parts were constantly in motion. As Mitchell puts it, "the two lines, the family and the vertical, and the social group and the horizontal, go on together, interacting but not identical" (2014, p. 11). They interact and resonate constantly within oneself.

In very simple terms, just as Mitchell posits that the rich social life rescues the child from the trauma of the vertical family dynamic and the loss of special identity, so the use of horizontal or lateral social supports during the doctoral process compensates somewhat and provides a containing resource for the humiliations and challenges of the student role.

Research as "me-search"

As I reflect in a general way on my doctoral journey and the use of this combination of third spaces, I would say that I have been deeply involved in a process of gradually growing a new professional identity boundary for myself. This process is a natural one, and takes place for all of us who are active professionally. However, undertaking a doctorate (no matter at what time of life) creates extraordinary conditions and challenges that force one to examine existing assumptions about knowledge and practice and, by its very existence, expands one's intellectual horizons. Tchelebi (2015) has aptly characterised this process as "me-search".

Petriglieri and Petriglieri (2010) offer the interesting notion that business schools can serve as a kind of "identity workspace" (p. 44), where one is gradually able to develop a new professional identity. They define identity work as an ongoing process that "involves individuals crafting, protecting, and modifying their views of themselves, as well as gaining social validation for those views." (2010, p. 45). They note that this work does not take place in isolation, but within a certain containing context. They also point out that "identity work is stimulated by moments of identity destabilization and experiences of uncertainty, confusion, and anxiety" (2010, p. 45). I think this very much captures my own experience over this time.

Although I cannot truly say that I experienced UWE as an "identity workspace", I do believe that the combination of horizontal and vertical third spaces did serve that containing function. I join the above authors in defining "a holding environment as a social context that reduces disturbing affect and facilitates sense making" (Petriglieri & Petriglieri, 2010, p. 50).

One way of thinking of this process is that one is creating a skin around oneself that is continually porous and up for negotiation, what Armstrong (2007, p. 204) terms a "'boundary of identity'" and Tietel (2002, p. 33) "a holding social skin". Tietel explores the concept of social skin in depth, and links it to one's earliest sense of being as an infant. One exists in a social skin, giving a passive "feeling of belonging and of being held, finally a feeling of being 'one'. [It] offers a context in which one feels contained and held" (2002, pp. 37, 38). When one, perhaps, falls out of the social skin of an organisation (as with retirement) these primitive feelings of losing one's skin can emerge. Here, one loses "the experience of a communal surface with one's team or organisation" (2002, p. 39).

This process, I believe, also takes place when one undergoes the profound experience of doing a doctorate, where the "pre-existing boundaries of identity" (Armstrong, 2007, p. 205) become threatened and questioned. One is in a constant state of leaving and becoming. This is consistent with Ogden's notion that the analytic third

> is gradually transmuted into forms of experience of self and other that can be . . . incorporated into one's larger sense of self (including one's experience of and understanding of how one has come to be who one is and who one is becoming). (Ogden, 1999)

In my own case, with years of involvement in Tavistock conferences (Miller & Rice, 1967), it has been my experience, as Armstrong (2007, p. 208) notes, that "there is something inherently difficult in resisting the pull towards thinking of hierarchy as the only possible form of organisation". This pull is also enacted in the student role during one's entire lifetime, and definitely revitalised in the doctoral experience. In fact, nothing could pull more strongly for the vertical. Ogden (1999) notes as well that the analytic third in the vertical spaces are more asymmetrical (i.e., like analysis), meaning that the analyst has more power and status in the relationship. The work of validating the horizontal (symmetrical) axes, therefore, does not come easily. As an older student, I had the luxury of reaching out very broadly for lateral support and perhaps the common sense to make active use of it. Nevertheless, intense childhood feelings were actualised.

Drawing on socio-technical thinking (Trist & Murray, 1993), I would cite the long time span (seven years) and the geographical distance between my home and the university as helpful to integrating this process of skin building. Like the analytic third, that is, a "jointly created unconscious life of the analytic pair" (Ogden, 2004, p. 167), it develops over time.

Going back and forth between these two axes made for an excellent balance, and I consciously made active use of them. I never lost my passion for my topic, while, at the same time, I was often very frustrated with the university requirements. I was very much held by this matrix of horizontal and vertical support and thinking systems. As my Director of Studies once commented, "It's almost as if there is a third space continuum from vertical to horizontal and from 'passing-oriented' (your supervisors!) to 'free-thinking'". I found it especially difficult to be a learner, on the one side, and a creative thinker, on the other. It is clear that no one person could have taken all these roles in supporting me. The multiplicity of resources was essential. And I certainly could not have done it alone.

Conclusion

In summary, the process of doctoral research is a "full body" experience, stimulating and utilising many aspects of one's being. Intellectual theory, the losses and gains associated with transitions in professional identity, the disappointments of being judged, and the great pleasures of creating and developing something "in the arms" of, so to say, many others have been some of the most important aspects for me. One does not undertake this alone or start from scratch. One enters a field and, and, as best as one can, finds one's way.

I very much hope that this chapter will be helpful to supervisors of mature students, who bring to the working relationship a very particular kind of transference. To these supervisors, I would suggest that you take the risk of sharing with your mature supervisees the complicated role boundary issues that you experience, that is, the part of the role that is there to encourage new thinking and the part of the role that is there is ensure that the university's standards and requirements are met. Through this disclosure, a new kind of third space can be forged that brings the student more constructively into the reality of doctoral demands and university pressures. In this way, the student would not be so dependent on separate third spaces to process this and would be less at risk of abandoning his or her studies.

I would also like to say to you supervisors that, in an ironic way, the older student might need more guidance with the basics than you might think. Since older students could be seen as already quite competent and professional, supervisors might underestimate their need for clear guidance and guidelines, such as what should be the content of each chapter and what is the acceptable format for bibliography. To the extent that these specifics can be defined at the beginning, I think the mature student will be less likely to feel disappointed and frustrated.

In terms of designing doctoral programmes, I very much favour community-building structures, such as bi-annual seminars and the role analysis group. These structures make it possible for supportive lateral relationships to be developed between candidates that can sustain them throughout the years.

To the mature student, I send you a special message. Be prepared for an experience that you never could have anticipated when you first started. While you may not "need" a doctorate for your professional career, you might find that the achievement of a doctorate profoundly changes you sense of yourself in relation to your professional world. And that is a great bonus!

References

Armstrong, D. (2007). The dynamics of lateral relations in changing organisational worlds. *Organisational & Social Dynamics, 7*(2): 93–210.
Benjamin, J. (2004). Beyond doer and done to: an intersubjective view of thirdness. *Psychoanalytic Quarterly, 73*: 5–46.
Clarke, S., & Hoggett, P. (2009). Researching beneath the surface: a psycho-social approach to research practice and method. In: S. Clarke & P. Hoggett (Eds.), *Researching Beneath the Surface: Psycho-social Research Methods in Practice* (pp. 1–26). London: Karnac.

Creswell, J. W., & Miller, D. L. (2000). Determining validity in qualitative inquiry. *Theory Into Practice*, *39*(3): 124–130.

Hirsch, I. (1996). Observing–participation, mutual enactment, and the new classical models. *Contemporary Psychoanalysis*, *15*: 359–383.

Hollway, W., & Jefferson, T. (2013). *Doing Qualitative Research Differently: A Psychosocial Approach.* London: Sage.

Miller, E. J., & Rice, A. K. (1967). *Systems of Organisation.* London: Tavistock.

Mitchell, J. (2014). Siblings and the psychosocial. *Organisational & Social Dynamics*, *14*(1): 1–12.

Ogden, T. (1999). The analytic third: an overview (accessed at: www.psychspace.com/psych/viewnews-795 on 29 January 2016).

Ogden, T. H. (2004). The analytic third: implications for psychoanalytic theory and technique. *Psychoanalytic Quarterly*, *73*(1): 167–195.

Petriglieri, G., & Petriglieri, J. (2010). Identity workspaces: the case of business schools. *Academy of Management Learning & Education*, *9*(1): 44–60.

Phillips, A. (2012). *Missing Out: In Praise of the Unlived Life.* London: Penguin.

Tchelebi, N. (2015). Research is me-search: a journey from research to practice & from practice to theory – and 'me'. Presentation to Doctoral Seminar, UWE, Bristol, 20 May 2015.

Tietel, E. (2002). Triangular spaces and social skins in organisations. *Socio-Analysis*, *4*: 33–52.

Trist, E., & Murray, H. (1993). Historical overview: the foundation and development of the Tavistock Institute. In: E. Trist & H. Murray (Eds.), *The Social Engagement of Social Science: A Tavistock Anthology, Vol. II, The Socio-Technical Perspective* (pp. 1–34). Philadelphia, PA: University of Pennsylvania Press.

Winnicott, D. W. (1971). *Playing and Reality.* London: Penguin.

CHAPTER EIGHT

Markers and milestones: learning to navigate the psycho-social research journey

Jane Woodend

Introduction

In this chapter, I describe in detail the process of constructing and conducting research. In so doing, I provide a guide for students starting out on their research journey. I use my own experiences as a researcher, new to the psycho-social approach, to illustrate some of my learning from practice. My aim is to bring to life the research milestones that you will be hearing about from your supervisors and peers: What exactly is epistemology? How might you attempt to be reflexive? Where do you find research participants? How do you go about collecting and analysing data? What are the practical implications for conducting ethically sound research? Through the journey, the theoretical and practical aspects of psycho-social research resonate, collide, and pull apart in the realities of the research situation. The psycho-social approach lends itself to the exploration of incredibly varied research questions. What is reassuring, though, is the commonality of the challenges that researchers face in organising, structuring, and implementing their research methods. I hope to demystify some of these challenges and help you think about how you might best approach them.

My research was concerned with my work as a psychodynamic counsellor. I wanted to explore the ending stages of counselling, because I found this aspect of my work hard to do. I worried that I was not doing a good enough job and that other counsellors found this easier than I did. After becoming a counselling supervisor, and then a service manager, I realised that very many counsellors found endings difficult. So, this got me interested in what it was about endings that seemed to create a challenge for so many of us.

Endings in counselling might be planned from the outset, negotiated through the course of the work, thrust upon participants due to external circumstances, or the work might end if the relationship between counsellor and client was not robust enough to be sustained. I used a psycho-social research methodology to gain a deeper understanding of the interaction between participants' internal worlds and the broader context of the social and cultural constructs around them. I look at the different aspects that comprised my journey through the research methodology in their chronological order.

The importance of knowing how we know

The research pathway starts with a research problem, which I have just described, and then moves through several phases, beginning with the theoretical and then moving inwards towards the practicalities of research, before moving back out to evidencing or developing theory. So, beginning with the theoretical, the first thing I needed to do was to define the epistemology, or theory of knowledge, that underpinned my research. In addition to completing a literature review, in which existing knowledge is mapped and critically evaluated, research should generate new knowledge. But what kind of knowledge is sought? How do we know what we know?

The sociologist Max Weber (1864–1920) articulated the differences between knowledge of the physical world and knowledge of human social action.

> He argued that by necessity of each of the sciences sought to obtain different kinds of knowledge. In the natural sciences, knowledge is of the external world which can be explained in terms of general laws, while in the social sciences knowledge must be of the "internal or

subjective states of individuals" in that human beings have an "inner nature" that must be understood to explain outward events that lead to their social actions in the world. (Morrison, 2006, p. 348)

So, how do we find out about the inner nature of man and the conse-quences for the social world?

One way we might approach this is through the study of her-meneutics. In relation to philosophy rather than religion, the diction-ary definition is "the study and interpretation of human behaviour and social institutions" (Hanks, 1986, p. 717). The word is derived from the Greek *hermeneus*, meaning "interpreter" and is of uncertain origin. The critical theorist Habermas turned to the German tradition of hermeneutics: the science of interpreting texts, which has its histor-ical roots in the work of Schleiermacher (1768–1834), who studied biblical texts in order to find their true meaning. Dilthey (1833–1911), whose work later influenced Weber, described our understanding having a fore structure that disallows pure knowledge. Dilthey considered other texts (outside of biblical texts) and artefacts, to be open to hermeneutic interpretation and then realised this might also be applied to human actions, which have meaning and a narrative structure just as a text does. Parker (2002, p. 147) helpfully elucidates the notion of what "texts" might be:

> It is useful, as a first step, to consider all tissues of meanings as texts and to understand which texts will be studied. All of the world, as a world understood by us and so given meaning by us, can be described as being textual and it is in this sense that, once this process of inter-pretation and reflection has been started, we can adopt the post-struc-turalist maxim "there is nothing outside of the text" (Derrida, 1976, p. 158)

Giddens (1984, p. 20) developed the idea of a "double hermeneu-tic", whereby lay concepts make their way into the social sciences, but that also social sciences concepts feed back into social life, making for a two-way relationship and one where research findings feed back into society, thereby changing it. Knowledge generated by hermeneu-tic research feeds back into its object of study, both consciously and unconsciously, which can create further alteration and change.

Another way in which we find out about the inner nature of man and the consequences for the social world is by considering cognitive interests. Alvesson and Sköldberg (2000, p. 124) give an overview of the work of critical theorist Habermas, who suggests there are three ways of looking at this:

- Technical cognitive interest concerns itself with the knowledge interest required to ensure human survival: how we produce food, treat disease, clothe ourselves, and so forth. This knowledge is drawn from the application of natural sciences.
- Historical–hermeneutic knowledge interest focuses on the transmission of meanings within and between contemporary cultures and across historical divides. Communication, language, and culture are used to foster shared understanding.
- Emancipatory knowledge interest is concerned with identifying and explaining the constraints that limit the potential of an individual or group.

Alvesson and Sköldberg (2000, p. 125) write,

> Psychoanalysis is regarded as the model for the emancipatory project. By way of self-reflection and the critical inquiry into ideas, perceptions, fantasies and so on, it is possible to counteract the psychological barriers that restrict man's potential. The intellectual insight thus acquired helps to combat repression.

So this helped me to locate the epistemology I sought to answer my research questions in both emancipatory knowledge and with historical–hermeneutic knowledge.

I felt there was another area of knowledge which I had first come across used technically in psychodynamic training, but which, when explored via an extended literature review, has important origins and extensions I had not previously seen, and which might make sense of some of the things that happened to me when I did research. Much of the work of counselling is concerned with feelings and emotions. There is also a state of being that we experience before we can clearly label a feeling and identify it as "upset" or "joyful", for example. This state is known as "affect". Affect is one of those words that has multiple meanings. So, in addition to my simple description of affect being a precursor state to labelling a feeling, there are other ways in which we might make sense of affect. We know that the moon affects the tides, or that diet affects health. This suggests that affect is a force of some kind. Another way to think about affect is on a societal level. For example, we can be affected by events such as the terror attacks in London and Manchester in 2017. Wetherell (2012, p. 2) suggests that thinking about affect in this way "leads to a focus on embodiment, to attempts to understand how people are moved, and what attracts them, to an emphasis on repetitions, pains and pleasures, feelings and memories".

A third construction of affect is presented by theorists who support the philosophies of Deleuze, Bergson, Spinoza, and Whitehead. For them, affect "slides over distinctions between human and non-human, animate and inanimate" (Wetherell, 2012, p. 3). This construction of affect challenges the way we have previously understood social institutions and the people who form them. They also describe a very different type of epistemology from Derrida's famous quote given above ("there is nothing outside of the text"). This quote seems to me to have a quality of being in denial of the "real" world, and ignorant of the affective realm. Life cannot be lived as if there were no physical reality to the world. Psychoanalytic thinking is permeated with notions of internalisation and somatisation, so attention to the affective is important for me. Indeed, underpinning my training is Freud's whole notion of drives and impulses, which are concerned with affect rather than thought.

So, there are different and complex ways of approaching affect.

> For those new to this area, or perhaps only beginning to encounter the importance of affect in your own work, this might entail a response to an imagined and perceived question, "what is affect?" However, a more cautious response might be to consider what different versions of affect do in our theorizing. (Blackman & Venn, 2010, pp. 8–9)

I was aware that my research would be located in participants' feelings and emotions related to endings, loss, mourning, and attachment. As a psychodynamic counsellor, I use my own feelings and somatic responses as useful data: to illuminate what might be happening in the client's inner world, to gauge my own reaction to the encounter, and to make sense of the dynamic between us. I anticipated drawing on a similar process within my research. The epistemology of affect was, therefore, central to my research.

One of the tasks of research is to define the parameters in which you are working. I came across a variety of definitions or explanations of affect, each with their own merits and drawbacks. In the end, I had to define my own conceptualisation of affect, which is that the non-verbal conscious and unconscious self and the physical self have responses to external and internal events that are registered by the individual at conscious and preconscious levels, but are not necessarily accessible in verbal terms. We are affected by events at a level that precedes giving meaning.

I was aware of my feeling of being on thin ice when I thought and wrote about affect, but I suspected this came with the territory. Hollway (2010) said, "The truth that emotion carries as its cargo . . . using one's subjectivity as an instrument of knowing will not be a popular paradigm". Affect is still conceptually confusing, so we need to resist the urge to rush towards a concept or method that defines it and, instead, think of researching affect as a developing craft. For me, affect needed to be worked with in both my research participants and within myself. Affect is to do with entanglement, is relational, is connective and intersubjective. I was trying to see what the participants' affective responses might tell me about endings in counselling, and also to see how my own affective responses might generate data for the research process.

My encounter with reflexive research

The model for accessing data produced from my own affective responses is through the use of reflexivity. Reflexivity means not just reflecting on my research findings, but reflecting again, at a secondary and then tertiary level: what informs my reflections and responses to my research findings? What might there be in my personal history and social context that lead me to certain conclusions? How does my relationship with my research participants, the data, and with the literature I encounter shape my interpretation of my findings? I will be consciously aware of some of these aspects, but others will be unconscious. Hollway and Jefferson (2000, p. 45) construe

> both researcher and researched as anxious, defended subjects, whose mental boundaries are porous where unconscious material is concerned. This means that both will be subject to projections and introjections of ideas and feelings coming from the other person.

This notion of the unconscious intersubjectivity between researcher and researched raises the importance of qualitative research being reflexive research in this context. I was familiar with the idea of individuals bringing their own personal defences to any encounter from my clinical work: the development of defences, what they might mean, and how to work with them formed a significant aspect of my training. However, I felt it unhelpful to automatically assume all my research participants, and, indeed, myself, would be both anxious and defended. I preferred to see what happened, to me and to the participant, in each encounter. Sometimes, I was aware of these aspects in the moment, at other times, they come into consciousness through engagement with the research material.

In order to produce good enough research, I had to allow that my understanding of endings through the research process was also mediated by my own personal history and affective responses to the research material. Research is a highly personal activity in which the research process allows something to be transformed within the researcher. Parker (2002, p. 190) states,

> In qualitative work, where an analysis of reflexivity is encouraged and where new forms of subjectivity are allowed to take shape in the course of the research, there is often a strong personal engagement with the material, a sense of being immersed, overwhelmed, and sometimes of being transformed by the subject matter.

By allowing the personal engagement to be known, indeed by facilitating one's awareness of it from the pre-conscious to the conscious, the personal investments in the research might be seen more clearly.

As described at the start of this chapter, I had a personal history of relatively few endings. I was aware of my own preoccupation with death, having experienced little of it. I knew that I was inclined, therefore, to respond to accounts of endings involving deaths as somehow more significant than other endings, as I was still rather in awe of those who survived bereavement. It was a couple of years into my research before I thought to document and reflect on my own experiences of ending in counselling as a client. I was rather shocked at how easily I had overlooked an obvious significant aspect of my personal history and the place this played in my research. This realisation led, I believe, to my being able to sit back and take all accounts of endings in a more even-handed way.

Here is how I approached reflexive research. First, I decided to keep a reflexive journal. I used this to record my thoughts, feelings, dreams, synchronicities, and other phenomena, in relation to my research. Synchronicity could be simply described as the experience of noticing meaningful coincidences. However, this rather reductionist rendering of it loses the richness and intriguing metaphysical qualities that Jung (1961) interpreted in synchronicity. Mathers (2001, p. 140) usefully suggests that "Synchronicity describes meaning raining all around us – irrigating, rather than flooding". An example of a synchronous experience in my research was my encounter with Roberta, one of my client research participants. In the interview with Roberta, the visceral theme of death was apparent from the start of our first interview. She had sought counselling to help her come to terms with a number of deaths, including the early death of her mother. Roberta described a poor working alliance with her counsellor, which left her feeling there was no point in continuing with the counselling. She decided to call it a day, but "because I found it difficult I did it in a very clumsy way. And it's stayed with me."

The "clumsiness" of the ending she then described seemed to me to be strongly paralleled by the clumsiness which accompanied other aspects of her story and also of my own clumsy start to the interviews: the train line on which I had been travelling to meet with Roberta had been closed due to a body on the line (another visceral death) and I had arrived late, panting and sweating on a hot day, having run from another station. The clumsy endings in Roberta's account included her parting from her mother.

> I'd been away from home for a year, and I'd gone back to visit Mum and I could see she was unwell but no one was saying anything. And as I was actually on the train going back to London . . . my father said, "Look, your Mum's ill and she's got what your Grandma had" [cancer]. And she'd come with us to the station in the car. And I'd walked to the train and that's the last I saw of her . . .

In the interview with Roberta, we were able to play with ideas of clumsiness, feeling childish, and with what Roberta had unhelpfully experienced as the smooth, resistant, professionalism of her counsellor. My own clumsy arrival had been experienced by Roberta as reassuring—I, too, was human like her. These apparent parallels, with things going wrong at stations, opened a space for professional and

personal relating to be engaged with in what was, for me, a very phys-
ically informed way. My sweaty, panting physicality did not allow me
to hide behind the veneer of the professional, impersonal researcher.
These aspects of my interview with Roberta were recorded and
explored in my reflexive journal and field notes.

My reflexive journal was, in practice, a notebook into which I
jotted any thoughts, feelings, dreams, and observations, and so I had
that which I felt pertained to my research. The notebook was marked
"Private!" and I carried it around with me in my bag. There was no
confidential data in it, in the sense of giving away information about
my participants, for instance. Looking back at the journal, I can see
how my mind was initially concerned with theory, then role, then
practicalities, and then back to theory again.

Second, I maintained careful fieldwork notes. My field notes were
in some way an extension of my journal, but with a particular focus
on my experience of events leading up to, during, and after each interview. I would note how my journey to the interview venue had been,
how I had been feeling, what my gut reactions and first thoughts were
on meeting my participant were, how I felt during the interview and
any stray thoughts or connections that had had come to me then, how
I felt after the interview, and then my journey home. The field notes
provided a practical account of what happened, but also enabled me
to retain odd synchronicities, my own affective responses, and to see
patterns emerge across the interview process.

Some thoughts on methodological design

How do you design a methodology that will enable you to answer
your research questions? My starting point for methodological design
was to consider my own experience of endings in counselling. I connected to a range of emotions. There was often the satisfaction of "a
good job done", the pleasure at seeing someone leave feeling much
better than when they first started counselling, and accepting their
thanks for my part in this change. This is the easily accessible component of endings. But other feelings emerged, that are perhaps less
acceptable and, correspondingly, less accessible. There can be feelings
of relief at no longer having to sit with a client with whom I felt out
of my depth, or useless to help, relief at the departure of a boring or

annoying client. Are these my own feelings anyway? Might they be, in part at least, a projection of the client's feelings? There can be concerns that the counselling engagement has, in fact, made things worse for the client—what responsibility do I hold in these cases? And there can be the ongoing feelings of sadness, loss, or abandonment that I feel after a particularly meaningful counselling relationship has ended . . . are my feelings congruent with my role as a practitioner or have I become too personally entangled with my client? The range of feelings, emotions, and actions that I might want to find out about as a researcher would encompass the conscious, the unconscious, things which participants might be willing to share, and things which they might not want anyone to know about.

I was aware that to research a phenomenon that included potential "failure" was a countercultural theme within the current development of counselling as a profession. Keen to show our effectiveness in a culture that requires evidenced outcomes, failures can become hidden. This meant that researching a topic where failure might be a component would need a methodological framework that could enable participants to feel contained and safe. If this were achieved, they would allow their ambivalent feelings, or partially formed responses, in their conscious and unconscious communications to be considered and reflected upon.

With these difficult emotions in mind, in addition to the more positive feelings people might want to express, how did I choose a participant sample and how did I engage in collecting data? There is a chicken and egg quality to these matters. The type of participant sample that you can get might shape the method of data collection, or your chosen method of data collection might lead you to a specific group of research participants. This is where there needs to be some play of ideas and juggling of research priorities, best done in consultation with your supervisors or research peer group. Often, there can be very pragmatic decisions that result in your research methodology going in one particular direction or another. What is important is knowing what you would like, realising what you can get, and then finding ways to either bridge the gap between these two realities or letting go of some of the original scope of your ideas.

The issue of ethics is present throughout clinical practice and also throughout research. The client–counsellor relationship is often thought of as confidential, and, although a client may give informed consent to his own participation in research, it does not follow that his counsellor will necessarily agree to participate. The notion of confidentiality is held dear within the profession and this incorporates the notion that the work undertaken is internalised and can continue after the termination of the actual counselling sessions. There is a view that to "intrude" on this, to re-examine the counselling relationship and process, changes the internalised relationship. I was concerned that, by inviting former clients and counsellors to revisit endings, in the interests of research, this might be seen as breaching confidentiality and potentially changing how clients had seen and internalised their counsellors. I provide more detail about how I managed the ethical components later.

Reflections on finding an appropriate method to collect data

I needed to find a way of collecting data about endings in counselling that would enable me to capture both conscious and unconscious material, allow the participants to feel secure enough to voice subversive or countercultural ideas or experiences, and maintain the ethical framework that supports good counselling and research practice. Through discussion with my supervisors, and through completing a research methodology module, I encountered a range of possible approaches. These included using grounded theory, interpretive phenomenological analysis, the biographical–interpretative method, free association narrative interviews, ethnographic approaches, photo-ethnography, and the use of poems and dreams in research. I decided to utilise the technique of free association narrative interviews (FANI) promoted by Hollway and Jefferson (2013). FANI evolved from the use of biographic–interpretative interviews, which require the interviewer to apply many of the skills central to psychodynamic counselling. For example, Wengraf (2001, pp. 125–126) draws attention to the importance of active listening:

> Your task is always to remain actively listening – interviewees will immediately sense when you have stopped listening to them, and this "no longer listening" will end or distort the expression of their gestalt – and always to be prepared to notice that the interviewee is needing support, not necessarily verbal, from you to continue in this often difficult task.

He goes on (2001, pp. 128–129) to list the positive and negative forms of active listening desired, many of which are identical to those found in counselling skills. For example:

> Do allow the interviewee the length of pause, of silences that they need to think through or recall material they are trying to access; if strong emotions arise during the interview, you should be prepared if necessary, to "mirror" them; don't console; don't give advice; don't suggest what the interviewee might next well talk about!!

I felt that FANI would enable me to use a skill set I already possessed, while giving me a chance to learn and integrate my "new", researcher skills. Wengraf (2001, p. 125) flags up the differences between a therapeutic and a research based interview:

> We deviate from the free association rule by framing the interaction as a research interview rather than a session of psychoanalysis or of therapy or of counselling. We also deviate because we start the first session by a request not for any free association but for a very specific type of account: a biographical narrative.

An important enactment of this distinction is that the researcher keeps their focus on the data and can point the interviewee back to the narrative when they dry up. Wengraf suggests (2001, p. 129) "You are doing research. Try to get more story/any more stories: . . . Any other things you remember happening? . . . Do you remember/recall anything else – without specifying what the storying should be about."

Another element of FANI that Clarke (2002, p. 174) cites is "Psychoanalytic interpretation does not take place within the interview but is confined to interpretation of the data collected". I am not in the habit of making frequent interpretations in my counselling practice, but the notion of these being off the agenda altogether needed to be absorbed. My initial belief was that I would have no problem with FANI, given my counselling skills and experience. As my understanding of the approach grew, I began to feel much more aware of the different stance I would have to employ in research interviews. This was going to be a challenge to me. When I actually came to do the interviews, I found that I did not consciously think about interpreting, or not interpreting, what was said in the moment. Looking at the subsequent transcripts, I can see that I did make some interpretations, which, to my mind, served to open up the participants to begin to make their own links and interpretations more freely in the interview.

My research design was based on undertaking two interviews each, with counsellors, supervisors, and clients who had ended their counselling, with a week between the interviews. I chose this design because of both methodological and ethical reasons. First, my research objectives were concerned with finding out about endings in psycho-dynamic counselling and in life more generally, in order to have a social context in which to set my clinical findings. I felt it was not possible to fully understand the meaning that participants attributed to their endings in counselling without having a sense of where this sat in relation to their life history.

I thought it would not be possible to gather this breadth of data within one interview. This gave me a clear sense of wanting to address endings in counselling at the first interview, with an opportunity to find out about other, more personal, endings in the second. There was also an issue here of the first interview being, potentially, less reveal-ing. I wanted my participants to feel secure and contained enough to bring their life stories of endings outside of the counselling setting and thought this was better served by their having had some experience of me and the interview process first.

The second reason was concerned with the ethics of opening up the counselling relationship for further scrutiny. If participants felt that there were adverse or disconcerting effects from revisit-ing their endings in counselling in the first interview, the second interview gave the opportunity for this to be aired, explored, and contained.

How I found the research participants

As a counselling service manager, I had access to a potential research sample from the number of clients, counsellors, and supervisors within the service. However, I felt uncomfortable with the possible dynamics that might result from me operating as a researcher within the service. I felt there was a capacity for ethical dilemmas to occur and for role conflicts to abound. Being an "insider" researcher—research-ing your own culture, environment, or group—has advantages and disadvantages. You might know the territory, but sometimes this can blind you from asking what I colloquially define as "the bleeding obvious". I chose not to research within my own organisation, but with other counsellors outside of my locality. But still I found that my shared professional knowledge with participants got in the way of my getting below the surface of their discourse on occasions. I found I had not asked questions that I knew the answers to and, thus, missed the opportunity to hear first-hand accounts of systems, processes, and ways of working that might helpfully have revealed something new to me. This is a limitation of being an "insider researcher". It is hard to balance this with the advantages of being an insider. Would those participants have agreed to take part if they did not know I was a counsellor, too?

So, I decided to find a counselling organisation outside of my own in which to locate my research. I needed a gatekeeper organisation through which I could contact and engage with potential research participants. I approached a counselling organisation (CO) based in London. The training and clinical approach of the counsellors and supervisors there was very familiar to me (my own training had been with one of their regional centres and accredited by them), so I knew I would be encountering the psychodynamic counselling model in which I wished to base my research. An advantage of going to a larger organisation was that they had structures in place that facilitated research: an ethics committee and a database of former clients who indicated they would be willing to be approached as research participants. As well as the practical advantages this offered me, I also felt contained and reassured by the way the organisation evidently valued the research process.

My method for identifying counsellors and supervisors was straightforward: in discussion with the CO, we agreed that both qualified and trainee counsellors would be invited to take part, in addition to all supervisors. I produced a brief, two-paragraph note of introduction to give an overview of the research project, which was to be emailed to these staff. I wanted to begin my research activities with counsellors and supervisors, honing my skills with fellow professionals before embarking upon client interviews. A separate letter was produced to be sent to former clients. I did not have access to the client database myself, but produced the letter that the CO could then forward.

A dry run at data collection

Before embarking on my actual data collection with "real" participants, I wanted to practise my research skills, and thought that my
own service was an appropriate place for this. I asked if colleagues
would be willing to be interviewed. This provided me with a chance
to hone my interviewing skills and also to create some background
information on the topic of endings. The interviews I undertook were
not recorded. I made field notes of my recollections of what was said
and my thoughts and feelings around the process each time were
recorded in my reflexive journal. My experience of these interviews
was that I had relatively little to do after my opening remarks. It felt
as if this produced a flood of material from each participant. This
surprised me, but proved to be a useful early research experience:
exactly the same thing happened in my actual research interviews, so
I was helpfully prepared for this and able to go with it.

I then approached three senior staff members with a request for a
similar pilot interview, but this time to make a digital recording and
transcript, so that I might begin to practise data analysis as well as
understand my own interview technique better. My approach was
more formal, in that I provided each interviewee with a written statement about my research, including details of how long the interview
might take and notice that it would be recorded and transcribed.
Interviewees were offered a copy of the transcript if they wished. The
statement informed them that I would ensure the transcript was
anonymous and would be kept in a locked cabinet, and that my digital recording of the interview would be deleted from my computer
when I completed my research. I let them know that the information
produced would be background material that would not appear in my
final thesis. I also asked for their consent for me to use excerpts from
the transcripts for training purposes.

These pilot interviews produced three experiences and transcripts
of surprisingly different content. My sense of these pilot interviews, in
conjunction with the range of responses I encountered in my non-
recorded interviews, was of the disparate nature of the data: an image
of a river separating out into a delta comes to mind. It is as if, in the
research process, I had been travelling on the somewhat winding
course of a river, contained on both sides by banks, until I reached
the point of engaging with participants, when suddenly everything

spreads out in a number of directions, at varying depths and to varying points. This suggested to me that my research findings might well not show a convergence, a single coherent line emerging, but could indicate major differences and experiences of isolation, otherness, or separation in relation to the research topic. This felt important to keep in mind, as the notion of getting a whole picture operates across each interview, and across the research project overall.

Having conducted my pilot interviews, I gave the go-ahead for the CO to send out my research details to their counsellors and supervisors. I waited, but I received no response to my request for research participants. After a couple of weeks, I checked with the CO administrative team, who confirmed the email had been sent. I felt deflated at the total lack of interest in my project. In supervision, we discussed what this absence of response might mean. Was I being treated as another trainee? Was there a split between the wish to be involved in research and the fear of what this might reveal, particularly given the close relationship between endings in counselling and outcomes? My supervisors urged me to take hold of my status as a researcher, rather than feeling apologetic for being a nuisance to the organisation, and chase up what was happening with more energy. They suggested I offer something to give some focus to my research: run an event, or attend a team meeting. I did not reflect on this, but acted on instruction. I rang the CO that afternoon, telling them to re-issue my email and ensure it was sent to all counsellors and supervisors, and I offered to run a workshop on endings for them. This was an important and formative experience within my research journey. It crystallised the shift in role to researcher for me, with an understanding that managing the relationship with my gatekeeper organisation was my responsibility. Within twenty-four hours, I began to receive expressions of interest from potential research participants and spoke to each person individually.

The importance of ethical issues and the "containment" of data

Ensuring that your research proposal has been scrutinised by an ethics committee serves several purposes. Most importantly, it means that the wellbeing and safety of your research participants has been given due consideration, and also the wellbeing and safety of you and any organisation with whom you might be working. It also creates a sense of containment and validation of your research work, which I found important in helping me make the role transition from counsellor to researcher. I presented my research proposal to both my university faculty research ethics committee and to the ethics committee at the CO.

Ethical consideration needs to be given to any potential risks associated with the research. For my participants, this first concerned the reopening of therapeutic issues after an episode of counselling had been completed and, second, how counsellors and supervisors might feel towards the agency in which they work. I was able to negotiate with the CO that they would take responsibility for offering an appropriate response in support of a former client, counsellor, or supervisor. For a client, this might be exploring the option of further counselling. For a counsellor or supervisor, this might be a meeting to discuss their work within the service and the support they received for this. I felt this measure offered appropriate protection to people involved in the research process from the CO.

I provided a participant information sheet for each participant. These sheets gave more information about the research process and about the potential risks of taking part, as well as the CO's agreement to take responsibility for appropriate follow-up if needed. I ensured that everyone who expressed an interest in taking part in my research received a participant information sheet and signed to say they had read it.

There are issues of confidentiality within the research process itself. For participants, knowing that what they say will remain confidential is very important. In order to maintain absolute confidentiality, I took a number of steps. First, although I required the assistance of the CO in identifying research participants, I did not tell them who responded to my request. I ensured that all participants' identifying information was stored in a locked filing cabinet, separate from the associated non-identifying information. I anonymised all participants using a simple approach: the first person I interviewed was given a pseudonym beginning with A, the second with B, and so forth. I made sure that all my data was stored in locked filing cabinets or with e-versions of transcripts anonymised and stored on my own password-protected home computer (not networked to others).

Only I and my professional transcriber had access to my data in raw form. I would send her a memory stick containing an interview by recorded delivery. She would complete the transcription and then return the memory stick, containing the digital recording and transcription, to me, also by recorded delivery. We communicated by email to say when the memory stick had been posted, so the recipient knew when to expect it. This proved to be a watertight system, with no material getting lost.

My supervision team, and the peer groups I used to help me analyse the data, were given copies of anonymous data, which were returned to me for shredding upon completion of the data analysis session. I undertook that in my selection of quotes from transcripts, and in any sections used from my accompanying field notes, in my thesis or in any subsequent publications, no personal description or details could give away the identity of any participants. Finally, I stated in my participant information sheets that all data would be kept for the duration of the PhD. Upon completion, all data was destroyed. In retrospect, I think a better approach is to obtain consent to keep all data securely for potential use in further research; you do not know what your data might produce or how you might value having it to use for future research.

(The practicalities of) interviewing and creating transcripts

It can take a lot of planning, communicating, and organising to find research participants and ensure that the necessary ethical requirements have been met. Once these tasks have been completed, it is important that you set up and structure the interviews to ensure that both you and your participants have an engaging and fruitful experience. This is about getting the physical environment, the timing, and the content right—not always easy! And, be warned, it can cost money to hire rooms, buy digital recorders, and perhaps pay for transcription services, so think about building this into your financial planning for your research.

I was lucky in situating my research within a counselling setting. It meant that I could hire the rooms at the CO and know that I had a quiet, comfortable, and relatively bland space in which to work with my participants. Knowing that you have your interview room secured for as long as each interview lasts is very important to enable you to feel contained. If you are feeling jumpy, not knowing how long you have or whether you will be interrupted, it is hard to create a calm and inviting space for your participant. I made sure that I had bottled water available and actively asked my participants if the room was comfortable for them and let them know where the toilets were should they need them.

I tried to ensure that my participants were fully informed about the research process and took part willingly at all stages of the research process. I did this by using an open and accessible communication style that invited questions and further debate via email, telephone, or face to face. Before commencing each first interview, I checked that the participant had read and digested the participant information sheet. I drew particular attention to the statement "It is up to you to decide whether to take part or not. If you do decide to take part, you will be given this information sheet and asked to sign a consent form. If you decide to take part, you are still free to withdraw at any time and without giving a reason." Then I asked each participant to sign two copies of a consent form prior to the first interview starting. The consent form iterated that participants could withdraw at any time without giving a reason, in addition to confirming they had read the information sheet and had had a chance to ask questions. All participants signed the consent form without question. They then kept one copy, with me taking the other. On completion of these administrative tasks, I began the interview proper, using the free association narrative interview method described earlier. Over the course of eighteen months, I completed thirty-eight interviews with nineteen participants: nine counsellors, six counselling clients, and four counselling supervisors, all involved with providing, receiving, or supervising psychodynamic counselling. I completed my fieldwork notes, as described earlier, before and after each interview. Each interview was recorded on a digital recorder.

The digital recorder was never allowed to contain interview recordings for longer than twenty-four hours. I felt aware that it contained precious cargo that could not be replaced if lost. As soon as I returned home from completing the interviews, I downloaded the interviews to my laptop and deleted them from the recorder. I made a back-up copy on an external hard drive, which was kept in a locked filing cabinet. Similarly, my field notes were transcribed by me on to the computer on my return home. This felt important, as it gave me an opportunity to revisit my observations and add any later thoughts to them. All of my interviews and field notes used the pseudonyms I had given to the participants.

Initially, I transcribed the interviews myself. Although a competent typist, I soon had to face the reality that I was not going to be able to undertake all the transcription myself, no matter how desirable this might be in terms of getting really familiar with the material. I had over thirty hours of recorded material, and a family and a job. I have described earlier how I sent copies of the digital recordings to a professional transcriber. On receipt of her transcripts, I would listen to the digital recording against the transcription to correct the occasional error and to experience the voices against the written copy. This gave me a chance to add in any additional details, such as "long pause", or "tone of voice suddenly drops". The transcription service was, for me, as a part-time researcher with a challenging job and family commitments, an expensive necessity. Without it, I do not believe I would have been able to complete this research project.

Learning about thematic analysis of data

As with research methodology, there is an array of approaches for analysing data. I found it interesting to note that research methods and data analysis are not more strongly aligned. Having considered various options of data coding and processing which are software based, and having struggled to fully understand what discourse analysis meant in practice, I opted to use thematic analysis, which Braun and Clarke (2006, p. 77) say is "a poorly demarcated and rarely acknowledged, yet widely used qualitative analytic method". I found, with thematic analysis, that research is an action learning process, whereby understanding and knowledge are generated through engagement with the task in hand. There is also the role of academic supervision in steering the researcher towards good practice through suggestion and passing on "the tricks of the trade".

Braun and Clarke (2006, p. 79) describe thematic analysis as

> a method for identifying, analyzing and reporting patterns (themes) within data. It minimally organizes and describes your data-set in (rich) detail. However, frequently it goes further than this, and interprets various aspects of the research topic (Boyatzis, 1998).

They go on to describe a common misconception of the approach: it is not about themes "emerging" from the data, which positions thematic analysis as "a passive account of the process of analysis and denies the active role the researcher always plays in identifying patterns/ themes" (Braun & Clarke, 2006, p. 80).

The first stage of thematic analysis is to immerse oneself in the data. In addition to collecting the data, via interviews and my own reflexive responses detailed in field notes, there is the issue of transcription. Ideally, the researcher transcribes their own interview recordings, but I have given my view on the practicality of this for part-time researchers. When the transcriptions are complete, the researcher needs to read and re-read the transcripts as well as checking these back against the digital recordings. From this initial immersion, the next step is to begin to code the data. This means working "systematically though the entire data set, giving full and equal attention to each data item, and identifying interesting aspects in the data items that may form the basis of repeated patterns (themes) across the data set" (Braun & Clarke, 2006, p. 89). Once the data has been coded it can be organised into themes.

What counts as a theme and how do you identify it? Braun and Clarke (2006, p. 82) suggest "a theme captures something important about the data in relation to the research question, and represents some level of patterned response or meaning within the data set". They go on to say (p. 83),

> Part of the flexibility of thematic analysis is that it allows you to determine themes (and prevalence) in a number of ways. What is important is that you are consistent in how you do this within any particular analysis.

My approach to identifying themes was to take a "bottom up", or "inductive", stance: to organise and make sense of the data without having categories in mind within which to fit it. Identifying themes is an iterative process of interrogating one's suggested themes. Is there enough data to support the theme? Is the theme discrete? Can two themes be more usefully combined under one heading? Does the theme contain sub-themes? Braun and Clarke (2006, p. 92) warn, "as coding data and generating themes could go on ad infinitum, it is important not to get over-enthusiastic with endless re-coding".

Having identified themes, I then based my analysis at what Braun and Clarke (2006, p. 84) describe as "a latent or interpretive level". This was in keeping with my psycho-social methodology, where the researcher looks beyond the surface content of what the participant has said. Braun and Clarke (2006, pp. 84–85) comment,

> in this form, thematic analysis overlaps with some forms of discourse analysis . . . where broader assumptions, structures and/or meanings are theorized as underpinning what is actually articulated in the data. Increasingly, a number of discourse analysts are also revisiting psycho-analytic modes of interpretation (eg Hollway and Jefferson, 2000), and latent thematic analysis would also be compatible with that framework.

These observations assured me that my mode of data analysis was appropriate for my particular research questions and compatible with work being done by my contemporaries.

How I approached thematic analysis

Using the method described by Braun and Clarke (2006), the first thing I did was to identify the data extracts that interested me. These I gave my close attention to and began to code. Although there are software programmes available for this, I undertook the task manually. I wanted the security that I felt would come from having a "hands on" relationship to my data, a direct and intimate engagement with the material. My method was to use the "track changes" function on the computer, so that I could highlight a section of text and then list my comments about the section. I did this in conjunction with listening to the digital recording. This enabled me to put a timing next to my comments (for instance, twelve minutes, thirty-seven seconds) so I could locate the point in the digital recording if I wanted to listen to it again.

Braun and Clarke (2006, p. 89) helpfully point out,

> Note that no data set is without contradiction, and a satisfactory thematic "map" that you will eventually produce—an overall conceptualization of the data patterns, and relationships between them—does not have to smooth out or ignore the tensions and inconsistencies within and across data items.

This awareness helped me retain and interpret the inconsistencies that were present.

Once I had done this for a whole transcript, I then started on the second interview for that participant. This enabled me to see the pair of transcripts as related data. It helped me to "tune in" to the discourses, tones, reflections, and references across the two interviews. There is also the important issue of retaining the *Gestalt* here. This is an identifying feature of the biographical–interpretative method, which has been carried forward into FANI: "the idea that there is a Gestalt (a whole that is more than the sum of its parts, an order or hidden agenda) informing each person's life which it is the job of biographers to elicit intact" (Hollway & Jefferson, 2013, p. 32). Retaining the *Gestalt* needs to be attended to not only in the interview process, but also in the data analysis process. If data is fragmented into coded sections and only considered in this way, then the overarching themes, tones, or story can be lost.

Once a pair of interviews had been considered in terms of coding data extracts, I re-read the transcripts. This bringing back together of the narrative alongside the coded extracts enabled me to identify and interpret what I perceived to be the broader themes in the data. I recorded this process by writing down what I thought to be a theme related to the first piece of coded data, then the next, and so forth. I found that extracts of coded data began to fit into earlier themes. Sometimes, these themes remained connected to only one data extract; others had many extracts clustered around them. Some themes with clusters remained clearly related to the central idea; others seemed to sprout sub-themes. And then there were themes that I was aware were not centrally located in the coded extracts, but came from my field notes and reflexive journal entries. This knowledge came from my own memory and experience of having met the participants and undertaken the interviews myself; this data would not have been present had I been working with data collected from other researchers. By reviewing and considering how the themes linked, I was able to engage in the iterative process of refining the themes by participant until I felt I had an accurate representation of my analysis of the data from their interviews transcripts, my field notes, and my reflexive journal.

I also needed a way of triangulating my data analysis, to make sure that I had not been reaching conclusions that were so highly subjective they might hold little value for the external reader. I did this through two main ways. The first was by presenting recorded extracts from my interviews, along with the corresponding transcript extract, to my supervisors. They would free associate to the material and play with ideas that linked to the material. The second method was to use a data analysis panel. I presented extracts from transcripts to my fellow students and let them free associate to the material. I would sit outside of this process and make notes about their comments. It was heartening to hear where their responses converged with my own analysis of the data, and illuminating to see new themes or concepts being picked up.

For each participant, I produced a "key themes" page detailing the themes I identified and showing which interviews the corresponding data extracts belonged to. Where we had listened to data extracts in supervision, and identified further themes here, these were identified on the key themes page.

Once I had completed this task across all participants (my inter-case analysis), I then needed to identify the themes across the partici-pants (cross-case analysis). My first attempt at cross-case analysis was very "hands on". I made copies of all my "key themes" pages and put the participant's initial against each theme recorded. I then cut up the pages to leave one theme per piece of paper (which I could track back to its origins by the participant initial). Then I sorted the pieces of paper, stacking similar themes in piles. In some cases, the piles com-prised themes that ran across participant groups; in others they were specific to participant groups. Having these initial groups enabled me to return to the process of reviewing and considering the "fit" of the themes against my research objectives, my epistemology, and the psycho-social theoretical framework within which this research is constructed. This activity sounds as if it took place over an afternoon. In reality, it was an extended exercise which included several super-vision sessions, reflection, and reworking over several months and was still being refined in the writing up stages of my thesis, during which time some of my thematic assumptions really began to be tested. I produced a final map cross-referencing the overarching cross-case themes by participants organised by group. From this map, I then began the final stage of my data analysis: writing up my findings by theme. The writing up stage of research is not to be underestimated, both in terms of the amount of time it takes and also of the process of active engagement with the material and with the literature review. This is where arguments are honed, a finer and deeper level of under-standing of the meaning of the data is wrought, and the solidity of the research findings are demonstrated. It is in the writing up process that the new researcher finally begins to feel she is on firmer ground and knows what she is talking about!

My reflections on data analysis

When analysing some of the transcripts, I initially found my proxim-ity to the interviewees got in the way of my being able to step back and make sense of the data. For a long time in the data analysis process, I kept getting caught up in wanting to give participants (clients in particular) their voice, to enable their story to be told. It took some pointed feedback from a tutor for me to really get the point that giving clients their voice was not the object of my research. This is reinforced by Braun and Clarke (2006, p. 80): "We do not subscribe to a naïve realist view of qualitative research, where the researcher can simply 'give voice' to their participants". I think my relative slowness in taking this point is to do with making the final shift into the role of researcher. Feeling confident in the role of researcher, and giving my opinion of what I inferred from the data and why, initially felt as if I was being arrogant: it was a much less comfortable position than that of giving someone else their voice. But, of course, it is not arrogant—it is the job in hand. By the end of the research process, I became much more at ease in this role.

The whole issue of role, confidence, and the merging of personal and professional life and the research process took some unpicking. I was lucky enough to be able to access a Balint-style group (named after the psychoanalyst Michael Balint (1896–1970), who pioneered this approach). This is where one researcher gives voice to his thoughts about one aspect of his work that is currently occupying him. The rest of the group listens in silence. After ten minutes, the group has a chance to ask any simple, clarifying questions they might have. The researcher then sits outside of the members of the group, who free associate to the material they have just heard. With assis-tance from the group facilitator, they hypothesise what might be happening in the research process and draw attention to verbal and non-verbal communications from the researcher that could get beneath the surface of the presenting issue. The researcher is then invited into the group to reflect on what he has heard and what meaning he draws from this.

For me, the Balint groups showed me how the personal has impacts, practically, consciously, and unconsciously, on how I positioned my research, my assumptions, and my investment in it. In turn, the process of undertaking research changed the person I was, which was one of my reasons for engaging in research; it would be disingenuous not to acknowledge this. So, it became very important to have some way of tracking my engagement and development, to be able to notice and own the effect one might have on the research process.

My conclusions on the research methodology

Perhaps the benchmark for reflecting upon the methodology I used for my research is to ask myself "If I were to pursue the same research questions again, would I use the same methodology?" For me, the response is yes, but with an additional focus.

Having set out my epistemological stall at the start of this chapter, I believe my research has found a good home in the psycho-social realm. Using FANI as my method for structuring my interviews has not been without its challenges: as a psychodynamic counsellor, I believe that many of my existing skills have been deployed to good effect. However, the closeness of the skill-set to that of the FANI interviewer also makes it difficult to make some of the small, but essential, differences necessary. I believe my research would have been stronger for my keeping a clearer focus on my research agenda and using some more specifically targeted, narrative-pointed questions in interviews, such as asking how the research participants felt their own life experiences had had impacts on their endings in counselling, and *vice versa*. This would have helped me knit the two interviews together more closely, rather than hoping that the links might be apparent.

Perhaps the one major change I would have made would have been to request a biographic-narrative interview for the second interview, rather than asking about endings more generally in life. This might have revealed more about participants' broader social and personal world within which to contextualise their reflections on endings in counselling, and might have allowed a stronger engagement with discourses of endings in society at large.

In terms of my data analysis, I am largely happy with what I found and how this was triangulated by my supervisory team and the data analysis panels I worked with. There can be a pull to get a broader consensus on whether an interpretation is "correct" or not, but this rather denies the importance of reflexive research: this was my research and I attempted to be open about my own investments in it and show something of my own autobiographical inputs to my engagement with endings. I came up with a final image of my research findings being like a crystal. There are many facets that give me different perspectives on my research topic. This is not be confused with "crystal clear vision". A filtering of my data would not give me a closer approximation to the truth; I needed to be able to let my gaze drift across a number of truths. In qualitative research, there is never just one answer.

So, what, at the end of my research, had I discovered? My research findings produced a distinctive history of how endings in psychodynamic counselling are constructed, with a focus on the acculturation of new counsellors affecting how they approach endings. I found that the adherence of new counsellors to a narrative of death, loss, and mourning in relation to endings appeared to lessen over time and to allow a broader interpretation of endings, with a greater association to attachment-based narratives of endings emerging.

Although not strongly linked, my research also suggested that the counsellors who experienced sudden, rather than timely, deaths in their biographies, and those who have no children, tended to use a narrative of death, loss, and mourning to frame their understanding of endings in counselling.

Finally, my research offered a unique view on how counselling clients experienced the psychodynamic counselling relationship. This raised sometimes uncomfortable questions about whether professional practices and expectations around endings might serve as a defence against the anxiety of managing this complex part of the counselling relationship and of counsellors' lack of awareness of the public's expectation of their role. These were not things that I had expected my research to reveal. But, after all, is that not one of the reasons we do research? To see if we can discover something that none of us knew?

References

Alvesson, M., & Sköldberg, K. (2000). *Reflexive Methodology*. London: Sage.

Blackman, L., & Venn, C. (2010). Affect. *Body and Society*, 16(1): 7–28.

Boyatzis, R. E. (1998). *Transforming Qualitative Information: Thematic Analysis and Code Development*. Thousand Oaks, CA: Sage.

Braun, V., & Clarke, V. (2006). Using thematic analysis in psychology. *Qualitative Research in Psychology*, 3: 77–101.

Clarke, S. (2002). Learning from experience: psycho-social research methods in the social sciences. *Qualitative Research*, 2(2): 173–194.

Derrida, J. (1978). *Writing and Difference*, A. Bass (Trans.). Chicago, IL: University of Chicago Press.

Giddens, A. (1984). *The Constitution of Society*. Cambridge: Polity.

Hanks, P. (Ed.) (1986). *Collins Dictionary of the English Language*. London: Collins.

Hollway, W. (2010). Researching affect and affective communication seminar series, 26 March, Cardiff University.

Hollway, W., & Jefferson, T. (2013)[2000]. *Doing Qualitative Research Differently*. London: Sage.

Jung, C. (1961). *Memories, Dreams, Reflections*, London: Fontana Press.

Mathers, D. (2001). *Meaning and Purpose in Analytical Psychology*, Hove: Brunner-Routledge.

Morrison, K. (2006). *Marx, Durkheim, Weber: Formations of Modern Social Thought*. London: Sage.

Parker, I. (2002). *Critical Discursive Psychology*. Basingstoke: Palgrave Macmillan.

Wengraf, T. (2001). *Qualitative Research Interviewing*. London: Sage.

Wetherell, M. (2012). *Affect and Emotion*. London: Sage.

CHAPTER NINE

Finding "self" when looking for "other": intrasubjectivity in the research encounter

Nadine Riad Tchelebi

W ith this chapter, I wish to share insights from the lived experiences of my own research encounters, as well as my learning from these. I intend to tell my research story in a manner that draws the reader "into a collective experience" (Butler, 1997, p. 928), focusing on the process of the research work itself, rather than its outcomes alone; those Eureka moments that advanced theoretical insight as much as my own personhood.

The discussion makes contributions in two realms: first, by sharing a selection of memoirs, the reader is presented with hands-on examples of how attention to self-experience can further the learning about the other. Second, the argument explores the theoretical underpinnings that support such research philosophy. Thereby, it adds to the body of knowledge on immersive research studies by claiming it is the process of comparing the "other-in-the-mind" to the "other-in-the-here-and-now", as I call it, that unveils pertinent insight.

More holistically, the account promotes the underlying principle that social science research is fundamentally "me-search" (Ely et al., 1991). The discussion evidences the importance of recognising one's own lived experience as primary data as a key capability of the qualitative enquirer. With that in mind, social science researchers are encouraged to pay attention to the *intra*subjectivity of the research encounter for understanding "other" through their "self", and to exploit their surprises and confusions during that encounter as an indicator for frame-breaking (Schein, 2010) of a basic assumption underlying their own understanding of self and other, engagement with the research, and, hence, the entire academic enquiry itself. Not least, the narrative also evidences how principally experience-led research can generate academically rigorous theory.

I first explore the incentive that gave rise to my original enquiry: the exploration of the so-called "us *vs.* them" mentality in organisations, before including an in-depth discussion on the underlying research principles employed. The account then moves on to a second case study, after which I conclude with a strengthened argument for the importance of intrasubjectivity during immersive research.

"Us vs. them": incentives behind the enquiry

When embarking on my research project, my tireless curiosity for studying the "us *vs.* them" mentality in organisations seemed to have been driven by a concise and particular experience: my being trained and employed as office staff, a so-called "clerical", in a manufacturing plant of a multi-national car producer. Clericals formed the "us" from *my* perspective and were supposedly opposed by the "industrials", which made up the manual labour power of the plant—"them".

During my years of employment, I was struck by the obvious enmity between task groups that led to the organisation's segmentation into opposing "camps", and it appeared to me as though the unity of the organisation portrayed to the outside world—through the slogan "Us at FutureCo"—was not reflected internally (FutureCo is a pseudonym). The organisational "falling apart" led to a great amount of mistrust and resentment between task groups which, in turn, hampered the organisation's ability to satisfy its members' need for identity and belonging as a result of a hostile climate for social relationships. I had plenty of opportunities to witness the conduct and consequences of "us *vs.* them", thinking both from a distance and through personal involvement. I learnt to mourn the canyons such dichotomised thinking created, the segregation and separation, accompanied by a degree of vanishing understanding and misperception for each other's differences and commonalities, and, last, the complete abandonment of the common goal: the organisational mission. Instead of a sense of "pulling together", a "magnetism" throughout the manpower due to shared interest in the success of the organisation, and the recognition, therefore, that working together would lead to that success, I experienced the compromising of human wellbeing in a workplace, where "silo mentality" and "blame culture" had long since demolished the spirit of creating something together.

I was beginning to enquire into the origins and true motives behind this group dynamic, which seemed to solidify itself in front of me as, first, an urge to differentiate one's self from the other, followed by an urge to derogate that other in comparison to self. In the following, I share memoirs from my daily lunch routine as a clerical.

> Five past twelve. I open the big double doors, and step into the huge dining hall that can easily seat 300 people. . . . I am greeted by a cool draft. Tunnel vision. The food counters are located half way down the walkway/runway. I continue to enter, hectic as usual, my high heels clicking on the concrete, fast paced and determined, while my gaze stares straight ahead. Despite my stubborn focus (I might be frowning), I cannot help but be distracted by the dynamics of the location, only a couple of seconds and metres into the hall. Something is tearing at my steady, straight walk. To my left, I have approximately five long table rows full of people, all dressed in the predominantly grey with bits of blue factory floor health and safety uniforms (overalls and jacket, fire proof), like a bunch of soldiers. Certainly, most of them are staring right at me, not necessarily into my face, and not necessarily with a smile. They are sitting rather chauvinistically, portentous. To my right, more people. The first few table rows empty—buffer zone—and then, a safe distance from these industrials, the clericals are sitting down . . . more scattered around than the large groupings of the industrials. No loud laughing, contained body language. Some with laptops, some writing, some discussing one-to-one what seems to be a business matter. All sophisticatedly dressed, in suits, just like me. . . . I feel much less noticed here, I do not "feel" any X-rays scanning me. I do not feel out of place . . . but, rather, a sense of belonging. Even before I get my food on a tray, I have made up my mind about where I am going to sit to consume it. . . . The divided atmosphere in the hall is so great that I do not really have a choice—it is not a question of choice in the first place.

However, there was one specific occasion when I did make a conscious choice: coincidentally, I have known one of the industrials privately; we went to school together. . . . Last weekend we made plans to meet up in the canteen, so I come looking for him. I wave when I spot him (is this appropriate?) and go to get my food, clicking on the concrete and all. As I return, carrying my tray, aiming my movements towards my friend, I feel something really unusual, unsettling. I feel as though I am breaking some kind of rule the moment I put my tray on the table and pull the chair out—directly opposite my friend and only a few metres away from the rest of "them". We are sitting in the buffer zone, in "no man's land". It feels as though I have upset the apple cart, and, as a response, the whole canteen stops talking, stops chewing, stops reading, stops breathing, and turns its frowning face at me, eyes squinted, mouths wide open in a state of horrified disbelief.

Following this one-sided experience from my own "one-of-us" perspective, I was keen to find out whether the "others"—the industrials—had similar experiences in their encounters with "us" from *their* point of view. I set up interviews accordingly. Respondents chose to emphasise the divide between "us" and "them" with the help of metaphorical expressions:

> There was this total wall between the industrials and the clericals! It was as though one would break a taboo if one sat down with them.
> Here [in the canteen], two worlds crash into each other.

It seemed that both parties of "us" and "them" were voluntarily choosing to maintain the distance between each other, albeit at an unconscious level:

> And then you don't want to behave different from everyone else, so you stick to your own squad.
> But these are normal codes of conduct here. No idea where they come from, it's like [the] Loch Ness [monster]—no one's ever seen it, but everyone believes in it.

It also transpired that these unwritten rules were a tool for reinforcing the division between "us" and "them"

> Once I was on an all-day training course in the IT department [which is clerical territory], and there we learnt together with the clericals. But we were not even allowed to take off our overalls.

Further confirming the division from *their* perspective, the industrials insinuated on a number of occasions a feeling of inferiority compared to the clericals. The rather drastic metaphoric comparison of the relationship to that between the Chinese and the Americans during the time of railway construction emphasises this feeling:

> Like in America, where all the Chinese were let down in baskets into the tunnels, and if the people on top didn't pull fast enough, then those down there exploded along with the bombs.

I elicited from these responses, with great astonishment, not only a confirmation of the above described segmentation dynamics, but also the lowering of the other's self-esteem that developed in parallel. In the same line of argument, friendly encounters with "us" were reported with surprise at exceptional treatment and great appreciation:

> That was quite something, if someone in a suit shakes your hand … I thought that was awesome.

Likewise, an interviewee's perplexity about the "normality" of interaction possible with a clerical stood out:

> The surprising thing is, if they talk to us, I experienced that myself—you can talk with them completely normally.

This thwarting of perception particularly intrigued me, given that no reference was made to any evidence explaining the felt superiority of clericals. In fact, I was a clerical; however, at the beginning of my career, I was predominantly occupied with making photocopies and adjusting my coffee-making skills to the preferences of my line manager, and I certainly earned far less than the average industrial. How this fits into the industrials' perception of my being a "metaphorical American", and, hence, somewhat "superior", I did not know.

*   *   *

With this awareness of my own motivation in mind, I was ambitious to research the theoretical underpinnings of the so-called "us" *vs.* "them" mentality. It was not until another year into my enquiry that I pondered upon further, more unconscious, motives firing my interest in this topic. I explored how my own life history could be related. My fierce dislike for ethnocentrism caught my attention first. Being of Middle-Eastern origin (the Orient) and having some level of insight into that culture as a "native" in the scientific sense of the word, but, on the other hand, having been born and brought up in Germany (the Occident), I have witnessed in both settings the "brick walls" between the "us" and the "them" that ethnocentrism erects among people. Fuelled by a lack of understanding for one another, and, more importantly, the failure to *acknowledge* that lack which typically compels us to judge the other, the "different from me", as being wrong (Capozza & Brown, 2000), is, to my mind, a larger-scale embodiment of the same underlying group dynamic I partook in at FutureCo.

I have come to believe myself to be in some kind of "privileged" position, having got to know from the "inside", as a member of two cultures, the Orient and the Occident. Whether this position is truly privileged is questionable, however, as it more likely describes a state of limbo. Volkan comments,

> If the ambivalence arises because the individual has identified with more than one . . . cultural group, it may become an issue in itself. When one is simultaneously invested in the relations of more than one group . . . his sense of self may suffer. (1988, p. 50)

Not only does my multi-cultural background provide a possible insight into my "us *vs.* them" interest, but I could also argue to be the very embodiment of this manifestation—I was created by "us" and "them". My mother and her family and my father and his family have been in deep animosity with each other since before my birth, and have not exchanged a single word with each other in over thirty-five years. I am the only link between these two frontiers; I am the *versus*. Experiencing, since the very first day of my life, this profound manifestation of "us *vs.* them", the strength of its boundaries, the depth of the canyons it creates, and having to straddle these boundaries without being caught up on either side, while also trying to satisfy my need for identification and belonging from both sides, might, in fact, have been the strongest, yet unconscious, drive behind my research enquiry. As Louis puts it, "I am an instrument of my inquiry: and the inquiry is inseparable from who I am" (1991, p. 365).

Why, then, have I decided to commit myself to an intense research project on the underlying dynamic of the "us *vs.* them" mentality? Was I hoping to heal the world? Maybe it was for purely egotistical reasons, since, if I could manage to reunite "us" with "them", I would no longer have the agony of choice.

Methodology: objective, subjective, intersubjective, and intrasubjective enquiry

The assumption developed in this chapter is that any journey into understanding human nature is also a journey into understanding one's self, for the world is not perceivable other than through one's own self *in relation* to the other (Chang, 2008). This assumption carries with it the importance of exploring with intensity the researcher's own perspective on, and relationship to, the phenomena under scrutiny, and the narrative so far has done that. Therefore, I do not claim to present an unbiased explanation of the "us" *vs.* "them" dynamic; my, now partly conscious, pre-existing antipathy to the concept might incline me to see "us" *vs.* "them" mentalities in social settings where others do not. With that, the chance of analysing a phenomenon that "only" exists within the mind of the researcher is an inescapable prospect of any qualitative enquiry. This is not to say, however, that the findings of such research are fruitless—quite the opposite: I argue that in order to understand any human dynamics on a critical level, researchers have to explicate that human dynamic "in-the[ir]-mind" (Armstrong, 2005). In the following, I will integrate this stance into a continuum of research philosophies with objectivity on one end, and intrasubjectivity on the other (Figure 1).

Objectivity

Advocates of the modernist school of thought have traditionally warned that researcher involvement with the subject under investigation is

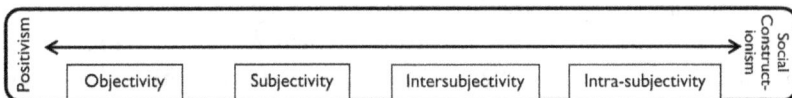

Figure 1. A continuum of research philosophies.

a threat to desired objectivity. Hammersley and Atkinson (1995) alert the researcher to not "succumbing to affect", and, in other words, Wax (1971) stresses the importance of avoiding "becoming the phenomenon". McCall and Simmons (1969) add accounts whereby immersive research is accused of bias, personal equations, and "hearsay" without rigour. Promoted predominantly by the Chicago School, the "pioneer" of sociological anthropology, the researcher was encouraged to maintain a separation towards the observed so as to not endanger the objectivity of the scientific enterprise. Pollner and Emerson (1983, p. 251) explicitly state that "the very notion of a science is possible only to the extent that these distinctions (between the observer and the observed) can be sustained". Later, symbolic interactionists acknowledged the affective role of the researcher, such as anxieties, confusion, or loneliness, but still regarded these as a hindrance to data gathering (Hunt, 1989). By assuming "neutrality", the researcher was expected to report from an Archimedean standpoint of objectivity in order to preserve the validity of the findings.

Subjectivity

Post-modernist advocates have argued that the fantasy of an "objective" stance denies the fruitful source of the researcher's own emotions for primary data. Kreb (1999), for example, introduces the term "edgewalker" to describe those researchers who have significant lived experiences with different communities through which they develop solid cross-cultural competence while maintaining a healthy understanding of self. Hence, a method that brings the researcher closer to gaining insight into, and from the perspective of, the subjects, to see with their eyes, to feel from their point of view, to understand their line of thoughts, was sought after. The task of interpreting that world could only be achieved through participation with those involved (Manis & Meltzer, 1967) and only if the language that was used to communicate its meaning was understood (Hall, 1976).

Drawing on principles of *Verstehen* helps clarifying this methodological stance. Primarily, *Verstehen* has a concern for the subjective state of humankind and the process by which people give meaning to the social world around them (Weber, 1962). It is the process of interpretative understanding through the empathetic examination of social phenomena, making empathy a key dynamic of sense-making. In

1924, Dilthey introduced *Verstehen* into sociology as a first-person participatory perspective in the theoretical frame of hermeneutics (Harrington, 2001) and, thereby, opposed the external third-person perspective of objective explanation (*Erklärung*). Here, subjectivity shifts with context (Schulte, 2000) and the meaning of behaviour is only interpretable within that context or shared framework.

Chang (2008) adds that this empathetic understanding entails an act of putting aside one's own framework and "seeing others' experiences within the framework of their own" (Geertz, 1984, p. 126). Similarly, in the Malinowskian–Geertzian sense, this empathetic understanding is achieved from the "native's" point of view, and not from self. Lingerfelder (1996) adds that researchers need to *deny* their own self so as to immerse with and in others. Along with that, the genuine effort to the *Verstehen* of others is believed to engender the crossing from self to other (Chang, 2008).

Intersubjectivity

Post-modern psychoanalysis has acknowledged the interconnectedness of self and other through principles of intersubjectivity and the "emotional turn" (Clarke & Hoggett, 2009). Benjamin (1994) defines intersubjectivity in terms of a relationship of mutual recognition, where each person experiences the other as a "like subject", another mind who can be felt with, yet has a distinct, *separate* centre of feeling and perception. While modern psychoanalysis has assumed individuals to be discrete entities that act externally upon each other (Schulte, 2000), post-modernity has witnessed a deconstruction of this "sovereign self" (Cavell, 1991) whereby the motivation behind human behaviour does not solely originate from an individual's inner world, but resides in a network of feelings and thoughts between self and other that make it part of the lived social world. In agreement, Coelho and Figueiredo (2003) stress the need to recognise otherness as one of the elements that constitute singular subjectivity and acknowledge this psychoanalytical notion as being in direct contrast to the "I" as a self-constituent unit and the classical subject–object opposition of modern thought. This post-modern development is also recognisable in Heidegger's (1993) notion of *Dasein* and *Mitsein*, of "being-in-the-world" *with* others.

However, the literature on intersubjectivity still demonstrates a degree of ambiguity with regard to the relationship between self and other. Although a deconstruction of the "sovereign self" might well be under way, the claim of seeing other as a separate entity seems to contradict this trend. Heidegger's notion of *Dasein* and *Mitsein* might actually contribute to this ambiguity, as it might, indeed, be *"Insein"*, "other-within-self", a perspective underlying the thoughts put forward in this chapter, that more appropriately resembles the relationship between self and other.

Intrasubjectivity

There is, then, an additional differentiation that I would like to draw the reader's attention to. Empathetic examination, as described by Weber (1962), above, calls for the researcher to "vacate" his own position and point of view so as to adopt the one of the other. This process has also been referred to as "going native" (Becker, 1958). It is important to note that such recommendation assumes that the other exists *outside* of self, which, in itself, alludes to some kind of objective existence of that other, an assumption that goes directly against the very intention of defining the social world as non-objectively constructed. This is an important notion to deliberate, certainly for the research encounter explored in this chapter, but also for immersive research designs in general. I propose an engagement with otherness that has long been employed in the clinical psychoanalytic setting and in systems–psychodynamic approaches to organisational consulting, but that has not yet been exploited for social science research (Skogstad, 2004): the psychoanalytic principle of "other-in-the-mind", as well as the idea of relatedness to that "other-in-the-mind". A summary of the key differences between this stance and conventional intersubjectivity is outlined in Figure 2.

The concept is borrowed from the developments around the term "Organisation-in-the-mind", which was first introduced by Turquet in 1974 and further conceptualised by Hutton and colleagues (1991), and Armstrong (2005). The authors explain that humans habitually construct organisational models in their minds that differ from the reality they act in. With that, "organisation", as such, does "not exist outside the mind at all—it is not a thing out there—it is a set of

Verstehen / Empathetic Understanding:	Other-in-the-mind:
• Crossing *from* Self into Other • Assumes Other exists independently from Self	• Crossing *through* Self into Other • Assumes Other exists independently from Self, but is only "knowable" through the representation of Other *within* Self

Figure 2.   Differences between conventional intersubjectivity and the psychoanalytic principle of "other-in-the-mind".

experiences held in the mind" (Hutton et al., 1991, p. 115). Similar to Hirschhorn's notion of the "workplace within" (1990), Hutton and colleagues go on to explain that organisational members introject some aspects of their environment that then become internal objects to which they relate. These internalised representations are more tale-telling of the thinker's psychic reality, rather than any objective external reality.

This lens for understanding the human world, which is that any social phenomenon—an organisation, a group, a nation of people, or similar—needs to, and, in fact, can only, be understood through its representation in-the-mind of the thinker who sets out to understand it, is also the lens that has led to the poignant insights generated during my own research endeavour. Shapiro and Carr (1991) add that reality is experienced in the interaction with the in-the-mind entities, which then also have an impact on our perception of our environment, as well as our behaviour within it. Hence, it is attention to the "other-in-the-mind" of self at the centre of the enquirer's awareness that generates insight for the enquiry itself. In the case of the research underlying this chapter, "other" was a group, "them", and "other-in-the-mind", or "group-in-the-mind", was exclusionary, closed-system-like, and defensive against "not me" (Winnicott, 1974), "us".

In the course of the ongoing discussion, I shall stipulate that it is, in fact, when "other-in-the-mind" clashes with "other-in-the-here-and-now" that in-depth insight can be gained about human dynamics. The development of events presented in the following portrays such a clash and, thereby, reminds strongly of Schein's (2010) notion of frame-breaking, whereby the researcher's very basic assumptions underlying the researched phenomena are shaken.

Letting go of "other-in-the-mind": the inclusionary other

During the primary data collection for my next case study, I was brought to alter my understanding of the "us *vs.* them" mentality and question, in particular, my understanding of its claimed innateness that I was originally set to prove right (see, for example, Allport, 1979; Berman et al., 2000; Duek, 2009; Gaertner et al., 2006; Gold, 2010; Hogg, 2001; Turner et al., 1987). I selected a convent community so that I could witness the "us *vs.* them" mentality of a group who did not come together only Monday to Friday, nine to five, but was permanently bound together. Additionally, the opportunity to study the "us *vs.* them" mentality in an environment that was, in itself, created for the very purpose of forming union, and, hence, directly opposing division, was intriguing. I wrote a letter that explained my intentions to six convents, of which one accepted me.

Five weeks participant observation took place in an enclosed and silent, UK-based, convent with a community of twenty-two professed Sisters. The convent community itself did not ask any further questions before my arrival but wished that, once I entered the enclosure, I should remain in it for the duration of my stay. My role in the community was treated as that of a postulant, a nun in the first of her seven years of formation, for which I was assigned a personal mentor. In the following, I present the first entry from my field notes in the hope of taking the reader with me into the enclosure.

> After a two and a half hour journey, the rest of it through idyllic countryside, I arrive in the village. I find the convent and drive straight past it. In a nearby car park, I stop to collect my thoughts. I stuff the rest of my favourite chocolate biscuits into my mouth, take a few deep breaths, and head back towards the convent. Beautiful building, incredible. Looks really old, authentic, but well maintained and looked after. . . . I step out of my car and approach what looks like the main entrance, a massive wooden door. . . . There is a bell, and a sign right above: "Worry not—you cannot hear the bell, but we can." OK, then, so I ring it. Nothing indeed . . . still nothing . . . minutes pass . . . I'm gazing around . . . then footsteps coming closer from beyond the wood. The door opens with a squeak, and I find myself staring at a nun. Oh dear. She stares back, mumbling a "Good morning". "Good morning", I answer, "my name is Nadine, I've come to stay with you for five weeks" (what else would I say). "Sorry, who?" she asks, and I repeat. After a few seconds of prolonged mutual staring, her face becomes softer, "Oh yes, oh yes, that's

right, that's right," she mumbles. "Do you have a suitcase?" I point to my car, and upon her request to bring my luggage, I get my two suitcases out of the boot. She pulls one of them, me the other. Up the three steps, through the wooden door and into a huge dark cold hall in which every move I make echoes with great awe. Another squeak, the door slams shut. Oh dear. I follow her through the hall, feeling small. At the end another door, "No entry—enclosure". Oh dear. The nun asks me to wait here and disappears. . . . A few moments later the door opens again, three other nuns emerge. "Good morning, Nadine, it is so nice to meet you—we are very pleased to welcome you—oh you must have left very early this morning—how long did the journey take you—we hope it was not difficult to find us—do you have all your luggage with you . . .", and each of them gives me a firm hug. I don't know what to say or how to behave. I feel awkward is an understatement. In we go, each of the nuns grabbing my belongings. Down another small corridor and into a larger hall with a staircase. . . . Echoes everywhere. There are lots of them whizzing about, all smiling at me, greeting without interrupting their calm haste. One of the three nuns shows me to my room—cell, they call it— I can't remember any of their names any more. There is a sign at the door "Welcome Nadine" with a picture of a flower. The room is lovely; simple, small, but all I need. Comfortable single bed with two pillows, small desk with chair, sink in the corner with soap and cup, a cupboard with three shelves and a curtain covering them, a granny-style armchair. A vase with fresh flowers on a bedside table together with a lamp and a kettle. I am given half an hour to unpack. Then I'm picked back up and given a grand tour of the house. I can't remember anything though, am completely lost—this place is huge, and it doesn't help that there are two floors and three different ways to get from A to B. On our way, we meet lots of other nuns, and the one showing me around knocks on their cell doors and every single one of them comes out. They welcome me, ask me questions, tell me something about them, crack some jokes (witty humour, great!), some anecdotalism, and long and firm hugs. I just got here, but I feel as though everybody is really happy to have me.

What struck me most was the unconditional trust I was offered by the community as a whole, and how quickly and thoroughly, from the first day onward, the Sisters "swallowed" me, integrated me into all aspects of their life without any signs of suspicion noticeable to me. In fact, I was so assimilated into the Sisters' daily routine (Figure 3), had I not pulled my weight, I would have caused a significant disturbance to their peace of mind; a responsibility I certainly felt on my shoulders

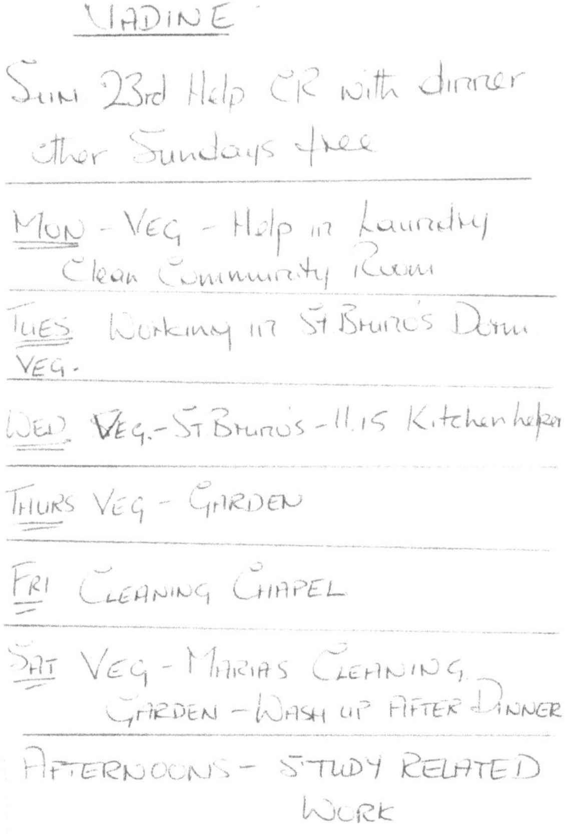

NADINE

Sun 23rd Help CR with dinner
other Sundays free

MON - VEG - Help in Laundry
Clean Community Room

TUES Working in St Bruno's Dorm
VEG.

WED VEG.- ST BRUNO'S - 11.15 Kitchen helper

THURS VEG - GARDEN

FRI CLEANING CHAPEL

SAT VEG - MARIAS CLEANING
GARDEN - WASH UP AFTER DINNER

AFTERNOONS - STUDY RELATED WORK

Figure 3. My timetable.

at all times, as peace of mind and routine seemed to be one of the cornerstones of the community's spiritual life. This is not to say that I felt to be an equal to the Sisters—it takes seven years of formation to become a professed nun of this order—but I certainly felt completely accepted, just the way I was—Muslim and all.

The experience of being fully integrated also meant being fully integrated in all aspects of convent life, including group conflict. On one occasion in particular, I had insight into the struggle one has to undergo in order to preserve the greater good.

> It's 6:30 p.m., but I have got absolutely no idea what day it is; I lost count a long time ago. I am completely agitated and emotional, I even feel like crying. . . . I feel hugely agitated by Sr X, and that probably since last

week, but today it reached the peak. Sr X was not present at the introduction for my social photo matrix. . . . So we agreed that I would fill her
in the next morning. . . . She really did not make any effort hiding the fact
that she can absolutely not be bothered with my project. When I said,
"Well, it would not really work if you only gave it five minutes to do the
photos," she answered, "Well, that is all the time I would spend on it."
I know she probably doesn't mean it, but I have noticed . . . that she can
be that stroppy with a lot of people. . . . Anyway, just an hour ago then
the final straw: I was standing in front of the notice board discussing the
SPM with Sr Y, . . . Sr X passes by and stops, and when Sr Y said, "She
is ever so good at explaining", Sr X answered, "Well, it's only in her own
interest." That infuriated me hugely. What an unfair and rude comment.
First of all, I never made a secret out of how helpful their taking part
would be for me; I have more than shown my appreciation. And second,
I think that I give something back, too, and everybody can see that I am
trying very very hard—I am literally breaking my back in the garden.
Anyway, this did give me a different flavour of community life, and I could
finally relate to what one of the nuns said a while back, that here you
cannot just run away from problems, you have to sort them out. And
that is quite literal: the strict schedule means that privacy can only take
a maximum of two hours at a time. I cannot simply decide to remain in
my cell and sulk. I have to pull my weight, pull myself together and do
my part for the community. If I didn't, it would unbalance the whole
group, that's for sure. This was the first time I felt a pressing on me and
an urge to go for a long walk, to have a time-out, just to get away. My
head was spinning. I really had to compose myself, was kind of shouting
at myself in my own head. I felt quite claustrophobic. I wanted to retreat
like a snail would into its own shell.

*   *   *

Temporarily joining the convent community signified a turning point
in my own understanding of what "group" actually meant—the
group that presented itself before me did not match my "group-in-
the-mind". My surprises during my stay in the convent can, among
other insights, be summarised into four particularities. These particularities, taken together, led to the Eureka-moment referred to by
Schein as frame-breaking (2010).

First, I experienced, for the first time in my life, some sort of immediate acceptance into a pre-existing system. I felt as though I was fully
*in*tegrated into the convent community, straight after my arrival. I did

not undergo any stage of transitioning into the group, during which I would have to metamorphose for the purpose of becoming one of "them". Of course, I had to adjust some of my habits, such as, to give only a few examples, I had to get up at an unusually early hour, do more physical work than I was used to, and struggle to remember to keep my voice down. Despite these behavioural adjustments to the convent's structural life, I felt a "good enough" member of the community just the way I was, without having to adjust any of the character traits that define my personhood. I felt appreciated in the authentic complexity that made up my identity. This experience resonated with a perplexing statement by one nun: "In here, I am truly free. In here, I can be myself."

Second, I observed the Sisters to be strongly heterogeneous and pluralistic in the way they presented themselves to me. This astonished me, since I expected a group that had spent so much time together to appear more similar to each other with regard to behaviours, opinions, and habits and display more conformity dynamics as the years go by. Instead, I found myself in the middle of a group consisting of unique and diverse individuals that were ready to assert themselves without hesitation whenever necessary.

Third, not only was the frequency of these assertions unexpected, but also the fact that they did not lead to any kind of conflictual group engagement; in other words, disputes remained on an individual level, between two disgruntled Sisters who would use their solitude time to first reconcile with themselves and consecutively with each other.

Fourth, and most significantly, I could not find evidence that would support the existence of any "us *vs.* them" dynamics during my stay. This is not to say that the Sisters felt no need to differentiate themselves from parties of opposing values—far from it; however, while representations of "them" and the wish to differentiate oneself from these existed, the *versus* to these did not. This insight moved me to alter my understanding of the "us *vs.* them" mentality, as I was now drawn to focus my attention to the meaning of "us" *and* "them". Even the devil, so it was portrayed to me, is an angel who lost his path, and, therefore, needs to be embraced in prayers: to quote St Augustine of Hippo, "hate the sin but love the sinner" (in Azkoul, 1991). The Sisters further explained that "Every encounter with difference is taken as an opportunity for reintegration. . . . We are constantly challenged to grow into integrated human beings that way"; "To be loving with one another is really the hallmark of our life. . . . Through any relationship we are growing through love into self-awareness. . . . Exclusion is against our principle of love."

Eureka: when "group-in-the-mind" does not match "group-in-the-here-and-now"

The narrative has made clear that insight in this enquiry was not brought on by the study of theoretical literature, but by the critical self-reflection on my own lived experiences as part of the human dynamic I set out to understand. This was not easy, and there is evidence in my field notes about my partly unconscious struggle to accept that my "group-in-the-mind" (group being "other") did not match what I was experiencing, which was the "group-in-the-here-and-now", although it was exactly this mismatch that unlocked key theoretical developments from the data (Figure 4). For a large proportion of my fieldwork, I was accompanied by the discomforting suspicion that I was failing as a researcher, because I became more and more convinced of missing out on those significant moments when, as I believed at the time, those unavoidable group manifestations of "us

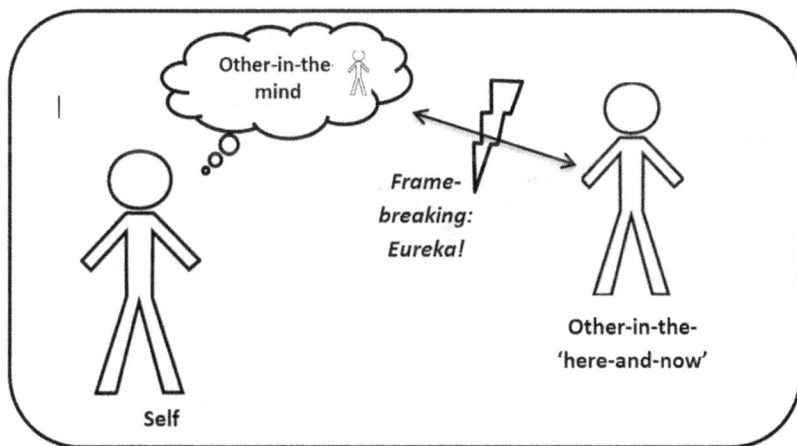

Figure 4.   The Eureka moment when the frame breaks the mismatch between "other-in-the-mind" and "other-in-the-here-and-now".

vs. them" that I had come to study were readily observable. I felt as though I was never in the right place at the right time.

It took me a long time to accept that this was a group other than my common understanding of "group"—other than my "group-in-the-mind". One that was always bound together by union, but comprises differentiated individuals. Only further into my stay did a coincidence make me realise that my worries about the Sisters hiding something from me were unsubstantiated:

> I am going for a walk in the back garden, taking a break from my obser-
> vations and reflections. Dusk has settled in, and when I turn the corner
> and my gaze falls back on to the convent building, I realise that I can
> look straight into most of the Sisters' cells. Despite the feeling of being
> intrusive, I continue to observe, and so I see that all that time, I had not
> missed out on anything, no hidden agenda—they are all there, by them-
> selves in their cells, either reading, writing, working through papers,
> sorting the room, or going for a walk on their own—just like me.

New definition of group

The self-critical recognition of my own "group-in-the-mind" and my ability to adjust this inner representation to the "group-in-the-here-and-now" enabled me to suggest some fundamental additions to the body of knowledge on group dynamics to date. To summarise, I could shift the commonly held belief from "the need to have an enemy is innate to humanity" (Erlich, 1997) to "the need for self-boundaries is vital for a healthy sense of identity", thereby limiting the need for an opposing "them" assumption to being provoked by projections of a group dominated by oneness-mentality (Turquet, 1974) (Figure 5). I came to argue that hostile opposition satisfies the need of a group with oneness-mentality for "self-cleansing" as a "suitable" other contains its psychotically split off and projected "bad" parts. In a group dominated by what I came to call unity-mentality, it is easier for individual members (Turquet, 1974) to maintain the balance between their idiosyncrasy and homogeneity needs. In a group dominated by oneness-mentality, individuality is lost and members are likely to become membership individuals, in which case the relationship to an other is characterised by "us *vs.* them". In a group with unity-mentality, however, "us *and* them" better describes the identification

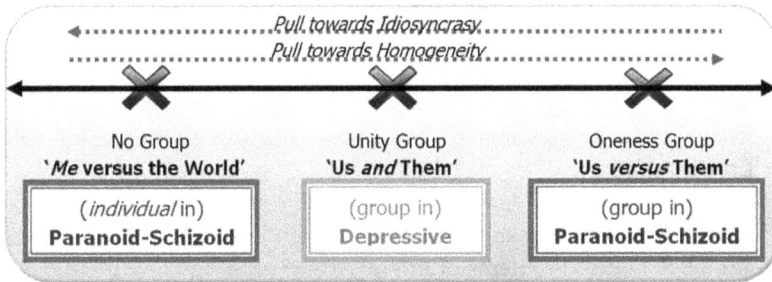

Figure 5.   Summative model of theoretical contributions.

process with the other. Hence, the "us *vs.* them" mentality is a salient characteristic of a group dominated by oneness-mentality and is exercised by the group as-a-whole, not by its individual members.

Concluding thoughts: "other-within-self"

This contribution has exemplified how principally experience-led research can generate academically rigorous theory. I have argued that critical self-reflection on my own lived experiences as part of the human dynamic I set out to explore led to the pertinent insight summarised in this discussion. With that, social scientists are encouraged to focus attention of their enquiry on those frame-breaking moments (Schein, 2010) that urge for the calling into question of an underlying assumption to their own perspective on the researched world; a degree of criticality reached by assuming an *intra*subjective stance for understanding other *within* self. In particular, this moment can be conceptualised as the clash between "other-in-the-mind" and "other-in-the-here-and-now". This call for introspection and for recognising "other-within-self" unpicks Ely and colleagues' notion that social science research is fundamentally "me-search" (1991).

The chapter offered my own research example when my "group-in-the-mind", built up through life experiences of exclusionary, closed, defensive, and blame-projecting systems, clashed with a "group-in-the-here-and-now", the convent community. *Eureka* was born out of the unexpected realisation of that "clash". I had come very close to overlooking it, because opening your eyes can be painful.

References

Allport, G. W. (1979). *The Nature of Prejudice*. New York: Basic Books.

Armstrong, D. (2005). *Organization in the Mind: Psychoanalysis, Group Relations, and Organizational Consultancy—Occasional Papers 1989–2003*. London: Karnac.

Azkoul, M. (1991). *The Influence of Augustine of Hippo on the Orthodox Church*. Thousand Oaks, CA: Edwin Mellen Press Ltd.

Becker, H. S. (1958). Problems of inference and proof in participant observation. *American Sociological Review*, 23(6): 652–660.

Benjamin, J. (1994). The shadow of the other (subject): intersubjectivity and feminist theory. *Constellations*, 1(2): 231–254.

Berman, A., Berger, M., & Gutmann, D. (2000). The division into us and them as a universal social structure. *Mind and Human Interaction*, 11(1): 53–72.

Butler, R. (1997). Stories and experiments in social enquiry. *Organization Studies*, 18(6): 927–948.

Capozza, D., & Brown, R. (Eds.) (2000). *Social Identity Processes*. London: Sage.

Cavell, M. (1991). The subject of mind. *International Journal of Psychoanalysis*, 72: 141–152.

Chang, H. (2008). *Autoethnography as Method*. Walnut Creek, CA: Left Coast Press.

Coelho Jr, N. E., & Figueiredo, L. C. (2003). Patterns of intersubjectivity in the constitution of subjectivity: dimension of otherness. *Culture & Psychology*, 9(3): 193–208.

Clarke, S., & Hoggett, P. (Eds.) (2009). *Researching Beneath the Surface. Psycho-social Research Methods in Practice*. London: Karnac.

Duek, R. (2009). Dialogue in impossible situations. *Organisational and Social Dynamics*, 9(2): 206–224.

Ely, M., Anzul, M., Friedman, T., Garner, D., & McCormack Steinmetz, A. (1991). *Doing Qualitative Research: Circles Within Circles*. London: Routledge.

Erlich, H. S. (1997). On discourse with an enemy. In: E. R. Shapiro (Ed.), *The Inner World in the Outer World: Psychoanalytic Perspectives* (pp. 123–142). New Haven, CT: Yale University Press.

Gaertner, L., Luzzini, J., Orina, M. M., & Witt, M. G. (2006). Us without them: evidence for an intragroup origin of positive in-group regard. *Journal of Personality and Social Psychology*, 90(3): 426–439.

Geertz, C. (1984). From the native's point of view: on the nature of anthropological understanding. In: R. A. Shweder & R. A. Levine

(Eds.), *Culture Theory: Essays on Mind, Self and Emotion* (pp. 123–136). Cambridge: Cambridge University Press.

Gold, S. (2010). The transfer of evil. Conference presentation at the 27th Annual Meeting of the International Society for the Psychoanalytic Study of Organizations, Elsinore, Denmark, 14 June.

Hall, E. T. (1976). *Beyond Culture*. New York: Anchor.

Hammersley, M., & Atkinson, P. (1995). *Ethnography: Principles in Practice* (2nd edn). London: Routledge.

Harrington, A. (2001). Dilthey, empathy and Verstehen: a contemporary reappraisal. *European Journal of Social Theory*, 4(3): 311–329.

Heidegger, M. (1993). *Basic Concepts*. Pennsylvania, PA: Indiana University Press.

Hirschhorn, L. (1990). *The Workplace Within: Psychodynamics of Organizational Life*. Cambride, MA: MIT Press.

Hogg, M. A. (2001). Social identity and the sovereignty of the group: a psychology of belonging. In: C. Sedikides & M. B. Brewer (Eds.), *Individual Self, Relational Self, Collective Self* (pp. 123–143). Philadelphia, PA: Taylor & Francis.

Hunt, J. (1989). *Psychoanalytic Aspects of Fieldwork*. London: Sage.

Hutton, J., Bazalgette, J., & Reed, B. (1991). Organisation-in-the-mind. In: J. Neumann, K. Kellner, & A. Dawson-Shepherd (Eds.), *Developing Organisational Consultancy* (pp. 113–126). London: Routledge.

Kreb, N. B. (1999). *Edgewalkers: Defusing Cultural Boundaries on the New Global Front*. Far Hills, NJ: New Horizon.

Lingerfelder, J. (1996). Training education students for multicultural classrooms. *Christian Scholar's Review*, 25(4): 491–507.

Louis, M. R. (1991). Reflections on an interpretive way of life. In: P. J. Frost, L. F. Moore, M. R. Louis, C. C. Lundberg, & J. Martin (Eds.), *Reframing Organizational Culture* (pp. 361–365). London: Sage.

Manis, J. G., & Meltzer, B. N. (Eds.) (1967). *Symbolic Interactionism: A Reader in Social Psychology*. Boston, MA: Allyn & Bacon.

McCall, G. J., & Simmons, J. L. (Eds.) (1969). *Issues in Participant Observation. A Text and Reader*. London: Addison-Wesley.

Pollner, M., & Emerson, R. M. (1983). The dynamics of inclusion and distance in fieldwork relations. In: R. M. Emerson (Ed.), *Contemporary Field Research* (pp. 235–252). Boston, MA: Little, Brown.

Schein, E. H. (2010). *Organizational Culture and Leadership* (4th edn). San Francisco, CA: Jossey-Bass.

Schulte, P. (2000). Holding in mind: intersubjectivity, subject relations and the group. *Group Analysis*, 33(4): 531–544.

Shapiro, E., & Carr, A. (1991). *Lost in Familiar Places: Creating New Connections Between the Individual and Society*. New Haven, CT: Yale University Press.

Skogstad, W. (2004). Psychoanalytic observation – the mind as research instrument. *Organisational & Social Dynamics*, 4(1): 67–87.

Turner, J. C., Hogg, M. A., Oakes, P. J., Reicher, S. D., & Wetherell, M. S. (1987). *Rediscovering the Social Group: A Self-categorization Theory*. Oxford: Blackwell.

Turquet, P. M. (1974). Leadership: The individual and the group. In: A. D. Coleman & M. H. Geller (Eds.), *Analysis of Groups* (pp. 349–371). San Francisco: Jossey-Bass Publishers.

Volkan, V. (1988). *The Need To Have Enemies and Allies: From Clinical Practice to International Relationships*. Northvale, NJ: Jason Aronson.

Wax, R. (1971). *Doing Fieldwork: Warnings and Advice*. Chicago, IL: University of Chicago Press.

Weber, M. (1962). *Basic Concepts in Sociology by Max Weber*, H. Secher & H. Secher (Trans.). New York: Citadel Press.

Winnicott, D. W. (1974). *Playing and Reality*. Harmondsworth: Penguin.

INDEX

For Product Safety Concerns and Information please contact our EU
representative GPSR@taylorandfrancis.com
Taylor & Francis Verlag GmbH, Kaufingerstraße 24, 80331 München, Germany